THE BLUE GUIDES

Albania
Austria
Belgium and Luxembourg
China
Cyprus
Czechoslovakia
Denmark
Egypt

FRANCE
France
Paris and Versailles
Burgundy
Normandy
South West France
Corsica

GERMANY
Berlin and Eastern Germany
Western Germany

GREECE
Greece
Athens and environs
Crete

HOLLAND
Holland
Amsterdam

Hungary
Ireland

ITALY
Northern Italy
Southern Italy
Florence
Rome and environs
Venice
Tuscany
Umbria
Sicily

Jerusalem
Malta and Gozo
Morocco
Moscow and Leningrad
Portugal

SPAIN
Spain
Barcelona

Switzerland

TURKEY
Turkey
Istanbul

UK
England
Scotland
Wales
London
Museums and Galleries
 of London
Oxford and Cambridge
Country Houses of England
Gardens of England
Literary Britain and Ireland
Victorian Architecture in
 Britain
Churches and Chapels
 of Northern England
Churches and Chapels
 of Southern England
Channel Islands

USA
New York
Boston and Cambridge

D0499370

Château des Duras, Rauzon

BLUE GUIDE

South West France

Aquitaine: Dordogne to the Pyrenees

Francis Woodman

A&C Black
London

WW Norton
New York

1st edition 1994

Published by A & C Black (Publishers) Limited
35 Bedford Row, London WC1r 4JH

A CIP catalogue record of this book is available from the British Library.

ISBN   0–7136–3910-5

Published in the United States of America by
WW Norton and Company, Inc
500 Fifth Avenue, New York, NY 10110

Published simultaneously in Canada by
Penguin Books Canada Limited
10 Alcorn Avenue, Toronto, Ontario M4V 3BE

ISBN   0–393–31188–0   USA

Maps and plans drawn by Robert Smith

Photographs by Francis Woodman

Francis Woodman lives in Suffolk and is an architectural historian specialising in the European Middle Ages. A panel tutor for the University of Cambridge Board of Continuing Education, he also teaches for the Bartlett School of Architecture, University College, London. Educated in Canterbury, he studied History of Art at the University of East Anglia and later at the Courtauld Institute of Art, where he gained his PhD. He was a Junior Research Fellow at Christ's College Cambridge and later a Leverhulme Trust Senior Research Fellow. His wide list of publications includes standard works on both Canterbury Cathedral and King's College Chapel, Cambridge. For many years, Francis Woodman has led art and architectural tours to France, Turkey and Greece.

Please write in with your comments, suggestions and corrections. Writers of the best letters will be awarded a Blue Guide of their choice.

Printed and bound in Great Britain by
Butler & Tanner Ltd, Frome and London

CONTENTS

Maps and plans

Acknowledgements

The author wishes to thank Charles Barbier and all his staff at Tourisme d'Aquitaine, Bordeaux, for their generous assistance with hotels, access arrangements and liaison with the many institutions, organisations and private individuals necessary for this book. Grateful thanks also go to Martin Johnson for his help in too many areas to list, and to Barry Cheeseman for much useful advice, information and support. It is impossible to thank by name the many individuals whose kindness made the research work so enjoyable. Tourist offices throughout south west France were always helpful and eager to assist wherever possible. Equally, thanks are due to the many property owners who allowed me total access to their houses and castles.

Thanks also go to Gemma Davies of A & C Black for her editorial skills, quick responses to problems and her general air of calm.

A Note on Blue Guides

The Blue Guide series began in 1915 with Muirhead Guide-Books Limited. The first edition of 'Blue Guide London was published in 1918. Finlay and James Muirhead already had extensive experience of guidebook publishing: before the First World War they had been the editors of the English editions of the German Baedekers, and by 1915 they had acquired the copyright of most of the famous 'Red' Handbooks from John Murray.

An agreement made with the French publishing house Hachette et Cie in 1917 led to the translation of Muirhead's London guide, which became the first 'Guide Bleu'—Hachette had previously published the blue-covered 'Guides Joannes'. Subsequently, Hachette's Guide Bleu Paris et ses Environs' was adapted and published in London by Muirhead. The collaboration between the two publishing houses continued until 1933.

In 1933 Ernest Benn Limited took over the Blue Guides, appointing Russell Muirhead, Finlay Muirhead's son, editor in 1934. The Muirheads' connection with the Blue Guides ended in 1963 when Stuart Rossiter, who had been working on the Guides since 1954, became house editor, revising and compiling several of the books himself.

The Blue Guides are now published by A & C Black, who acquired Ernest Benn in 1984, so continuing the tradition of guidebook publishing which began in 1826 with 'Black's Economical Tourist of Scotland'. The Blue Guide series continues to grow: there are now more than 50 titles in print with revised editions appearing regularly and many new Blue Guides in preparation.

'Blue Guides' is a registered trade mark.

The Tour de Vésone, Périgueux

INTRODUCTION

Aquitaine occupies the south-western angle or the bottom left-hand corner of France. An ancient name for a modern creation, the region was formed by the amalgamation of several Départements—Gironde, Dordogne, Lot-et-Garonne, Landes and Pyrénées-Atlantiques. Thus it encompasses many famous and historic titles within its boundaries, including the Périgord, Gascony, the Béarnais and the Basque country. It does not correspond exactly with the inheritance of Eleanor of Aquitaine, whose marriage to Henry II of England in 1152 began the English Empire in France not to mention three hundred years of trouble. More famously, modern Aquitaine includes some of the best known wine country in France, if not the whole world, including Bordeaux, Médoc, St-Émilion, Graves, Sauternes, and Barsac.

Not only is Aquitaine the land of wine but also quite literally the Land of Water. Flanked by the Atlantic and watered by the Pyrenees and the Massif Central, the region is sub-divided by one of the great river systems of western Europe. The Garonne is the principal river, rising far off in the central Pyrenees, and swelling into the great Gironde estuary with the help of the Dordogne. Other rivers flow from the lush north-western slopes of the Pyrenees, where icy torrents, or *Gaves*, tumble and rush even in the hottest of summers. Streams become rivers, still hurrying by, until, combining with the Adour, one of the loveliest of French rivers, they finally wind their way towards Bayonne and the sea. Rivers shape the countryside and many of the towns. Bordeaux, Périgueux, Agen, Bergerac and Pau all have handsome waterfronts while Bayonne is made by its twin rivers. Not surprisingly, watersports and boating activities feature strongly in the region's attractions.

A holiday in Aquitaine can be what you want it to be. The region has enormous beaches, mountains, caves, National Parks, wonderful walking country and spectacular drives. Its unique position offers access to a rich variety of neighbours, including northern Spain. Perhaps the main attraction to visitors is the rich and often violent history, expressed by hundreds of monuments from pre-history to the present day. South West France is a world centre for the study of our earliest ancestors. Caves and grottos were shaped, sculpted and painted, bringing us face to face with our most distant past. Prehistoric evidence apart, the natural wonders of Aquitaine are irresistible and easily accessible. More recent history is brought vividly to life by the medieval towns and castles which seemingly dot every hill and valley. The *bastide*, the planned and fortified town, is a constant feature of the region, commonly associated with a nearby medieval castle. The English and French fought over Aquitaine for centuries, building rival castles and competing towns and bequeathing one of the largest collections of medieval fortifications in Europe. In calmer days, many castles were rebuilt as elegant and imposing châteaux, whose conical and whimsical roofscapes pierce the sky. The south west seems to specialise in the more intimate country house, many still furnished and often inhabited by the families who built them.

The church too has left its mark upon Aquitaine. The kings of both England and France and their political allies vied to build splendid churches and monasteries. The cathedrals of Bordeaux, Bayonne and

Périgueux are all major works of architecture, while abbeys and priories are to be found in abundance. Tragically, the 16C Wars of Religion were fought most bitterly over the soil of Aquitaine, and the ruined state of church and castle more often recalls Protestant England than Catholic France.

The towns of South West France are very varied but nearly all delightful. Stone architecture is dominant, except in Bayonne which is heavily timbered. Bordeaux became rich in the 18C and refurbished itself with gusto. But it is perhaps the little towns and villages that linger in the mind, not just the famous names of Domme, Montpazier and Beynac, but also the quiet and unexpected ones such as Rions, Hastinques, St-Maurin, and the quite different but utterly disarming villages of the Basque lands.

Historical Introduction

Early-medieval France consisted of a King holding directly a Royal Domain, roughly the modern Ile de France surrounding Paris, and exacting authority over the great fiefdoms, that is the dukedoms and other territories, whose rulers owed homage and service to the King. Under Charlemagne, died 814, **Aquitainia** lay south of the Loire, excepting only the Mediterranean coast. The Treaty of Verdun, 843, broke up the Carolingian Empire amongst Charlemagne's quarrelsome grandsons, Francia falling to Charles the Bald, died 879. His ineffectual successors found it hard to wrest power from the local lords, who in practice ruled as petty kings. The Duchy of Aquitaine was one such area, at times consisting of much of south-western France plus Poitou, the Angoumois and parts of the Auvergne. Ecclesiastically, medieval Aquitaine had a metropolitan see at Bordeaux, whose territory extended north almost to the Loire, while the rest of the duchy was split between the metropolitans of Auch, Narbonne and Bourges. Modern Aquitaine contains most of the medieval duchy of that name, including the Agenais, Béarn, parts of Bigorre and about half the Dordogne.

In the 12C the Duchy passed to **Eleanor of Aquitaine**. Normally, French territory could not be held by a woman, though medieval Aquitaine, Brittany and Flanders were exceptions. The King of France, Louis VI, anxious to extend his real as well as supposed territorial authority, married Eleanor, daughter and heiress of Duke William of Aquitaine, to his son and heir, the future Louis VII, thus hoping to bequeath a greatly enlarged royal possession. Unfortunately, Louis VII was not for Eleanor, who found him deeply boring and sexless. While this was the experience of most married women in the Middle Ages, Eleanor's spirit and independent streak determined that she would do something about it. What she did rocked the Christian world and shaped the future of Aquitaine for three centuries. In 1152 Geoffrey Plantagenet, Count of Anjou, came to court with his 19-year-old son Henry. Eleanor, already 30, fell hopelessly in love with the boy, and decided there and then to elope with him. Louis fumed at first but upon reflection accepted that his loathing for his wife was such that he would release her, even at the cost of her enormous dowry. Thus, Eleanor got rid of her dull Louis, and married Henry. Within two years, Henry was King of England and thus began the **Plantagenet Empire in France**. Guienne and Gascony were united to form an English duchy of Aquitaine, and though in principal Henry still owed allegiance to Louis as his liege lord, the Kings of England considered Aquitaine as theirs. Henry already owned Anjou, to which he added Maine, Lorraine and Normandy. By 1160, he was ruler of an empire stretching unbroken from Scotland to the Pyrenees. Yet Eleanor's behaviour should have warned Henry about the people of his southern duchy. They were headstrong, fiercely independent and quarrelsome, some would say ungovernable. Technically, the King of England may have been their lord, but heaven help the king that tried to impose his will. In 1169, Eleanor gave Aquitaine to Richard, the future King of England, who, as Duke, paid homage to Louis of France in 1170.

Evidence suggests that the English gained little financially from their possession, while Aquitaine profited from being a producer of agricultural surpluses and a great exporter of wine. There was, however, a price to be paid. Successive kings of France eyed this lost region, together with the powerful county of Toulouse to the east. Toulouse toyed menacingly with the neighbouring powers in Spain, posing the threat of total secession from their notional allegiance to France. After a rather messy war between Henry III of England and Louis IX, the Treaty of Paris, 1259, ceded large areas of the Dordogne to the English, including the cities of Périgueux, Limoges and Cahors. However, the treaty was unpopular, the French quickly regretting their generosity, and the area became the scene of continual local fighting. This became more serious in the reign of Philip IV (le Bel; died 314), who struggled for a dozen years against the armies of the English Edward I.

War became the constant way of life for the whole region, with the **Hundred Years War** (1337–1453) merely a more intensive period. In the 13C Aquitaine was reorganised by the English, Guienne being lopped from Aquitaine and united with sections of the Bordelais, Périgord, Limousin and Quercy. In 1327, sections of Aquitaine were ceded back to the French but a few years later, Edward III of England made his claim to the vacant French throne by right of his mother, the murderous Isabella. The French would not accept the King of England as their king, effectively adding France to his Empire. The throne was offered to someone else. For the next 120 years, the rulers of the two kingdoms slogged it out, usually over the soil of south-western France. Towns, castles and whole regions changed hands in a seemingly endless cycle of siege, battle and intrigue. Finally, in 1453, the last English troops were defeated in Aquitaine, and Charles VII took the whole region as spoil.

This did not suit everyone. The peoples of Bordeaux and Bayonne, and others loyal to the old regime were persecuted and penalised. Bordeaux remained obstinate for centuries. The French kings were not subtle in their actions, levying crippling taxes which compounded the economic woes.

But the repercussions of the English defeat were as nothing compared with the religious turmoil of the 16C. Trading links with Flanders proved important in the spread of Protestantism in south west France. Not just the ideas of Luther, but the more radical Calvin and Zwingli. French Protestants, known to history as the Huguenots, combined much of the zeal and absolutist faith of their northern counterparts and the new religion spread rapidly across the region. Some towns proved most responsive—Bordeaux, Bergerac etc. while others remained staunch bastions of the old faith. The dynastic problems of the French crown did not help matters, kings dying childless in rapid succession. Catherine de Medici, mother and virtual ruler over her numerous royal offspring, fought to maintain the unity of the kingdom and its Catholic faith. In the troubles that led to the terrible **Wars of Religion**, both sides schemed, both sides committed atrocities, neither side acted with any spirit of Christian charity or understanding. When actual war broke out in 1572, much of Aquitaine was Huguenot, including the Béarnais and its Protestant rulers, the Albrets. Their rise to prominence stemmed from the marriage in 1527 of Henri d'Albret, styled King of Navarre, also Lord of Béarn, Count of Foix and Bigorre, to Marguérite d'Angoulême, sister of Francis I. Their daughter and heiress, Jeanne, married Antoine de Bourbon, a direct descendant of Louis VIII, died 1226, thus creating an alternative line for a French throne rapidly running out of claimants. Jeanne was a convinced Huguenot, a faith she passed on to her son and heir, Henry Bourbon. Henry married Marguérite de Valois, sister of Charles IX, died 1574, and was eventually named heir to the last of the Valois kings, Henry III, died 1589. This makes the succession of the Bourbons from Pau sound easy. It was not. There were dreadful massacres, violent uprisings, families were torn apart, towns and villages burnt, and trade ruined. The lasting legacy in Aquitaine is the shortage of religious art and objects from the whole period before c 1570, the great number of repairs and reconstructions evident in the region's religious and other buildings, and the spate of new châteaux built or rebuilt after the war ended in 1589.

The 17C proved no less eventful, Aquitaine being caught up in the general discontent with the increasingly centralised and absolute monarchy of Louis XIII. Uprisings, known as the *Frondes*, caused disruption of life and trade, and brought the power of the French kings and their proxies to bear on the whole area. Castles were smashed and populations punished. Yet Aquitaine survived the **Thirty Years War** virtually unscathed, and lay apart from the warring terrain of Louis XIV's belligerent reign. In the 18C much of Aquitaine grew rich in contented obscurity. Aristocratic familes milked the land and its peasants, towns steadied and trade flourished. **Bordeaux** became the dominant regional centre, expressing its wealth in considerable works of town planning and expansion. Slavery added to its income, and of course, the wine trade continued to enrich the country landowners. If the French aristocracy did not foresee the events of 1789, then for much of the time they never noticed the peasants nor had they the slightest interest in their welfare. But the **Revolution** that shook the world was not led by the peasantry but by the urban middle classes. Bordeaux played a crucial role in the Revolution, its moderate deputies, called the Girondists, attempting to rein in the more radical and murderous elements. In the short term they lost both their cause and their heads, but in the longer term, their brand of moderation won the day. But not without yet another great war.

The **Napoleonic Wars** affected Aquitaine because Bordeaux was a major port, and because the region lay on the main route to Spain. The moment Spain and Portugal became involved, and the English under Wellington began campaigning in Iberia, Aquitaine was at war. In 1813, Wellington crossed the Pyrenees to confront the French army under Soult. Defeated at Bayonne, the French scattered but Bayonne held out tenaciously behind its impressive Renaissance walls. Only after Paris had fallen to the Allies did Bayonne make terms.

For the first half of the 19C Aquitaine settled back into its rural calm. Wine production increased, the classification of the wines was established and international trade grew. Then came **phylloxera**, a disease capable of wiping out a region's entire wine production. It did this to Aquitaine. The only solution was to start all over again with clean stock, mostly imported from vines grown from plants originally exported from Aquitaine to America. It took half a century to recover the trade but production has never regained the volume of the early 19C. In other respects, Aquitaine gained a new industry, **tourism**. The coastal towns were the first to grow, especially Biarritz, much favoured by the court of Napoleon III and his Spanish wife, Eugénie. Then it was the turn of the mountain spas, to be followed in the 20C by winter sports and summer beaches. The discovery of gas around Pau in 1951 and the development of the petro chemical industry represents the one major industrialised element in what has remained a predominantly rural region.

Art and Architecture

Aquitaine is home to one of the world's most important collections of **prehistoric painting and sculpture**. Of 172 recorded sites in France with surviving rock painting or decoration, more than 100 occur in southwestern France, with the Dordogne and the Pyrenees showing the greatest concentrations. The practice of cave or shelter decoration stems from the Upper Palaeolithic peoples, hunters and gatherers living nearly 40,000 years ago. Harsh climatic conditions, particularly following the last Ice Age, caused them to find shelter in caves and cliffsides, usually close to water. The apparent inaccessibility of many of today's sites reflects their great age—the rivers have gone on carving away at the landscape, leaving the early settlements high and dry.

Cave art reflects the life of the artists, concentrating on the animals of the era, most notably the bison and the horse, possible hunting scenes, sometimes patterns and, rarely, human representation. The purpose for the designs can only be guessed at. Paint pigments come from natural sources—red, brown and yellow from ochres of iron oxide, while manganese dioxide or simple charcoal could be used as black. The presence of the latter has assisted with radiocarbon dating. Recent research suggests the presence of a binder, perhaps talc or a potassium variety. Paint was applied with the fingers or a simple brush. Some evidence suggests that it could be blown through a tube or direct from the mouth, while other surfaces indicate dry powder blown from the hand. Occasionally, several colours are used together, while at Lascaux, the painters took advantage of the natural colours of the rock surface. Most schemes combine painting with engraving while some sites also contain sculpture, or at least animals and other forms are created in part taking advantage of the natural formation of the rock, while in other sites, deep relief was created with the use of primitive picks. Carved objects were also found, though these are now to be seen only in museums. In Aquitaine, most of the sites date from the period known as Magdalenian, currently put between c 19,000 and 10,000 BC. Even in the darkest caves, artists worked by the limited light of small oil lamps, many of which have been discovered in the Périgord.

The Roman period is represented in painting, sculpture, mosaic art, and architecture. The Tour du Vésone (Périgueux) is one of the best preserved centrally planned temples in France, while civic fortifications can be found in Périgueux, Bayonne and Dax. Villas have been excavated in Périgueux, Plassac and Sorde-l'Abbaye, with accompanying mosaic floors and painting fragments. The collections in Bordeaux are especially fine. The Palais Gallien, also in Bordeaux, represents the only large section of an amphitheatre still to be seen. Good Roman museums can be found in Bordeaux, Périgueux, and the local collections at Arthous, Plassac and Sorde-l'Abbaye.

Medieval architecture is represented by churches, castles and domestic buildings. While several of the pilgrimage routes to Spain crossed the region, Aquitaine has no surviving examples of the standard Romanesque pilgrimage church. It has, however, oustanding examples of a quite different design, the domed church, and there is evidence of more than sixty of these in south west France. St. Etienne in Périgueux may be the earliest, St-Front is certainly the most ambitious. The churches are basically unaisled, with big square bays, pointed arches and giant stone domes on pendentives. Some, like St-Avit-Sénieur, have lost their domes but the distinctive plan remains. The cathedral of Bordeaux may have been another example though the surviving Romanesque work is ambiguous. Other outstanding Romanesque churches survive at Layrac, Moirax, Oloron-Ste-Marie and St-Sever. Sculpture is best seen at Aire-sur-l'Adour, Blasimon, Bordeaux, Hagetmut, La Sauve, Morlaas and St-Sever.

The Gothic period is dominated by the cathedral of Bayonne, a northern French piece transposed to the south. It is a fine work if a little mechanical. The same cannot be said of Bordeaux cathedral, which is a delightful mess, style piled upon style and a mass of stitched-up compromises. This additive approach is perhaps the result of English influence, though surprisingly, the medieval architecture of Aquitaine remains strongly French. By contrast, St-Michel in Bordeaux is a set-piece of late-Gothic, where variety is a stylistic ploy. Minor Gothic works can be seen in the many abbey buildings, Arthous, Blasimon, Cadouin, St-Amand-de-Coly etc. Aquitaine is not rich in Gothic sculpture, though St-Seurin, Bordeaux proves an exception, while the other churches in that city preserve large numbers of alabaster works which may be English.

Castles form a huge block of the region's medieval buildings, with Castelnaud, Beynac and Biron being perhaps the finest. Others from the late Middle Ages are more house than fortress—who could forget the shock of les Bories or the domestic charm of Morlanne.

Medieval towns abound, with Monpazier, Périgueux, St-Macaire and Sarlat grabbing the limelight. Courtyards are characteristic features, usually containing stair turrets and occasionally open wooden landings. Stone is the *lingua franca* of the region, though timber-framing dominates the Bayonne region and some of the Basque villages. Brick is rare in most of Aquitaine, though see the châteaux of Pau and Morlanne and the great brick friar's church at Agen—the latter perhaps not surprising as Agen is near to the major brick zone around Toulouse.

The Renaissance spread into Aquitaine in the early years of the 16C. Its influence can be seen on hundreds of town houses from Bordeaux to Sarlat, while particularly swish examples occur in Périgueux. The best Renaissance château must be Puyguilhem from the earliest phase, Lanquais from the later 16C. Both Pau and Hautefort look terrific from the outside. Notre-Dame in Bordeaux is perhaps the region's best Renaissance church. The city also boasts the finest **Classical** domestic buildings, the 18C Grand Théâtre being outstanding, while Renaissance fortifications are well seen at both Bayonne and Blaye. The Basque country has its own distinct architectural traditions, with characteristic, unaisled but galleried churches, and large, composite houses placed gable-end to the street.

Nineteenth-century work is less formidable, though the severe restoration of many earlier buildings has left an indelible mark. The most sensational contemporary work must be the interiors at Roquetaillade by Viollet le Duc, while Bordeaux railway station stands in the proud French tradition of style and function.

Modern architecture tends to be found on the fringes of towns, the Cité Mondiale des Vins et Spiritueux on the Bordeaux waterfront being a notable exception.

Glossary

Ambulatory, curving aisle around apse of church

Atlantes, supporting columns or members in male form

Apse, semicircular termination of church plan, ususally to east and containing altar

Archivolt, series of carved mouldings surrounding a door or window

Aumbry, small wall-safe near altar, for storing sacred vessels

Bailey, outer enclosure of castle

Barrel vault, semicircular tunnel vault, round or pointed

Bartizan, small turret corbelled out, usually on a defensive angle

Bastide, planned, fortified town, often enjoying tax privileges. Common in southern France and Aquitaine from the 13C

Bastion, projecting fortified tower, curved, polygonal or square

Billet, a roll moulding usually applied to arches in staccato fashion

Cabanos, name given to small dry-stone circular huts, commonly roofed with corbelled domes

Chevet, French term for apse and ambulatory, often with radiating chapels

Colombages, French for half-timbered

Corbel, stone block cantilevered from wall to act as support

Flamboyant, style of Gothic architecture current in France c 1400–1550

Fronton, exterior wall, usually pink, for the playing of paloto

Garde-robe, medieval name for a lavatory

Glacis, sloping or stepped descent of wall, commonly within a window opening

Groined vaults, intersecting squares of tunnel vaults creating diagonal stress without structural ribs

Lauzes, roofing fabric derived from split or frost shattered stone

Lierne, short rib in Gothic vaulting, neither springing from the wall nor intersecting at the centre

Machicolations, parapets supported by brackets on the outside of castle walls and towers, with openings in floor through which to drop missiles

Pendentive, curved triangular wall forming transition from wall or corner support to the base of a dome

Pilaster, half-pier or column built into wall or major support

Piscina, small cupboard or niche for washing the sacred vessels during mass.

Rayonnant, style of 13C Gothic, characterised by overlaid tracery patterns and refined details, common around Paris and royal projects

Squinch, small arch forming triangular bridge, cutting the corners of a square shape to create an octagonal base for a dome.

Stellar vaults, rib vaults creating a star-burst pattern with tiercerons and liernes

Tierceron, additional rib in Gothic vaulting, not intersecting at the centre

Transverse arch, in stone vaulting, the arch crossing the space at right angles to wall and defining the vault bays

Tribune, the vaulted middle storey of a church interior

Triforium, a passage cut within the thickness of a wall, usually the middle storey of a church interior

Tympanum, area between square-topped door or window and round or pointed arched surround. Commonly decorated

Voussoir, one of a series of blocks forming an arch

Bibliography

General
Three Rivers of France: Dordogne, Lot, Tarn, F.White, Faber & Faber

Art and Architecture
The Dawn of European Art: an introduction to Palaeolithic Cave Paintings, A. Leroi-Gourhan, Cambridge University Press
The Cave Artists, A. Sieveking, Thames & Hudson
Carolingian and Romanesque Architecture, K. Conant, Penguin Pelican
Gothic Architecture, L. Grodecki, Faber & Faber
Art and Architecture in France, 1500–1700, A. Blunt, Penguin Pelican

History
The Capetian Kings of France, Fawtier, Macmillan
The Norman Empire, J. La Patourel
The Hundred Years War, E. Perroy
Gascony, England's First Colony, 1204–1453, M. Labarge
Concise History of France, Marshall Davidson, Cassell

Works in French
Pays et Gens d'Aquitaine, Larousse (Reader's Digest)
La Côte Basque, Le Pays Basque, J. Casenave, Editions Lavielle
La Vie Intellectuelle en Périgord, 1556–1880, P. Barrière, Delmas
Histoire du Périgord, Privat
Périgord, A. Maurois, Hachette
Itinéraires Romans en Périgord, Zodiaque
Pyrénées romanes, Guyenne romane, Editions Desclee de Brouwer
Le Guide de Châteaux de France; Gers-Gironde, Hermé
Oeuvres romanesque, F. Mauriac (literature)
Cuisine Landaise, E. & J. de Rivoyre, Editions Denoël
Cuisine et Vins en France, Larousse

Using this Guide

South West France is a large and varied region, ranging from the rolling countryside of the Périgord to the stony heights of the Pyrenees. It has many famous and distinct parts, such as the Dordogne, and it will only be the traveller with much time and transport who could hope to cover most of the area in a single visit. The guide is laid out to reflect this fact, and that a number of towns and centres make themselves obvious as bases. Therefore, this Blue Guide will concentrate on those centres, providing additional excursions that can be made from them but returning each time to base. Of course, any of these routes can be subdivided depending on time and inclination, and some will cut straight in half to be spread over two days while others offer the possibility of a mid-stream overnight halt. In addition, some cross-country routes are included, especially if they make sense within a short holiday. Again, most of these cross routes will also cut into sensible chunks for a day-return visit.

Climate

It is difficult to generalise about the climate of south west France given that the region includes some of the highest mountains in Europe, a long coastal strip on the Atlantic, and inland areas as varied as the Garonne valley and the Périgord. Aquitaine is the land of water. It is lush and full of rivers. All that water comes from somewhere, and the short answer is the sky. Much of the region, especially the west, is lashed by Atlantic rain, even in summer. The mountains make it worse and cloud-bursts flooding towns are not uncommon, particularly in spring and early summer. The enormous development of winter sports in the Pyrenees tells its own story—the winters are cold and hard, there is a lot of snow, and the spring is late. Away from the mountains, the winters are relatively mild, more so towards Bordeaux where the temperature rarely drops below 10 degrees C. Summer highs are around 25 degrees C and the area is seldom humid. However, the Dordogne can be bitter in winter and can often disappear beneath a lingering cloud of damp fog. Even in summer, the Dordogne can develop a shroud of dank cloud, lowering the temperature and the light. It can stick around for days on end. Fogs of another kind can affect the Landes, dust-storms. Fine clouds of wind-blown sand blow east from the coast and inland areas, sometimes penetrating as far as Agen. The best times to visit are May and June, despite the risk of a soaking, and late summer into autumn. Avoid July and August; this is nothing to do with the weather, but Aquitaine is simply overrun.

Highlights of the region

Pays. Double asterisk: the valleys of the Dordogne, Adour and Vézère, the Gaves de Pau, d'Aspe, d'Oloron and Nive, the Gironde estuary, the forests of the Landes, the mountains and passes of the Pyrenees. Single asterisk: the valleys of the Isle and Dronne, the Bassin d'Arachon, *la côte d'argent*, the coast at Biarritz, the pays d'Albret and the Périgord.

Cities and larger towns. Double asterisk: Bayonne, Bordeaux and Périgueux. Single asterisk: Agen and Pau.

Smaller towns and villages: Double asterisk: Aïnhoa, Beynac, Brantôme, Espelette, Monpazier, Sarlat-la-Canéda, St-Émilion, St-Jean de Côle, St-Léon-sur-Vézère, St-Macaire, St-Maurin. Single asterisk: Aydius, Domme, Labastide-d'Armagnac, Salies-de-Béarn and Sauveterre-de-Béarn.

Prehistoric sites. Double asterisk: Les Eyzies-de-Tayac. Single asterisk: Lascaux II.

Roman sites, monuments and museums. Double asterisk: Périgueux, Plassac and Sorde-l'Abbaye. Single asterisk: Bordeaux, Dax, Bayonne.

Medieval churches. Double asterisk: Bayonne, Bordeaux and Périgueux. Single asterisk: Aire-sur-l'Adour, Artous, Bazas, Blasimon, Cadouin, Hagetmut, Moirax, Oloron-Ste-Marie, St-Sever, la Sauve and Uzeste.

Later churches. Double asterisk: Espelette. Single asterisk: Aïnhoa, Bordeaux and Roquetaillarde.

Castles and châteaux. Double asterisk: Blaye, Castelnaud, Lanquais, Morlanne, Puyguillhem and Roquetaillade. Single asterisk: Beynac, Biron, Bourdeilles, Cadillac, Hautfort, Losse, Pau and Villandraut.

Civic buildings. Double asterisk: The Grand Théâtre, Bordeaux. La Réole.

Museums and art galleries. Double asterisk: Bayonne, Bordeaux and Périgueux. Single asterisk: Agen.

Getting there

Tourist Information

The French Government Tourist Office produces annually a Reference Guide for the traveller in France, and for the cost of postage (at the time of writing £1.35) will send a 24-page brochure on Aquitaine. The London office is at 178 Piccadilly, W1V 0AL. Tel. 071-493 7622, fax 071-493 6594. In the USA you can contact them at 610 Fifth Avenue, Suite 222, New York NY 10020-2452. Tel. (212) 757 11 25, fax (212) 247 64 68. In Canada the address is 1981 Avenue McGill College, Suite 490, Montreal QUE H3A 2W9. Tel. (514) 288 42 64, fax (514) 845 48 68.

French Government Tourist Offices, local travel agents, and national newspapers are the best sources of information about the range of inclusive and accommodation-only holidays available. Several companies offer cultural tours with expert lecturers. These include Page and Moy, 136–140 London Road, Leicester LE2 1EN (tel. 0533 552521, fax 0533 549949), Specialtours, 81a Elizabeth Street, London SW1W 9PG (tel. 071-730 2297, fax 071-730 3138), Prospect Music and Art, 458–458 Chiswick High Road, London W4 5TT (tel. 081-995 2151, fax. 081-742 1969), Martin Randall Tours, 10 Barley Mow Passage, London W4 4PH (tel. 081-995 3642, fax 081-742 1066), Swan Hellenic, 77 New Oxford Street, London WC1A 1PP (tel. 071-831 1515, fax 071-831 1280).

Air

It is possible to fly direct from London Gatwick (British Airways, 081 879 4000, Euro Express tel. 0444 235678) to Bordeaux or from London Heathrow (Air France 081 742 6600) to Toulouse. Flights also connect Bordeaux with Manchester while flights direct to Lourdes leave from many UK airports. From Paris, flights connect with Agen, Bergerac, Biarritz, Bordeaux, Pau and Périgueux. Bordeaux Mérignac airport lies some 6km west of the centre. There is a bus service. Air Inter local number, 56 13 10 10.

Rail

The best railroute from Paris is the direct TGV service from Montparnasse, arriving in Bordeaux in under three hours. The only problem is crossing Paris if you are coming from the UK via the Channel Tunnel/ferry and the Gare du Nord. Montparnasse is the least well served Paris station by public transport, the metro being a long walk. Allow at least 30 minutes longer than you anticipated. Paris–Bordeaux trains continue to Bayonne, Biarritz and the Basque border towns en route for Spain. From Biarritz and Bayonne, a further service, with TGV, connects with Orthez and Pau. The Bordeaux–Toulouse service stops at many towns along the Garonne including Agen. Bordeaux is also connected with Bergerac and Périgueux, whence a rather roundabout route also connects with Les Eyzies and the Dordogne.

French Railways have an information office in London, 179 Piccadilly, London, W1V 0AU. Tel 071-409 3518.

Car

Currently, crossing to France with the car involves either a ferry trip via Dover or Folkestone, or a longer trip via one of the south coast ports. P&O (tel 0304 203000) and Sealink Stena (tel. 0233 647022) cross from Dover to Calais in 75–90 minutes. Hoverspeed Seacat (tel 0304 240241) from Folkestone reaches Boulogne in roughly 45 minutes. Eurotunnel's Le Shuttle cross-channel car passenger service carries cars, motorcycles, and coaches on a rail 'loop' between Folkestone and Calais 24 hours a day, every day of the year. The crossing time between platforms is about 35 minutes. The French terminal connects directly with the Calais–Lille–Paris motorway.

Driving from the UK to Aquitaine and the Dordogne is complicated by Paris. The new motorway bypassing the capital passes east, connecting with the infamous Autoroute du Soleil heading south. The motorway for Bordeaux, the A10, heads south west from the capital, necessitating a one-third circuit of the *péripherique*, not everyone's favourite occupation. An alternative is to cross from Portsmouth to Caen and head south cross-country, picking up the motorway system on the Loire.

Motorway connections within Aquitaine are good, with the A10 from Paris and the north, the A62 along the Garonne towards Toulouse and the Mediterranean, the A63 crossing into Spain and the A64 from Bayonne to Pau and beyond. The N10 between Bordeaux and Bayonne has yet to be upgraded as motorway all the way but is still a reasonably quiet route. Bordeaux will soon have a complete motorway ring.

Touring the region

Car

Like anywhere in Europe, traffic conditions in the south west range from delightful to dreadful. The *pay* motorways are surprisingly empty, except around Bordeaux, which are free and clogged. The Périgord country roads can be blissful, though the classic Dordogne area suffers from a surfeit of caravans. Some of the towns have rather horrendous approaches, full of DIY stores and traffic lights. Good map-reading skills are a great help as routes to historic centres are often not the most obvious ones.

If you arrive in Aquitaine by air or train, then hiring a car is the best option, though probably more expensive than driving from the UK. Car hire is available from many centres, especially Bordeaux, where major firms congregate around the central railway station. Do not drive in Bordeaux. Petrol costs more than in the UK, though Diesel is cheaper. Supermarkets offer the best prices and will take British Visa cards. Sundays are a problem as nearly all petrol stations are closed. Many also close at lunchtime and on Saturday afternoon. Always have a full tank by Saturday morning. The worst bottlenecks at present include the Pont d'Aquitaine at Bordeaux, leading to the A10 and the road from Périgueux to Bordeaux, the N89, which is a slog. The bypass soon to open around Libourne may ease another bad spot.

In general the roads are good, even in remote areas. Quite often, even the main routes have little traffic though heavy lorries often plod along quite unsuitable back roads. The Michelin Green Routes are always worth investigating. The mountain roads in the Pyrenees should be approached with great caution. Weather conditions are volatile and as a rule, if you can not see the peaks, do not go near them. Tourist Offices en route post weather and road conditions for the week. Read them. If a road is clearly closed for bad weather, stay away.

Parking is no great problem in the smaller towns. Many, like Agen, have large free parks, close enough to the centre to walk. In others, pay parking might have to be used, though it is often free for several hours around lunchtime. Avoid underground or multi-storey car parks as theft is rife. Pau has parking problems, if staying check that your hotel has its own space. Most central hotels do not. The worst problem is Bordeaux for, though huge car parks line the riverside, they are expensive and not intended for tourist use. If you have to park, try the northern sector of the Esplanade des Quinconces, intended for longer-term parking, or park out of the centre and take a bus in. Few hotels in the centre have parking, indeed some are almost impossible to reach unless you are on foot. If you intend renting a car from Bordeaux, pick it up only on the day you intend to depart. Having a car in Bordeaux is more trouble than it is worth.

Public transport

In towns, it is usually necessary to purchase bus tickets before boarding. Check locally. *Tabacs* and news-stands are the commonest outlets. Tickets must usually be punched using a special machine located near the back door. This dates and times your journey. It is an offence not to date-validate your ticket in this way. Some towns allow multiple journeys on a single stamped ticket within a fixed time. There are many rural bus services across Aquitaine, though times and routes often change and it is wise to enquire locally. Most places are connected, even remote villages, although some routes only operate during school terms. Taxi prices are about the same as in Britain and should always be metered. Only use taxis licensed by the local authority, there are many cowboy drivers touting for trade, particularly at railway stations.

Train services are as above. Stations will accept British Visa cards and often tickets can be purchased from automatic machines, though at present they will not accept British Visa cards. Many machines also supply time-table information. As with buses, tickets must be validated at the start of your journey. This is usually done by inserting the ticket into an orange box near the platform entrance. Only if the box clicks and snips a portion of the ticket has it been sucessfully validated. Check the back for a printed date to make sure. Fines may be imposed by inspectors who detect unvalidated tickets on a train. They have no mercy on hapless tourists.

Cycling

Aquitaine is mostly good cycling country. The Landes is generally flat while the river valleys provide relatively easy access into the interior. The Pyrenees is specialist territory. Cycling is much encouraged in France and as a sport is more highly regarded than in the UK. French motorists are generally more considerate to cyclists than you might expect, but beware of the many non-French drivers who are not. Special routes for walkers and cyclists are marked everywhere. Lists and details of routes are often collated and published by region—see *Les topo-guides randonées pédestres* at VTT, *la Régie départementale du tourisme de la Dordogne*, FF50, the free *Guide des landes 'Découverte à pied, à vélo'*, from the Tourist Offices in Landes, and *Lot-et-Garonne, 89 itinéraires cyclo*, again on offer from the tourist offices in the region (FF30). For general cycling information contact the Fédération Française de Cyclotourisme (FFCT), 22, Résidence La Brédinière, la Brède, 33650. Tel 56 20 34 96. The national organisation is at 8, Rue Jean-Marie Iégo, 75013, Paris. Tel 45 80 3 21, fax 45 88 01 41.

Special package deals are available for cyclists including route maps, booked accommodation (half-board, 2-star, assistance and sometimes baggage transfers. Contact the relevant regional tourist offices, asking for details of Randonées VTT.

Passports

These are still necessary despite EC attempts to abolish them. Crossing from France into Spain rarely involves any formality, indeed, on the mountain roads you will probably not realise you have done it.

Money

Currently, the franc is strong, making Aquitaine rather pricey. Smaller towns still offer outstanding value both in hotels and meals. Even in Bordeaux, hotel prices are well below the British norm. Fixed-price menus are usually a bargain.

Credit cards. American Express, Carte Bleue (Visa/Barclaycard), Diners Club and Eurocard (Mastercard/Access) are widely accepted in shops, hotels and restaurants. Some of these can also be used at petrol stations. It is important to check the receipt as in France no decimal point is shown between *Francs* and *centimes*.

Unlimited currency may be taken into France but must be declared if bank notes to the value of 50,000FF or more are likely to be re-exported.

Information Offices

Tourist offices, or *syndicats*, exist in most towns and in many villages. For details of these, see the individual entries in the routes. They can provide you with information on accommodation, restaurants, entertainments and local transport.

The main offices are in the various *départements* and are:

Dordogne, Office Départemental de Tourisme de la Dordogne, Loisirs

Accueil Dordogne, 16, Rue Président Wilson, 240009 Périgueux Cédex. Tel 53 53 44 35, fax 53 09 51 41.

Gironde, Comité Départemental de Tourisme de la Gironde, Loisirs Accueil Gironde, 24, Rue Esprit des Lois, 3 3000 Bordeaux. Tel 56 52 61 10, fax 56 81 09 99.

Landes, Comité Départemental de Tourisme des Landes, 22, Cours Victor Hugo BP 407, 40012 Mont de Marsan Cédex. Tel 58 06 89 89m fax 58 06 90 90.

Béarn, Agence Touristique de Béarn—Maison du Tourisme, Rue Jean-Jacques de Monnaix, BP 816, 64008 Pau Cédex. Tel 59 30 01 30, fax 59 02 52 75.

Pays Basque, Agence de Tourisme de Pays Basque, BP247—64108 Bayonne Cédex. Tel. 59 59 28 77, fax 59 25 48 90.

Lot-et-Garonne, Comité Départemental de Tourisme du Lot-et-Garonne, Loisirs Accueil Lot-et-Garonne, 4, Rue André Chénier, BP158, 47005 Agen Cédex. Tel 53 66 14 14, fax 53 68 25 42.

The Office de Tourisme at **Bordeaux**, 12 Cours du Juillet, 33080, tel. 56 44 28 41, the offices at the railway station and the airport, and also the Office de Tourisme at **Biarritz**, Square d'Ixelles, 64200, tel. 59 24 20 24, are open every day and will make hotel bookings the same day or up to eight days in advance for a small fee.

Two large National Parks exist within or partly within Aquitaine. For further information contact the **Parc National des Pyrénées**, 59, Route de Pau, 65000 Tarbes, tel 62 93 30 60 and **Parc Régional des Landes de Gascogne**, 33830 Belin-Beliet, tel 56 88 06 06.

Maps

Michelin produce the standard maps for the region in their 1/200000 series. These have all major and minor roads, monuments and places of interest, indications of terrain and recommended picturesque 'Green Routes'. Four maps are needed for complete coverage—234 (*Aquitaine*), 235 (*Midi Pyrénées*), 239 (*Auvergne Limousin*) and 223 (*Poitou-Charentes*). There is also the comprehensive Michelin *Road Atlas of France* (published in the UK by Hamlyn), updated most years, and avoiding the awkward folding and refolding of individually large single maps. The Institut Géographique National also produces a series covering the area to a scale of 1/125000, with a multi-language text. These have especially useful symbols for sporting activities. One map covers the whole of Aquitaine (*Région Aquitaine*) while other maps cover the individual *départements*—Gironde, Dordogne, Lot-et-Garonne, Landes etc. They have clearer coverage of train routes than Michelin. Their more detailed maps include *Bordeaux/Périgueux* (47), *Périgueux* (48), *Bordeaux/Landes* (55), *Agen* (56), *Bayonne/Landes* (62), *Bayonne/Pau* (69), *Pau/Pyrénées* (70). Available at tourist offices.

The Conseil Général of Gironde have produced a series of walking, cycling or hiking maps for several areas including La Haute Lande Girondine (includes Villandraut and Uzeste), le Pays de Podensac (directly over the river from Cadillac), le Pays de Langon (including Roquetaillarde), le Pays de Saint-Macaire and le Hait Entre-Deux-Mers. Apart from the easy to read maps with their symbols for features of interest, the text (in French, but not difficult), includes useful addresses, equestrian and other sporting centres, accommodation and restaurants, camp sites etc. Maps are free, ask at tourist offices.

Accommodation

In 1994, Aquitaine could offer more than 1500 **hotels**, over 300 of which were not officially listed. France operates a system of star rating for its hotels, no stars at all being the simplest. Many country and village establishments fall into the latter category, though they often prove perfectly adequate for a short stay. The star system seems quite arbitrary, and can depend more on local room shortage than actual comfort. Stars are no guide to prices or comfort, particularly in the two and three-star range. Often, you are better off at a cheaper two-star than at a more expensive three. Prices, which should be posted outside or at least in a window, are for the room, not per person. Check if it includes taxes. Prices must be displayed within the room by law. Some hotels such as the *Logis de France* offer half-board, room, breakfast and dinner. Sometimes this represents a good deal, especially if the food comes recommended. On other occasions, a cheap room rate is accompanied by an expensive and obligatory dinner. The best deal is always a hotel without a restaurant, leaving you free to choose the evening meal you want. Hotels rarely include breakfast in the room price. See whether it is worth the money—it rarely is. No hotel will quibble if you ask to see the room before deciding. Check for noise, a narrow street with late-night traffic or the ubiquitous disco. Some of the finest hotels in the region prove noisy disasters, particularly at weekends. All-night parties, discos or late-night basement clubs can transform your idyllic surroundings into a vision of hell. Wedding parties are the worst, still going strong in the early hours. Ask at reception before deciding.

Bordeaux has special problems if you are arriving by car. Few hotels have parking and if they do, you will have to pay a high price for it. Public parking is extremely difficult to find, expensive and risky. If you have to stay in Bordeaux with a car, try hotels further from the centre and use public transport. Ideally, stay in a nearby town with a direct train connection and save yourself a lot of hassle. Pau has similar problems.

Hotel lists are available from the French Government Tourist Office in London, or from Tourisme d'Aquitaine, Rue Réne Cassin, 33049 Bordeaux Cédex, tel 56 39 88 88, fax 56 43 07 63. Lists of the *Logis de France* can be gained by writing to the Féderation Nationale des Logis de France, 83 avenue d'Italie, 75013 Paris, tel 16 1 45 84 70 00.

Gîtes, or **self-catering accommodation**, usually rural, can offer economic solutions to family holidays. There is an official booking service requiring a small annual fee. Details from the French Government Tourist Office in London. In addition, Aquitaine offers **Chambre d'Hôte** (bed and breakfast), and farm accommodation, usually signposted as *Bienvenue à la ferme*.

Details of all these, plus speciality food outlets and rural activity holidays can be had from the Chambre Régionale d'Agriculture (CRAA), 57, Cours Xavier Arnozan, 33000 Bordeaux, tel 56 51 19 343, fax 56 48 25 35. Individual area addresses are, for Dordogne, Chambre d'Agriculture de la Dordogne, 4–6 Place Francheville, 24016, Périgueux Cédex, tel 53 09 26 26, fax 53 53 43 13, for Landes, Relais des Gîtes de France, Chambre d'Agriculture des Landes, Cité Galliane, BP279, 40005 Mont-de-Marsan Cédex, tel 58 46 10 45, fax 58 06 87 05, for Lot-et-Garonne, Agriculture et Tourisme, Chambre d'Agriculture du Lot-et-Garonne, 271 rue Pechabout, BP349 Agen Cédex, tel 53 96 44 99, fax 53 68 04 70, and for Pyrénées-Atlantiques, Association des Gîtes et de l'Accueil à la Ferme, 124 boulevard Tourasse, 64078 Pau Cédex, tel 59 59 80 13.

Opening times

There are 65 **museums** listed in Aquitaine. Many are closed on Tuesdays though this is by no means uniform. Most close at lunchtime, 12.00–14.00. In winter, closing time is generally 17.00. In summer, April to November, it is usually 18.00. Some museums have very civilised evening opening and some have free days. Smaller museums may open only in season, that is in July and August. This particularly applies to local and private museums. Always check with a tourist office before making a special trip to a particular museum or gallery.

Monuments such as **châteaux**, have a variety of opening times. State-owned buildings tend to close between 15 December and February, though not all. Most close for lunch (12.00–14.00) and many open earlier in the summer months (09.00 rather than 10.00) and stay open longer in the evening. July and August can see some monuments open until 19.00. Enquire locally. Private monuments such as lived-in châteaux can and do make up their own opening times each season. Most are open only in the afternoon and on certain days. Many restrict opening to July and August.

Prehistoric monuments again vary in their opening times. Lascaux II shuts down in January, and closes on Mondays and lunchtimes for the rest of the year except in July and August, when it stays open all day, every day. Combarelles opens every day except Wednesdays and holidays, but for strictly limited times, while Font de Gaume opens all year round except Tuesdays. Careful planning is neccessary.

Churches are a minefield. The French still insist on locking nearly all major churches for at least two hours if not more in the middle of the day. Assume that they all do it and be pleasantly surprised by those that do not. St-Etienne de la Cité, Périgueux, is often left open but precious few others. Minor, though no less interesting churches range from being open all hours to being firmly locked. The latter can usually be overcome by asking around. This tends to be a good way to see odd and unexpected places. Donations are usually expected if someone has to come with you.

Festivals

January — Gironde
Salon des Antiquaires, Bordeaux

February — Gironde
Promenade des Boeufs Gras, Bazas

March — Dordogne
Festival de Danse Choregora, Périgueux
Festival de Musique des Collégiens, Périgueux

April — Gironde
Flower Festival, Bordeaux
Brocante de Printemps, Bordeaux
Open weekend for wine châteaux, Médoc
Foire aux Chevaux, Cardillac

April — Pays Basque
Salon des Antiquaries, Biarritz
Fêtes Musicales, Biarritz
Foire aux Jambons, Bayonne

May — Dordogne
Festival l'Esprit des Voix, Périgueux
Foire aux Potiers, Bussière Badil

May — Gironde
Foire Internationale, Bordeaux
Mai Musicale, Bordeaux

May — Pays Basque
Mai du Théâtre, Hendaye
Foire Exposition, Bayonne

June — Dordogne
Musiconcerts, Périgueux
Jazz Festival, Terrasson
Concours de Chiens, Mussidan

June — Gironde
L'Été Girondin, Gironde
Vinexpo, Bordeaux
Feu de la St-Jean, Pauillac
Fête de la St-Jean, Carcans Ville
Feux de Garonne, Bordeaux
Fête de la Jurade, St-Émilion

June — Landes
Feria, Aire sur l'Adour
Feria, St-Sever

June — Lot-et-Garonne
Foire à la Tourtière, Penne d'Agenais

June — Béarn
Pau Festival
Festival de Musique Sacrée, Nay
Festival de Théâtre de Pau, Pau

June — Pays Basque
Fêtes Patronales de la St-Jean, St-Jean de Luz
Fêtes Patronales de la St-Jean, Hasperren

July — Dordogne
Festival du Pays d'Ans Périgord, Hautefort
Festival le Temps de Domme, Domme
Festival Musical du Périgord Noir, St-Léon-sur-Vézère etc
Festival Musique Espérance, Bergerac
Festival Musical du Périgord Pourpre, Monpazier
Festival d'Orgue, St-Cyprien
Musiconcerts, Périgueux
Festival Musique au Pays de Bessède et des Bastides, Monpazier etc
Festival Musique en Sarladais, Sarlat
Festival de Danse, Brantôme
Été Musical en Périgord Pourpre, Villamblard
Festival des Jeux de Théâtre, Sarlat
Foire aux Vins, Sigoules

July — Gironde
Fêtes Patronales, Carcans Ville
Foire aux Vins et Produits Regionaux, Pole de Maubuisson
Fête du Lac, Pole de Maubuisson
Jazz and Wine, Pauillac
Festival de Musique Classique, Soulac
Foire Gastronomique, Lac

July — Landes
Feria, Mont de Marsan
Feria, Hagetmau

July — Lot-et-Garonne
Festival de Jazz en Villeneuvois, Villeneuve sur Lot
Festival de Musique en Guyenne, Monflanquin
Festival Musique en Albret, various in Pays d'Albret
Festival Gascon, various in Pays d'Albret
Marché Mediéval, Vianne

July — Béarn
L'Été en Pau, Pau
Fête de Monein et du Jurançon, Jurançon
Feria d'Orthez, Orthez

July — Pays Basque
Présentation de la Force Basque, Espelette
Championnat de Force Basque, Baigorry
Festival International de Folklore, Biarritz
Rencontres Internationales de Piano, St-Jean de Luz etc
Festival de Jazz aux Remparts, Bayonne
Fête du Thon, St-Jean de Luz
Fête du Chipron, Hendaye
Foire Gastronomique et Artisanale, Sare
Foire Gastronomique et Artisanale, St-Etienne de Baigorry
Foire aux Fromages et Produits Régionaux, St-Jean Pied de Port

August — Dordogne
Festival Musique en Périgord, Audrix Paunat
Festival Musique en Périgord Vert, Piégut Pluviers
Brocante, Foire aux Vins et Fromages, La Coquille
Salon des Antiquaries, Mussidan
Bourse aux Armes Anciennes, Neuvic

August — Gironde
Fête Champêtre, Carcans Ville
Foire aux Vins et Produits Regionale, Pole de Maubuisson
Fête de l'Océan, Carcans Océan
Journées des Vins et des Produits Régionaux, Lacanau
Foire Gastronomique, Soulac
Festival Musique et Artistique, Uzeste
Festival du Théâtre, Blaye

August — Landes
Feria, Dax

August — Lot-et-Garonne
Foire Internationale de la Poterie, St-Avit
Festival Musical de Duras, Duras
Journées Mediévales de Monflanquin, Monflanquin
Festival Musical de Bonaguil, Bonaguil
Réconstruction Historique, Marché, etc., Laroque Timbaut
Music Festival, Nérac

August — Béarn
Fêtes Traditionelles, Laruns

August — Pays Basque
Fêtes Traditionelles, Bayonne
Fêtes Basque, Hendaye
Fêtes Patronales, St-Jean Pied de Port
Fêtes Patronales, Ascain
Championat de Force Basque, St-Etienne de Baigory
Gant d'Or de Cesta Punta, Biarritz
Foire aux Fromages et Produits Régionaux, St-Jean Pied de Port

Foire Gastronomique et Artisanale, Sare
Foire Gastronomique et Artisanale, St-Etienne de Baigory
Nuit de la Sardine, St-Jean de Luz

September — Dordogne
Salon des Antiquaries, Périgueux, Montignac
Marché aux Cèpes, Périgueux, Montignac
Cémice Agricole Traditionelle, Vergt
Marché aux Noix, Brantôme etc

September — Gironde
Ban des Vendages de la Jurade, St-Émilion

September — Lot-et-Garonne
Foire aux Pruneaux, St-Aubin

September — Béarn
Fête du Sel, Salies de Béarn
Foire de l'Automne, Pau

September — Pays Basque
Championat du Monde Professionel, Sport Basque, Biarritz
Fêtes Traditionelles, Sare
Festival International Cinema et Culture de l'Amérique Latine, Biarritz
Concours International de Danse Classique, Biarritz
Festival de Musique en Côte Basque, Bayonne etc
Festival 'Htza Pitz' des Contes et Conteurs du Pays du Monde, Hasparren
Fête du Ttoro, St-Jean du Luz

October — Dordogne
Festival Sinfonia en Périgord, Brantôme etc
Foire aux Plantes Vertes, Neuvic sur l'Isle
Foire aux Chataignes, Montignac etc
Marché aux Gras, Montignac, Périgueux, Sarlat, Thiviers etc
Marché aux Truffes, Brantôme, Périgueux, Sarlat, Sorges

October — Gironde
Journées Nationales de la Brocante, Bordeaux
Salon du Livre, Bordeaux
Festival du Jazz, Bordeaux

October — Béarn
Master de Guitar, Pau

October — Pays Basque
Festival de Théâtre Franco-Ibérique, Bayonne

November — Dordogne
Foire aux Dindons, Varaignes

November — Béarn
Salon du Livre, Pau

December — Dordogne
Salon du Livre Gourmand, Périgueux
Marché aux Dindes, Terrasson/Montignac

December — Gironde
Sigma — Festival d'Art Contemporain, Bordeaux

Markets

Most small towns have street markets one or two days a week, often in the morning only. Some of the best in the region are the Tuesday, le Bugue, Wednesday, Sarlat and Montignac, Friday, Brantôme, Montignac and Ribérac, Saturday, Sarlat and Bazas, Sunday in St-Cyprien. See entries under individual towns. Larger towns have daily markets, usually under cover in purpose built accommodation. Notable are the central markets of Bordeaux, the markets of Agen, Bayonne, Pau, and Périgueux (which also has a major Wednesday market). Many sell local produce including canned *pâtés*, wrapped in home-made labels. These are often the best buys. Markets are also some of the few places other than supermarkets where it is possible to buy wine. Again, the supply tends to be local. Wine shops and off licences are rare in Aquitaine.

Sporting activities

Given the vast geographic spread of Aquitaine it is not surprising that the sporting opportunities appear limitless. What follows is merely an outline. For many, Aquitaine means one of two things—sea or snow. The enormous beaches offer **surfing**, **swimming**, and **windsailing**, especially in the Arcachon region. For more information contact the Fédération Française de Surf, Plage Nord Boulevard Front de Mer BP28, 40150, Hossgor, tel 58 43 55 88, fax 58 43 60 57. **Canoeing** and **white-water sports** are also extensively available. Contact Fédération Française de Canöe Kayak, 87, Quai de la Marne BP58, 94340 Joinville de Pont, tel 48 89 39 39, fax 48 86 13 25.

Winter sports are big business in Aquitaine. Seven major centres operate: Artouse-Fabrèges, Gourette and Pierre St-Martin for downhill skiing, and Iraty, Pays de Cize, Issarbe and Le Somport for cross-country. Details from the two relevant tourist offices, Béarn, Agence Touristique de Béarn, 27, ter Rue J. J. de Monaix, 64000 Pau, tel 59 30 01 30, fax 59 02 52 75, and Pays Basque, Agence de Tourisme du Pays Basque, 1, Rue de Donzac, BP 811, 64108 Bayonne Cédex, tel el 59 59 2 77, fax 59 25 48 90. Both offices will also provide details for summer mountain activities.

Sport of a more relaxing nature is also found in abundance. **Golf** is a growth industry, having started in the region in 1856. Aquitaine now boasts 53 courses of International status. Information and golfing pack from tourist offices. **Horse riding** is also popular, many centres offering equestrian packages—see Ferme Equestre, details from the Chambre Régionale d'Agriculture (CRAA), 57, Cours Xavier Arnozan, 33000, Bordeaux. While not strictly sport, **canal-boat holidays** are very popular, Aquitaine having a considerable network of well-maintained waterways. A multi-language guide to six routes, covered in great detail, is available from tourist offices. Guide Vagnon de Tourisme Fluvial is published by les Editions du Plaisancier, book 7, Canaux du Midi. Boating is available in many centres, especially along the Dordogne.

For many of these, and other sporting activities, two addresses should be noted. **Comité Régionale Olympique et Sportif d'Aquitaine**, 5, Cours de Verdun, 33000 Bordeaux, tel 56 52 80 90, and **Centre d'Information Jeunesse Aquitaine**, 5, Rue Duffour Dubergier, 33000, Bordeaux, tel 56 48 55 50.

Camping

Camping is extremely well organised in Aquitaine and an increasingly popular option for families with young children. Many camp sites exist close to the centre of small towns and villages and 'ready-made' tent holidays are numerous. A number of British firms specialise in tailor-made camping holidays, including cross-Channel fares, overnight stops and fully fitted tents on approved sites upon arrival. Allow at least one stop-over en route. Up-to-date lists of camp sites may be obtained from the **Fédération Régionale Aquitaine de l'Hôtelerie de Plein Air**, 21, Rue de Grassi, 33000 Bordeaux, tel 56 51 00 50.

Naturism is especially promoted within the regions, with six holiday centres, three in the Gironde, and one each in Dordogne, Landes and Lot-et-Garonne. Further information from **Fédération Française de Naturisme**, 65, Rue de Toqueville, 75017 Paris (1). Tel 47 64 32 82, fax (1) 47 64 32 63.

Beaches

Aquitaine has a huge and relatively undiscovered coastline, stretching 270km from the Gironde estuary to the Pyrenees. Much of it is lonely and undeveloped, and relatively free from the horrors of the package beach holiday. The climate has something to do with this—the wind blows, as does the fine sand, and the sea can be intimidating. The Gulf of Arcachon provides the one major interruption to the general sweep of the coastline, and has been developed for a number of watersports activities. The tidal range means that for much of the day, water is hard to find. At the tip of the Côte d'Argent, Soulac-sur-mer offers a quiet almost Victorian seaside holiday while at the southern extreme, Biarritz and the coastal towns towards Spain come close to a vision of the Costa Hell. The development of Biarritz is the one major blot on the coastal scenery. Many of the beaches in the area are commercialised, and many are simply bad. For the rest, small villages offering accommodation may be found, especially towards the south, but essentially, the coast is for the independent traveller and camper and long may it remain so. Windsurfing and surfing are major attractions on nearly all the undeveloped stretches of coast, while a number of centres, such as Claquey and Hossegor, offer boating and other watersports activities.

Wine

Grapes were introduced into Aquitaine by the Romans, who cultivated the slopes around St-Émilion and along the left bank of the Gironde, the modern area known as Graves. Until the 18C and modern bottles and corks, wine could not be aged and thus Aquitaine specialised in light, fresh reds known as *clairet*. The English acquisition of the duchy saw real expansion in production, the climate ensuring an easy supply which outstripped the price and variable quality of English wine, whose production went into serious decline. Bordeaux, Liborne and Bergerac grew prosperous on wine exports and the profitability of the English trade must have been a factor in the region's persistent loyalty to the English Crown.

The 18C revolution in the maturing of wine saw the rise of a new product, a distinctly heavier red with good ageing quality. Some wines popular in previous centuries fell into neglect as stronger and dryer reds came to dominate the market. In 1855, the *cru* system came into being, classifying the top Bordeaux and ensuring quality. The familiar *appellation d'origine contrôlée* arrived in the 1930s, made necessary by the great explosion of wine production across the whole region.

The **principal regions** (see map) follow the valleys of the Garonne and Dordogne, with important zones flanking the Gironde. Many areas produce both red and white. Any vineyard offering *dégustation* may be visited, sometimes for a small charge, and the wine tasted. Often, the whole operation is free and surprisingly good-natured. There is no obligation to buy though most locals will purchase direct from the producer. Hence the absence of wine shops in most towns. Remember, Bordeaux wines are heavy and high in alcohol. They will affect your driving and put you quickly over the limit.

The main *appellations* along the Gironde and the Garonne are, on the left bank, with Médoc, Haut-Médoc (reds), Graves (mostly dry whites), and the Sauternais, famous for sweet dessert wines such as Sauternes and Barsac. Across the Gironde, you get the Côtes of Bourg and Blaye, with dry whites and rather robust reds. From north of the Dordogne come Fronsac, Pomerol and St-Émilion, and many smaller *appellations*, with reds seemingly irresistible to today's British traveller. Between the Garonne and the Dordogne, Entre-Deux-Mers and Graves-de-Vayres (dry whites), and the sweet whites of Ste-Foy-Bordeaux. Flanking the north bank of the Garonne, are the Premières Côtes de Bordeaux (reds), though Cadillac, Loupiac, Ste-Croix-du-Mont and Côtes de Bordeaux-St-Macaire produce sweet whites.

Other wines from Aquitaine are less august though more easily affordable. Best known is Bergerac, producing the rather hard and steely reds and consumed in most parts of the Dordogne. The area also produces the intensely sweet and punguent whites of Mombazillac, a cheaper alternative to Sauternes. To the south, Côtes de Duras, with both red and white, is an increasingly familiar name in British highstreets. The area around Nérac produces Côtes de Buzet, a newly fashionable wine, both red and white, while in the adjoining area, there is Côtes de Brulhois, another distinctive red. In the deep south, the reds of the Madiran age well and are relatively cheap. Next door, in Tursan, there is yet more red.

South of Pau and into the Pyrenees is Jurançon country, best known for whites including a sweet dessert wine. Downstream are found the reds of Béarn, produced in several patches. The main wine from the Basque country is a red from Irouléguy.

The most famous spirit of the region, Armagnac, comes from around the village of that name, and is a smooth and potent brandy. Prunes soaked in Armagnac is the food of the gods.

Most wine towns have a *maison du vin* or equivalent, offering information and occasionally a tasting. Many feature display boards giving information on the local châteaux open to the public and their visiting and tasting times. These tend to vary by the season so check before setting off.

Musées de la vigne et du vin may be found as follows:

Musée des Chartrons, 41, rue Borie, 33000 Bordeaux. Tel 56 44 27 77.

Ecomusée du Libournais, le bourg, 33570 Montagne. Tel 57 74 56 89.

Château Mouton-Rothschild, 33250, Pauillac. Tel 56 59 22 22.

Château Loudenne, St-Yzan du Médoc, 33340 Lesparre. Tel 56 09 05 03.

Château Maucaillou, 33480, Moulis en Médoc. Tel 56 58 01 23.

Les Chais Ryst-Dupeyron, 12, Cours du Médoc, 33300 Bordeaux. Tel 56 39 53 02.

For information on visits and *dégustation*:

Conseil Interprofessionnel des Vins de Bordeaux: CIVB, 1, Cours du XXX Juillet, 33000 Bordeaux. Tel 56 00 22 66.

Bordeaux Tourisme Animation, 12, Cours du XXX Juillet, 33000 Bordeaux. Tel 56 79 05 39.

Counseil des Vins du Médoc, 1, Cors XXX Juillet, 33000 Bordeaux. Tel 56 48 18 62.

Maison des Vins et du Tourisme du Médoc, La verrierie, 33250, Pauillac. Tel 56 59 03 08.

Office de Tourisme, Place des Créneaux, 33330 St-Émilion. Tel 57 24 72 03.

Les Côtes de Castillon, 6, Allées de la République, 33350 Castillon la Bataille. Tel 57 40 00 88.

Maison du Vin des Côtes de Bourg, 33710, Bourg sur Gironde.

Syndicat viticole de Blaye, 11, Cours Vauban, 33390 Blaye. Tel 57 42 91 19.

Syndicat viticole de l'Entre Deux Mers, 1, Cours du XXX Juillet, 33000 Bordeaux. Tel 56 81 66 42.

Maison des Vins de Graves, 33720 Podensac. Tel 56 27 09 25.

Syndicat viticole des l'ères Côtes de Bordeaux, Place de l'Église, 33360 Quinsac. Tel 56 20 85 84.

Maison de la qualitié (for Bordeaux and Bordeaux Supérieurs), 33750, Beychac et Caillau. Tel 56 72 90 99.

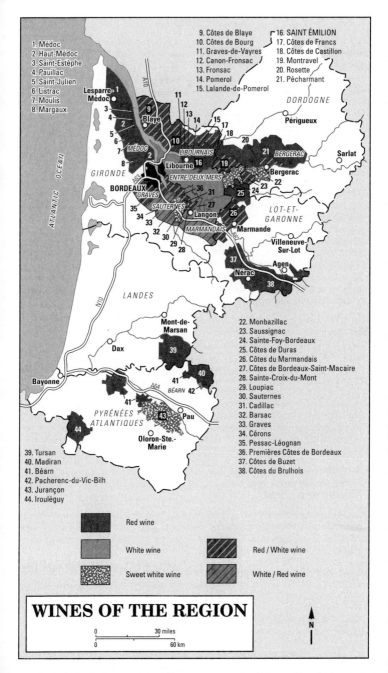

1. Médoc
2. Haut-Médoc
3. Saint-Estèphe
4. Pauillac
5. Saint-Julien
6. Listrac
7. Moulis
8. Margaux

9. Côtes de Blaye
10. Côtes de Bourg
11. Graves-de-Vayres
12. Canon-Fronsac
13. Fronsac
14. Pomerol
15. Lalande-de-Pomerol

16. SAINT ÉMILION
17. Côtes de Francs
18. Côtes de Castillon
19. Montravel
20. Rosette
21. Pécharmant

22. Monbazillac
23. Saussignac
24. Sainte-Foy-Bordeaux
25. Côtes de Duras
26. Côtes du Marmandais
27. Côtes de Bordeaux-Saint-Macaire
28. Sainte-Croix-du-Mont
29. Loupiac
30. Sauternes
31. Cadillac
32. Barsac
33. Graves
34. Cérons
35. Pessac-Léognan
36. Premières Côtes de Bordeaux
37. Côtes de Buzet
38. Côtes du Brulhois

39. Tursan
40. Madiran
41. Béarn
42. Pacherenc-du-Vic-Bilh
43. Jurançon
44. Irouléguy

Red wine

White wine

Red / White wine

Sweet white wine

White / Red wine

WINES OF THE REGION

0   30 miles
0   60 km

N

Food

In the battle for the hearts and stomachs of the French, the Périgord is a major combatant. The high quality of the food, the balancing of the menu and the skilful preparation make eating out in the area one of its major attractions. For what you get, the price is not high. What the Périgord lacks is a good local wine but with Bordeaux on the doorstep who should worry? It is a pity therefore that so much indifferent Bergerac is served. If much of the food of Aquitaine seems familiar, it demonstrates the far-reaching influence of the region's gastronomy on the whole of France. The greatest difference across the whole area comes in the Basque country, where the food is sharper, spicier and often red. A menu in Basque becomes a mystery tour.

Classic amongst the dishes of Aquitaine are *confit* and *magret de canard* and *pâté de fois gras*. *Confits* are sections of meat, usually from duck, cooked and preserved in their own fat. *Magrets* are breast of either duck or goose, surprisingly lean and barely cooked. Whatever the rights or wrongs of pâté production, the birds live outdoors and run free. Promotional material suggests little reluctance on the part of the greedy geese to accept the feed, indeed they fight over it. The resulting pâtés are extraordinarily rich and fine textured, and usually accompanied by a sweet white wine. If the *pâté de fois gras* of goose is beyond your pocket, try the duck version, *pâté de fois gras de canard*.

Chicken, usually *au pot*, is exceptionally fine. French chicken is truly free-range and tastes almost gamey. Often it is extensively and expensively stuffed, particularly with ham. Turkey can be another gastronomic rediscovery for the jaded palate. Wild boar is sometimes offered in the Basque region. Lamb reared on the coastal saltflats is another speciality and like many red meats, is often served *à la bordelaise*, in a thick wine based sauce with shallots and bone-marrow. *Bazas* is generally considered to produce the best beef in southern France. The Basque lands produce *axoa*, chopped veal with peppers, and *tripotxa*, a pudding made from baby lamb or veal. Wild pigeon is often cooked in Armagnac and served with prunes. Quail and partridge and other wild birds are hunted, though many species are now protected, at least theoretically.

Charcuterie of all kinds fills the markets; look out for hams, especially *jambon de Bayonne*, which despite its name comes from around Orthez. It is usually served solo.

Mushrooms are a regional speciality, including *cèpes*, *bidaous* and *morels*. Often, woodland mushrooms are combined with potatoes to form *pommes sarladais*. If you see it on the menu, order it! Truffles also feature in many dishes.

Soups of bewildering complexity are a feature of the whole region. Most favoured is *garbure*, a meat and vegetable concoction ladelled on to slices on bread. It should be thick enough to require a knife and fork, and the locals are not averse to thinning the remains with a glass or two of wine. Other variations on the theme include *estouffat* (beef and bacon), *ouliat* (garlic), *civet* and *daube*, the latter with strong red wine based stocks. The

Basque country has its own distinctive soups with unpronouncable names—*ttoro* (fish) and *elzeckaria* (basically vegetable).

Seafood and all kinds of fish feature strongly, with oysters (*huîtres*) from Arcachon heading the list, which may also include lamprey, *pibales* (elver) and crayfish. Do not be surprised if you order oysters in Bordeaux and find them accompanied by grilled sausage. That is the way they are eaten. In Basque territory, expect to find hake *koskera* and plenty of tuna dishes.

Of all the **fruits** grown, prunes are the most common especially around Agen. What the French can do with a prune beggars belief. Yet the area is also concentrating upon the dull kiwi fruit, and large areas of kiwi orchards now flank the banks of the Garonne. Walnuts form the basis of many desserts, and are extensively used in salads, usually with *gesiers* (gizzards).

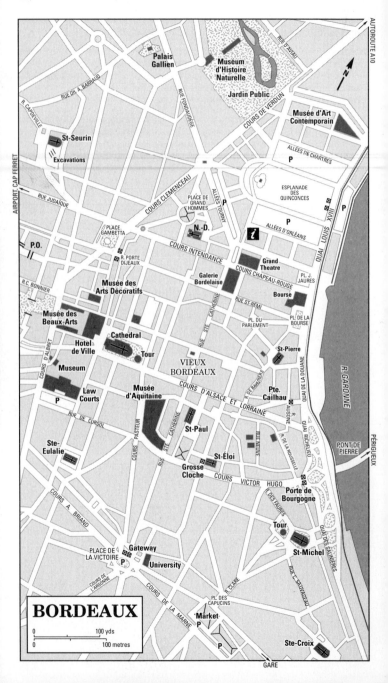

BORDEAUX

1

Bordeaux

Hotels/Rest. Tourist Information Bordeaux, 12 Cours du 30 Juillet, tel 56 44 28 41, fax 56 81 89 21. Aquitaine Region, Rue René Cassin, tel 56 39 88 88, fax 56 43 07 63. Gironde Département, 21 Cours de l'Intendance, tel 56 52 61 40, fax 56 81 09 99.

Festival. Two weeks in May, **Music Festival**, organised by the Grand Théâtre (tel 56 48 58 54). Horseshow, also May. **Opera** at the Grand Théâtre in season.

BORDEAUX (pop. c 220,000) is a large, bustling town and busy sea-port. You do not want a car in Bordeaux. Parking is impossible, and when available, it is expensive. The traffic system seems a mystery even to the inhabitants. Either go by plane/train and hire a car when you leave, or stay outside the centre and walk or use public transport.

First impressions may not be favourable. The surrounding country is generally flat and uninteresting, save for the direction of Libourne, where the ground rises, providing distant and dramatic views. Dismal suburbs, unfinished motorways and complex railways encircle the historic city. The ring road system (*rocade*) has yet to be finished but will be a great improvement. The walk in from the impressive station quickly exposes the town's basic problems—too much traffic very badly managed, dog mess, some highly questionable modern planning and above all, inner city decay. Such problems can be resolved and no doubt one day will disappear. Efforts are being made and much of the historic centre is being scrubbed and the general environment improved. But Bordeaux has a long way to go.

None of this should deter a visitor from seeing the town, which has an outstanding ensemble of historic buildings, good museums and excellent shops and restaurants. In addition, Bordeaux forms a natural centre for the whole region. Communications are good, and the surrounding sites varied and of great interest.

History. Bordeaux began as *Burdigala*, founded in the 3C BC by a Celtic tribe from northern France. It flourished by trading tin. The town was captured for the Romans by Crassus in 56BC. The Gallo-Roman town stood about the area of the Grand Theatre, an oblong settlement narrow end-on to the river. The two principal streets are represented by the present Cours de l'Intendance, and Rue Ste-Catherine crossing it. The town was seriously damaged in the Barbarian incursions c 270, after which it was fortified. By the 7C at least three churches are known. Bordeaux passed to the future Henry II of England upon his marriage in 1152, it being the property of his wife, Eleanor of Aquitaine. It remained with the English crown for the next 300 years. A new, longer wall was built in 1227 incorporating the adjacent suburbs such as La Rousselle, and yet more extensive fortifications were built in 1327, when the city expanded to take in areas such as Ste-Croix. After the fall of Bordeaux in the 15C following a prolonged siege, the French surrounded the city with forts, not to protect Bordeaux but to control it. Even in the 16C the population did not regard themselves as French. Though predominantly Catholic, a considerable Huguenot community existed by the outbreak of the Wars of Religion: some 300 Protestants were slaughtered here in 1572. The Bordelais remained unsettled throughout the 17C when it was the principal centre for the *Frondistes*, and saw uprisings in 1648, 1653 and 1675. Later, it was at the forefront of the Girondist movement, an attempt to tone down the revolutionary zeal of the new French Republic. Yet through all this, the city remained a great sea-port and trade centre, the most important in the region, with wine, spices and slaves forming the basis of its wealth. The town spread far beyond its medieval walls, encouraged by a law forbidding foreigners, Protestants and Jews from residing within its limits. The 18C saw attempts to regularise and organise the old city. Much of it now has a grid plan, with the occasional errant medieval street barging through. The principal contributions to the replanning of the city was the area around the Royal Square (Place du Parlement) in the 1670s, and the new developments centred upon the Place de la Comédie in the 18C. Thus in Bordeaux two main periods of history present themselves to the visitor—the Gallo-Roman and medieval, and the period from Louis XIV to Napoleon.

There being no obvious starting point for a tour of Bordeaux, this circular route will begin and end at the Cathedral. The **CATHEDRAL OF ST-ANDRE** is a weird building, aggressively restored in the 19C by Abadie, who destroyed its cloister and who is generally regarded as an architectural baddy hereabouts. It is now stranded on an island site, best seen from the Hôtel de Ville to the north east though the surrounding trees hinder any clear understanding of the architecture and its development. There is plenty of both. Basically, an aisleless 12C Romanesque church was extended east in the 14C with the transepts straying into the next century. The nave was partially rebuilt but mostly adapted, which accounts for the messy interior and for the strange cliff-like nave exterior which lacks any vertical alignments. The upper levels of the nave, seen between huge flyers, have early plate-tracery c 1200 to the west, changing to bar tracery c 1220 from the third bay.

The nave north wall, east end, retains a curious door, the 13C **Porte Royale**, with Reims-like nodding figures, a tympanum with Christ in Majesty and Angels holding the symbols of the Passion, but the central column (trumeau) figure is lost, as is the top of the arch. Above, is a row of bishops, and to the right a distinctly Renaissance buttress.

The **north transept façade** is flanked by towers sporting spires. The right tower west wall contains a blind window fit for Tewkesbury c 1320. Did English Decorated come first to Bordeaux and only later influence northern France? Other tracery hereabouts suggests Barcelona, particularly the concave star pattern. The north transept portal has an ungainly Ascension, the lower Christ figure intruding uncomfortably upon the upper. This is accompanied by a long and silly Last Supper. Pope Clement V, formerly bishop here, appears on the trumeau, while rather fey figures fill the jambs. The Annunciating Angel was the best of the lot but is now damaged. The intersecting tracery above is interesting and the upper rose distinctly Flamboyant.

The concave star tracery occurs in the 14C **choir and radiating chapels**, while the panelled buttresses have sculpted figures between the columns, very English. The buttress to the right of the axial chapel is treated as a

The south transept exterior of the Cathedral of St-André, Bordeaux

tabernacle, with a female figure and a male carrying a mason's level, possibly a portrait of the architect. The red-tiled chapel roofs strike a distinctly southern note amid all this northern Gothic.

The **south transept exterior** has two stumpy, unfinished towers and a rose window with very English Decorated tracery. The sculpted door beneath has socle figures showing the Life of St. Andrew. The archivolt figures resemble contemporary work in Norwich. The nodding ogee canopies on either side once housed more figures.

Inspection of the **interior** should start at the west end. The **aisleless nave** has three horizontal divisions, the lowest is Romanesque, with wide arches enclosing shallow apses. The details suggest a date around 1140. Work of the same date occurs stranded in the middle storey, west end.

Both the upper levels are 13C Gothic, the vaults somewhat later. Some of the western bays have huge shafts acting as vertical bay dividers, their character changing as they rise. The middle storey has windows, there being no aisles. The tracery infill is earlier to the west than east, indicating the direction of the rebuild. There is a wall passage. The easternmost bays are 13C from the ground up but all the vaults look late, perhaps 15C and of a piece. What saves the interior from being just a mess are its grand proportions and spaciousness. The **organ loft** over the west entrance is early Renaissance, with characteristic Florentine foliate detail, busts in roundels and angular angels with wreaths. See also two scenes, 1531, from the demolished screen. The wooden organ case has Atlantes figures.

In the fifth bay on the right is a big Crucifixion by **Jordaens**, 1635 and clean. Some of the figures seem tipsy, and if Mary Magdalene were able to stand, she would be 25 feet high. Opposite, is an 18C marble inlay pulpit.

The nave is wider and lower than the transept opening and choir, causing difficulties when it came to knitting the whole together with vaults. The **14C choir** has an eclectic plan and elevation, quoting both northern and central France. Double aisled and dirty, the choir is further darkened by 19C glass. It was begun by Bishop Bertrand de Got, 1300–05, later Pope Clement V. The style is basically 13C Rayonnant but minor details betray its later date: the moulded sections in the aisles and arcades that just die away and the use of shields as bosses in the aisle vaults, presumably once painted. There are five radial chapels, the axial with a 17C screen—wreaths, balusters etc—plus contemporary stalls placed against the 14C wall arcades. The wall passage at the base of the windows is a Reims/Champagne feature. The left-hand chapel contains **English Notting-ham alabaster panels**; a Resurrection and an Assumption with donor, 1390s. Directly opposite stands another Nottingham figure, St. Macaire, c 1420. The chapel beyond the north choir aisle has a Virgin and Child, probably of English alabaster, 14C and painted. Relics beneath the altar include those of the Englishman, St. Simon Stock, who died in Bordeaux. From the start, Bordeaux announces its English inheritance.

The north transept west wall has a large pierced-work canopied tomb from the 14C while the south transept has fragments of medieval glass in the clerestory. Both ends have rose windows with some late-medieval glass.

The detached **Tour Pey-Berland**, mid-15C, became a shot tower post 1789, and is now topped by an unfortunate gilt figure of 1863. There is a fine view from the top (usually open, fee).

Across from the west front stands the **Hôtel de Ville**, originally built as a palace for Archbishop Rohan in 1782, by the architects Bonfin and Laclotte, who were required to provide an unusual number of bedrooms for the prelate's 'nieces'. Protected from the street by an open colonnade, the buildings around the courtyard have a rusticated base supporting a giant order of Ionic pilasters and a central segmental pediment, classic 18C Bordeaux. The rear, seen from the Musée de Beaux Arts, recalls Queen's Square, Bath. To visit the garden and gallery, take the Rue Hôtel de Ville, last in a long succession of names—see the carvings at the far end—and then Rue des Ramparts. Left into Rue Montbazon past typical 18C Bordeaux buildings, stone-faced, with large shop entries and small side doors leading to upper residences.

Rue Bouffard (first right) houses the **Musée des Arts Décoratifs**, No. 39, formerly the 18C Hôtel de Lalande. The collection includes glass, enamels, porcelain and furniture, shown in elegant period rooms (pm only, closed Tuesdays, fee).

A left turn at the bottom of Rue Montbazon into the Cours d'Albret brings you to the **MUSÉE DES BEAUX ARTS**, a fine collection, well shown but hot (closed Tues and lunchtimes, fee, Weds free). The entrance hall features **Rodin**, seated nude, a project for a monument to Whistler of 1906 and two rather fascistic female nudes by Charles Despiau. The main collection, hung in chronological order, contains **Perugino**, Virgin and Child between saints, dirty but Raphael-like features, **Veronese**, the Holy Family with St. Dorothy, recently cleaned, the Virgin in Dresden colours, **Palma Vecchio**, Man with Letter, **Breughel**, a Village Fête with dancing, men peeing, ugly women and indiscriminate kissing, a rather sploshy Martyrdom of St. George by **Rubens**, with especially good damask, a double portrait by **Van Dyck** of Charles-Louis and Robert Simerin, a portrait of Anton Fugger by **Hans Maler** plus a number of other Dutch works. Of special interest is the Man with Books, by **Lavinia Fontana**, died 1614, daughter of Prospero Fontana. The picture is very Rubens, with dark colours and a through-view. There is also an unpleasant **Titian.**

Later pictures include **Thomas Lawrence**, portrait of John Hunter of Gubbins, Hertfordshire whose dog obviously died of obesity, **Sir Joshua Reynolds**, portrait of Baron Rokeby, the Primate of Ireland, whose facial colours and blue neckband make him the *tricolour* personified. **Benjamin West** has two interesting religious works in polychrome. Women artists are further represented by **Marianne Loir**, died 1781, portrait of Madame de Châtel.

The gigantic ploughing scene by **Vincent** is unintentionally funny while the quite dreadful political painting by **A.J. Gros**, Departure of the Duchess of Angoulême from Pauillac, blends post-Revolutionary ardour with 19C religious sentiment. Other 19C French works include several by **Delacroix,** especially his Arab with Horse, **Millet's,** Ceres d'Été, whose huge, widespread breasts are like headlights. **Corot** steals the scene with his Bath of Diana, though it is the picture that needs a clean. Modern artists include **Oskar Kokoschka,** View of Notre Dame de Bordeaux, 1925, **Matisse,** and **Picasso,** Olga reading, and a curious sculptured reclining nude by **Joseph Rivière**, died 1961, and a swimming pool monument for Albi (Hitler meets Henry Moore).

Regaining the Cours d'Albret, a few minutes walk north passing the **Musée Art Deco** (closed Tues, fee), which contains precisely that, enter the Rue l'Église and a rather scruffy area with some deeply unwise recent redevelopment. At the Rue Judaique, a diagonal turn to the left leads into the Place des Martyrs de la Résistance and the important church of **ST-SEURIN**. The original early-Christian church of St-Etienne was rededicated to the local 5C Bishop St. Seurin who had been buried in the surrounding cemetery.

The flank of the church forms the north side of the small triangular place, beneath which lies the palaeo-Christian cemetery (open Tues and Sat afternoons, guided tours only, apply at the tourist office). The rambling but interesting church dates from the 11C with many additions. The **south face** includes an unfinished transept, and beneath a porch, an elaborate sculpture cycle. There are three doors, the central one trilobe headed, with many figures placed between columns. The centre door has 12C figures on the right (SS. Paul and John?) and 13C ones on the left including St. Peter. The tympanum with its 13C Christ in Majesty plus angels with symbols of the Passion are all contemporary with the creation of the door. The left door has the Adoration of the Magi, the Dream of the Magi etc c 1170, set in a later arch. The right-hand tympanum has what looks like the life of St. Seurin.

The **west front** was altered in 1828. Basically 11C with a 12C tower, various 19C additions have given it the look of Poitiers. All the external sculpture is fake. The tower looks genuine. Inside the porch, cumbersome 11C capitals have scenes of Abraham and Isaac, monsters, pecking birds, and St. Seurin on his deathbed.

The gloomy church **interior** is dominated by giant drum piers, which are evidently 18C recasing over Romanesque work. The vaults are 13C restored after 1698. The aisles were always narrow, and have a variety of window designs from the 12–15C. In a low chapel to the left of the entrance, there is a 14C Virgin and Child in alabaster, which might be English. The Child holds a bird which claws at the Virgin's breast through a slit in her garment. The little chapel of St. Etienne (south side) contains a 7C sarcophagus and a 13C altarpiece. The organs over the west door are from 1771/2.

There is a **south transept arm** but no partner. A Gothic bay precedes a square, vaulted Romanesque chancel with original capitals. The altar stands over the early Christian sarcophagus of St. Seurin. The stalls are 16C with misericords and end-figures under canopies. To the left is a 15C stone bishop's throne with a very fancy fretted canopy, while opposite, a collection of what look like English alabaster panels, c 1400, newly framed. They include a pope and many saints, all set beneath canopies and with traces of red and gold paint. The Annunciation and Crucifixion are particularly fine.

The **north chapel**, 1424–44, has a fantastically decorated reredos wall and altarpiece, including some figures around the sacristy door. The altar houses another collection of English alabaster scenes from the Life of the Virgin, c 1400, all mis-arranged in a new frame. Flanking them to the north is an early Renaissance tomb. The south transept contains the tomb of Bishop Sault of Dax, died 1623.

The entrance to the **crypt** is via the nave aisle (ring at the sacristy if closed). The crypt is an interesting shambles. It has an undatable aisled structure with many re-used Roman and Merovingian pieces and painted capitals. The floor is broken to expose parts of the early cemetery. Sarcophagi abound; the decorations include a pecking bird motif and zig-zag patterns.

A detour heading further north from the church will bring you to the so-called **Palais Gallien**. Leave St-Seurin and walk north-east up Rue Capdeville, then turn right on Rue Dr. A. Barraud (bus stop Palais Gallien).

This substantial fragment of the town's 3C amphitheatre is named after the fictitious wife of Charlemagne. Among rather tatty surroundings, you see the monumental north entry, plus adjoining arcades preserving two of the original three storeys together with the attic design. The construction shows typically Gallic small stonework, interlaced with brick bands over a concrete or mortared rubble core. The shape and something of the size can be appreciated (reconstruction model in Musée de l'Aquitaine). The extra-mural amphitheatre was devastated in the barbaric raid of AD 276. A shorter return may be made via Rue Abbé de l'Epée, rejoining the Rue Judaique.

From St-Seurin, return to Rue Judaique and turn left. Much of the street was plush 18C but is now run-down, see No. 20. Many of the original ground floor fronts are intact, but the whole street looks piecemeal and speculative. By contrast, **Place Gambetta** is Louis XV and all of a piece. Giant arcades combine ground and mezzanine floors, fancy first floor windows and Mansard roofs. The entries have unsupported stone stairs and cast-iron banisters, while the rear yards are tiny. The pretty informal garden marks the site of the guillotine, which claimed more than 300. No. 57 is the Casa de Goya, where the painter died in 1828 (open weekdays and Wed am). In the south east angle, a stone gate carries the royal arms and the date 1748. Passing through, enter Rue Porte Dijeaux (No. 86 has a good 18C façade) and catch the view of the Cathedral down Rue Vital Carles. Two blocks on and a left turn takes you to the intersection with the Cours Intendance, the principal street of 18C Bordeaux. Crossing and continuing straight ahead you reach the Place de Grand Hommes, an elegant 18C circus, tragically infilled with a multi-level covered shopping precinct where a market recently stood. Taking Rue Diderot from the south-east angle of Place de Grand Hommes, and then Rue Mablit, you come to Place du Chapelet and the church of **Notre Dame**, 1684–1707 by Michel Duplessy, with its fine Bernini-like façade bulging into the pretty square. The interior is all stone, the elevations quoting St. Peter's in Rome, while the aisles have memorable porthole openings above the transverse arches. Good ironwork.

Opposite the west door, stands the attractive Hôtel du Nice et du Commerce, four storey, c 1720, while left of the church, pass through the Passage Sarget, 1878 and very Parisian.

Turning left along the Cours Intendance, see No. 13 on the left, the Hôtel de Verthamon, 1829, by Alexandre Poitevin. Further along on the same side is No. 5, the Hôtel Acquart, a wealthy merchant house with an elegant façade of 1785 by Louis Combes, sculpture by Deschamps. Turn left and enter Place de la Comédie, and see Nos 1–5, the Hôtel de Roly, a speculative development by the Count Roly, designed c 1780 by Bonfin. Continue north and you are on the Allées de Tourney, an elegant avenue planned in 1745. The view ahead towards the Place de Tourney reveals the statue of Louis de Tourney, Intendant of Guyenne 1743–58, responsible for planning this part of Bordeaux. The area has a variety of period buildings, see No. 1, Place Jean-Jaurès on the triangular site off to the right and across the road, the Hôtel Boyer-Fonfrède, 1776 by Victor Louis, while across the Cours de 30 Juillet, No. 12, is a neo-Classical design of 1820, now the **Office du Tourisme**.

This street leads into the **Esplanade des Quinconces**, an early-19C garden containing the reconstructed **Monument aux Girondins**, 1894–1902, by Victor Rich and Jean Dumilatre. This elegant ensemble, with its beautiful bronze figures and fountains, commemorates the local 'moderates' of the

French Revolution executed in 1792. Demolished for scrap in 1943, it was rescued and re-erected in 1982. North of the gardens stand huge warehouses for the wine trade. Return past the tourist office to the **GRAND THEATRE**, 1773–80, designed by Victor Louis, the most important historic building in Bordeaux (tours most days, not Sun, rehearsals permitting, leaving at 10.30, 15.00 and 16.30. Mid-Sept to end June, Sat at 15.00 only. Ask at the tourist office or at the box office). Standing on the site of a Roman temple demolished by Louis XIV, and looking quite like it, the theatre dominates the area. Long and perhaps too broad, the fine colonnade is topped by figures of the Muses and Graces. The interior is truly grand. When the French Government abandoned Paris for Bordeaux in 1870 it became the National Assembly of France.

The **great stairhall** is naturally-coloured stone. On either side rise splendid elevations, rusticated with columns above. A monument refers to Louis XVI and is dated 1780. The stair splits beneath a brilliant dome, lit both from above and laterally. At first floor level, each side has matching T-plan vestibules, richly decorated and covered with yet more domes. From here, passages provide access to the house, while other doors lead into a series of public rooms. The foyer above the main entrance is a long room, broken by small terminal pavilions. It was the model for the Paris Opera. As yet unrestored, it seems rather dingy. The coved ceiling is covered with 19C paintings and gilding. Two side chambers at right-angles still have 19C decorations over original wood carved interiors. The auditorium is surrounded by unexpectedly spare passages featuring exposed unadorned stonework and elegant spiral stairs. The multiplicity of doors relates to the arrangement of the house, which has many boxes.

The **auditorium** is D-plan, slightly more than semicircular, and smaller than expected though quite sumptuous. It is painted predominantly in blue and gold, the regal colours of France. The pit is surrounded by the rusticated basement of the tiers, which have three levels of which only the first has continuous seating, the others being independent boxes. There are fine Corinthianesque columns, heavily ornamented, and painted curtains and doors to the back walls. The painted dome has allegorical scenes and a large chandelier. Three elliptical half-domes cover a gallery, and the coat of arms of Bordeaux hang over the prosceneum arch.

Cross the Cours Intendance by the side of the theatre to the corner of the Rue des Piliers-des-Tutelle and the Galerie Bordelaise (one block back), filled with the sort of small shops seldom found in English city centres. To the west and north lies the principal shopping district of the town. Through the arcade and beyond, a left enters Rue St-Rémi, off which, at the third left (200m) Rue Jouanet preserves a tiny medieval church and a fine façade, No. 13. a classic early 18C house with shopfront and door to upper lodgings. Rue St-Rémi ends at **Place de la Bourse**, 1733–51, by Jacques Gabriel, and the river. The square is like a mini-Versailles, with grand end blocks, applied columns and pilasters and eye-hole windows. The south end contains the *douane* of 1738, now a Customs Museum (closed Mon and lunchtime, and weekday holidays, fee), an odd subject for a museum and of rather limited appeal. Some of the interiors are fine. To the north of the square is the *bourse*, completed in 1749. The central fountain (1869) replaces a destroyed figure of Louis XV. The majestic riverside is thought to be fit only for car parking.

Leave Place de la Bourse via the Rue François Philippart, which runs south

The great stairhall of the Grand Théâtre, Bordeaux

and parallel with Rue St-Rémi. The Rue François Philippart was cut through the medieval maze in 1750–55 and exemplifies the subtle handling of the 18C planning. Older streets crash in at odd angles and are highlighted and made into features by curving blocks and major balconies. Commonly, such interruptions are handled with great aplomb and sometimes made into surprise features, recalling some expert politician scoring points off a heckler. At the far end, enter **Place du Parlement**, a pretty, irregular 17C square with basket-handle windows and a fountain. Planned in 1670, it was the Royal Market for Bordeaux. The shop-fronts survive and the roofs peep through stone balustrades. There are many restaurants. Rue de Parlement St-Pierre exits from the left corner alongside the grumpy lion. It leads to the church of that name and returns to medieval Bordeaux. Here was the Roman port area. **St-Pierre** is late Gothic, with a pretty façade. Inside, is an Angevin hall church. Opposite the south angle, the Rue de la Devise contains the Hôtel de Sèze, No. 12 (left), a 17/18C block with an interesting courtyard, a fine stair and through the rear window, a fancy fireplace. To the rear of St-Pierre are 16C houses with original shop-fronts and four-square windows.

Rue des Bahutiers leading south from the church has many interesting façades—No. 13, dated 1687 on the corner niche, No. 17, No. 25 and No. 49, a complete mid-16C house with moulded window frames, a restored shop-front and crocketed gable. Turn left into Rue du Palais-de-l'Ombrière and see the **Porte Cailhau**, an odd-shaped river gate with characteristic pointed roofs (restored). It was built by Charles VIII in 1494 to commemorate his Italian triumph at the battle of Fornova. The town-side carries his arms beneath a canopied tent, while the river side has the figure of the King plus Cardinal d'Epinay and St. John the Baptist. It stands on the site of the gateway to the former palace occupied by the Black Prince. The interior contains a display of the gate's history.

The Rue Ausone leading south has attractive buildings, once you have crossed the busy Cours d'Alsace Lorraine, including No. 23, heavily rusticated, and the neo-Classical No. 39. Retracing the Rue Ausone towards Alsace Lorraine, a left into Rue de la Porte-St-Jean will avoid the traffic and keep you in pre-19C Bordeaux. At the top, runs the Rue de la Rouselle and directly opposite, at Nos 23/25, is the **birthplace of Montaigne**. The family chapel is presently inside the garage. The street curves right to a junction with Rue Neuve, still predominantly 18C if a little scruffy. Half-way down Rue Neuve, the Impasse Rue Neuve contains the Maison de XIVe Siècle, which is exactly what it says, and perhaps the oldest recognisable domestic buiding in the town. The stone elevations have twin-light Gothic windows. A little further along is the Maison de Jeanne de Lartigue, which once belonged to Jeanne, wife of Montesquieu, a 16C building with exterior galleries.

Passing back to the Rue Neuve and proceeding on to the far end, a right into Rue Renier and a left almost immediately into the Rue Bouquière will bring you to the Rue Victor Hugo (at the end and still out of sight, the Porte de Bourgogne, 1751 by Portier, leading to the Pont de Pierre, 1811 by Claude Deschamps). Proceeding left towards the gate and river, cross the street and enter the Rue Faures, whence you will quickly arrive at the church of **ST-MICHEL**, one of the great sites of the town. The church stands on a slope, the east end dropping towards the river. The west front and detached bell tower (not open) form part of a picturesque quarter, almost a separate town centre. There is a bric-à-brac market most mornings, and a clothes market at weekends.

St-Michel recalls St. Mary Redcliffe, Bristol, in both style and brassiness. A blousy, confident building, it includes almost all styles of late-Gothic.

The Place du Parlement, Bordeaux

Begun c 1350, it was badly damaged in the German bombardment of 1940. The west front is unfinished—it was to have a porch. The church is very wide and while the nave has rather wild Flamboyant tracery, including *fleur de lys*, the earlier choir is more sober. The transept portals are partly 1776.

The English influence is strong, particularly in the east end. The cathedralesque interior is sometimes gloomy. The choir arcades recall 14C England with their tall pedestal bases and Decorated tracery. The high vault is also patterned *à l'anglais*. The High altar base (also 14C?) is medieval and painted.

The flat **east end** exudes polygonal chapels, see the Evangelists in the spandrels of the south chapel wall arcades. The modern glass behind the High altar is by Max Ingrand. In the north aisle, the first chapel, has 16C glass in the top and a modern Agony in the Garden below. The chapel is dominated by a huge 16C sculpted Deposition in contemporary dress. The second chapel has early Renaissance glass plus donor, Marquis Henri de Mons. The glazing shows Notre Dame de Bonne Nouvelle and the Tree of Jesse. The altar is also 16C. One window in the north transept has 16C glazing.

The **nave** is the result of a series of builds and was still incomplete in 1557. The last east chapel on the north side houses a vast late Gothic/early Renaissance altarpiece with twisted columns, shell canopies and figures. On the altar, there are Nottingham alabaster scenes. In the aisle opposite, is a stone *pietà*, 16C and rather stiff but then it would be.

The **south west chapel** near the west door has a stone St. Ursula, 16C, sheltering the people beneath her cloak. The second chapel on the south, vaulted in 1548, contains a huge Louis XIII wooden altarpiece, very Bernini, with candlesticks by Pascal de Chabirol.

There is much post-war glass throughout by Couterant, Ingrand and Godin. The 150m free-standing **belfry**, begun 1472, was extensively re-stored and completed by Abadie. It has a stair turret zipping up one side and huge seated figures on the buttress tops. The tower contains strangely preserved bodies found in the medieval cemetery, put here from shortage of space.

The quartier St-Michel feels different from the rest of Bordeaux, perhaps more provincial, and in part, very run down. The Rue C. Sauvageau leads south-east from the church towards **STE-CROIX**, a major Romanesque building but another victim of Abadie. Ste-Croix was the town's Benedictine abbey though nothing remains save the church. Basically 12C, it has particularly fine east apses, the central polygonal, with good capitals. The west front needs sorting out. The upper sections and sculpture looks like Abadie, the left tower and the mounted St. George certainly are. Otherwise it is good 12C work, elaborate and recently cleaned. The capitals, barley-sugar columns, the figures of Avarice and Luxury and the gymnastic voussoirs of the central door are very fine.

The **interior** is very light and very odd, a sort of architectural jumble sale. The flat east wall with its three chapels and transept arms are spacially unrelated to the nave. The chapels have been much restored. The north transept contains a fine 15C abbot's tomb. The Romanesque crossing piers have interesting capitals, which depict Abraham and Isaac, Daniel, and Christ amongst the Doctors. The nave piers are inconsistent, beginning with Romanesque, then Gothic c 1200 (going with the vault), then 17C(?) boxing something earlier. The six-part vault covers the nave in two strides, quite ridiculously stretched, and hacks merrily across the clerestory windows.

Beside the church is a miniature Arts and Crafts presbytery, while behind stands a curious 18C sunken fountain built into a fragment of the 14C city wall.

The Rue de Hamel opposite the west front winds through to the Place des Capucins and the main markets of Bordeaux. The whole area is richly 18C and is beginning to be gentrified. The market buildings are modern. The Rue Bergeret opposite ends at the Rue Leyteire and the route continues across the road as the Rue Causserouge to the Rue du Mirail, much of the time maintaining the 18C theme. Arriving at the Rue du Mirail, with some very grand hôtels, is the view of the **Grosse Cloche** (right), a veritable symbol of Bordeaux. Formerly the Porte St-Eloi, it was rebuilt in the 15C and restored 1876/7. The low gate is topped by an enormous number of mouldings cut though the thickness of wall. Two fat round towers flank the gate with wall walks slung between, and of course, a clock. The Wagnerian roofs are 19C. Next door is St-Eloi, reconstructed in the 15C and built into a section of the 13C city wall. It has a little eastern octagonal tower and pretty 16C façade, but is commonly locked. The dismal area fronting the Grosse Cloche (currently under reconstruction) is in marked contrast to the interesting Rue St-James within, preserving houses from the 16C.

Back at the gate, walk west along the Cours Victor Hugo to the junction of Cours Pasteur and the **MUSEE D'AQUITAINE**, an ambitious museum tracing the human history of the region from prehistory up to the 20C. Finds and displays cover many districts and aspects of the area, and are arranged chronologically and with some flair. Unfortunately, not everything is labelled. The **ground floor** begins with prehistoric finds (25,000 year old relief sculptures and reconstructions of wall paintings from the Dordogne), Bronze Age (a gold torque, coins), and a major Roman collection with altars, sculpture, architectural elements, a reconstructed section of the town wall with many re-used architectural fragments, mosaics, bronzes and a model of Roman Bordeaux (see the 17C prints of the lost temple on the site of the Grand Théâtre). Individual sections are devoted to aspects of Roman life—family, religion etc. and early Christian art and burials.

The section on **Medieval Aquitaine** includes the English occupation, and has Nottingham alabasters amongst a small collection of medieval figure sculpture, Romanesque capitals and a large traceried wheel window. A gallery devoted to the Friars in Bordeaux leads to the 16/17C collection (Gothic pierced-work wooden window shutters, early Renaissance retable, tombs, bust of Cardinal François de Sourdis, 1622, by **Bernini**).

The **first floor** covers many topics from 1715 to the present day with the help of models and montages (trade and navigation, 18C agriculture, Bordeaux's maritime links around the world, specific regions within Aquitaine including the Béarnais, viniculture etc.). The 19C is reached with barely a mention of the Revolution, a curious oversight given the important role played by Bordeaux. The last 100 years lack vital areas—the railway and transport, war and the German occupation.

Leaving the museum, a right along Cours Pasteur returns you to the Cathedral. Turn right on Cours d'Alsace Lorraine and you intersect Rue Ste-Catherine, the principal and longest shopping street in Bordeaux (pedestrianised).

2

Bourg and Blaye

This circular route heading north and west of Bordeaux provides a variety of sites and landscapes. It is easily accessed from Bordeaux and offers an escape from the city's bustle into gentle countryside, with long stretches of riverside, a short boat ride, woods, lakes and the sea. It includes isolated buildings, small towns, abbeys and churches and a major Roman site.

Leave Bordeaux by the A10 (direction Saintes) and, once clear of the busy Pont d'Aquitaine, exit at Junction 30a, St-André de Cubzac on the D670. Cross the little town and head for the 669 (direction Bourg).

Once on the 669, the countryside opens up and Bordeaux is quickly forgotten. At **St-Gervais** (3km) on the right is a small three-cell Romanesque church with a decorated apse and a nice quiet stop. From behind the church, a detour on the D137 passes through St-Laurent d'Arce to the N137, where you follow the signs for **Magrigne** and a rare Templars Chapel. If you spot the chapel off the road to your left you have missed the turning. The Templars were one of the knightly religious orders founded during the Crusades to protect the Holy Places in Palestine. They grew rich from endowments, principally property, and aroused the envy of kings throughout Europe. With Palestine lost once more to Islam, they had little to do but lots of money to do it with. The Templars were suppressed in the early 14C. This church was undoubtedly attached to a retirement home for elderly or infirm knights. The chapel is an oblong box standing isolated in a field. No other buildings survive though corbels along the side walls indicate their former presence. There are no side windows. The interior (key from house opposite) is stark and impressive. Three windows light the east wall, one the west. The pointed barrel vault just cuts the windows and could be later. The dates are c 1160 for the shell, and c 1180 for the vault. The medieval altar retains paint fragments while to the right is a severe piscina. Throughout the simple interior are consecration crosses in red paint. The side walls have benches. To the north is an 18C pulpit, and there is another possibly medieval altar on the south side.

Heading back towards Bourg along the N137 to Blaye, turn left at Pugnac on the D249 towards **Tauriac**, a pleasant spot boasting a characteristically Bordelais Romanesque church with its square, two-storey west front, arcaded and with columns at each end, heavy cornices, interlace capitals and sculptured corbels, topped off with a bellcote. There are two free-standing sculptures, a man on horseback and an Agnus Dei, the latter possibly Carolingian. The curiously squat interior is the result of a massive raising of the floor level.

The D133/D669 brings you to **Bourg** (6km), an interesting small riverside town and wine centre of Roman origin. (Tourist Office, Hôtel de la Jurade, 33710. Tel 57 68 31 76, fax 57 68 30 25. Market around church, Tues. am.) Parking at Place F. Jeantet by the Maison des Vins (information board on local châteaux) and glimpses of the river below. The town is mostly pedestrianised and has some historic buildings.

The main street, Rue Valentin Bernard, leads to a little square, Place de la Libération, dominated by the 19C market hall and a rather odd clock-tower. The latter belongs to the Hôtel de Ville and tourist office. Behind, a small garden is reached by a flyover bridge, looking down on to the steep steps of Rue de la Gouttinière which passes beneath. The garden has views of the river and the town walls. The church is 19C and dull but passing round the far side and turning left, the entrance of the *citadelle* leads to another garden and the 18C pavilion where local Côte de Bourg may be tasted (closed Mon). It stands on the site of the Archbishop of Bordeaux's summer residence. The view of the town from the terrace is much photographed.

The Place Libération can be regained by taking the Rue du 4 Septembre in front of the church. On the opposite corner of the square, the Rue Cahoreau drops away, passing beneath the rugged 13C town gate and into the Place Eugène Marchal and the little Cours du Port. The Rue de la Fontaine on the right leads, as its name suggests, to a spring emerging from the rock, while from here, the picturesque view includes a 19C Moorish house. The stairs from the fountain lead back to the town gate and once through, a little stair right leads in a circuit until you land on top of the gate for another view. The street opposite returns to the main street, with a view of the late Gothic Museum in the distance.

Proceeding west from Bourg, a turning right almost immediately is sign-posted for the **Crypte Romain**. Finding this Romanesque fragment is almost as interesting as the monument itself, the lane dipping and twisting until you feel quite lost. You then follow a signpost left and park, apparently in someone's field. What you see is a low rubbly wall a foot or so high. Enter and you are in a small church. The apse was raised over a crypt which survives. (If locked, enquire at the adjoining house.) The little crypt is entered through a low doorway with interlace capitals. It has a four-bay barrel-vaulted interior linked in double bays with alternating piers, and narrow vaulted side-aisles. The capitals are crude though vigorously carved, some appropriately decorated with grapes, others with palmettes. The whole thing is c 1030 and thickly covered in rich green moss. Would it be so interesting if it were scrubbed and beneath a standing church? Perhaps not, but then you found it, others did not.

Returning to the main road out of Bourg, a left at Pain de Sucre leads to the alternative and more attractive **Corniche de Gironde**. At times beautiful and hair-raising, this road bounces along beneath sudden rocky outcrops with ancient cave dwellings, and offers occasional stretches of river bank. The elaborately decorated little Romanesque church at **Bayon**, heavily restored, has a curious trefoil plan. Eventually the corniche returns to the main road.

At **Plassac** (6km), a sudden left in the village is marked *Fouilles Archéolo-gique*. This is one of the best Roman sites in Aquitaine, discovered in 1883. Turn into the village and go round the back of the little church and park. To the north of the church lies a huge and disorganised site, being a **Roman villa** in three phases dating from the entire Roman period. The house began on an artificial platform close to the river, but was redeveloped repeatedly, each time getting larger and further from the original site. It finally covered 6000 sq m. Needless to say, the excavated remains are puzzling, though the **colourful mosaic floors** close to the church are clear enough, especially the patterned floor over a hypocaust within a polygonal apse, and the star patterned floor disappearing beneath the north wall of the church. The Roman drains still work though the site is threatened by the rising water table. Opposite, the little museum is a gem and a model of clarity. Site plans and reconstructions flesh out the remains and finds. The ground floor has more mosaics and there are stunning **painting fragments** in the third Pompeian style of c AD 30–40. See especially a cupid riding a flying swan and the columns sprouting various animals. Upstairs, the more domestic finds include loom weights, ironwork, coins, stamped pottery and small bronzes.

The main road then enters **Blaye** (3km) along the riverside. (Tourist Office, Allées Marine, 33390. Tel 57 42 12 09.) Another famous wine centre, Blaye (Roman *Blavia*) is dominated by a great **fortress** which guards the Gironde and a little harbour creek. The town is ordinary but park by the creek (the tourist office is under the trees). When you enter the château the place is transformed. The magnificent Renaissance walls of 1689 are by Vauban and are, as the approach to the Porte Dauphin confirms, quite forbidding. Within, the rambling rural settlement comes as a great surprise; this was the medieval town all but swept away by Louis XIV.

The road leads on up to a medieval gate and the ruined 14C **Château des Rudel**. Little survives but the relics are impressive. It once defended the medieval town and within its walls Roland was buried after the Battle of Ronceval, 778. Here too was born Jaufre Rudel, the famous 12C troubadour, who died in the arms of his 'lover from afar' Princess Mélissande of Tripoli. Climb the bank behind and the tower provides a good view of the surviving medieval towers and of Vauban's principal outwork before the Porte Royale. The rest of the enclosure is green and leafy, and has buildings dotted about. (Campsite and two-star hotel.)

The little museum in the Pavilion de la Place, the former prison of the troublesome Duchesse de Berry, has plans and drawings of Vauban's work, while rustic lanes lead past flower-decked cottages. It is a delightful place for wandering and has good riverside views. Near the Porte Dauphin lies the Bastin St-Romain, a medieval gate caught up in Vauban's scheme, with dank passages and dripping chambers. See it now before it is sanitised but take a torch.

Blaye is the most convenient point to cross the Gironde, the car and passenger ferry taking about 20 minutes. The crossing meanders around mud banks and islands and affords good views of the fortress. The south bank is in châteaux country and boasts many famous names. It is best to drive around and spot them at random as many are open for tasting and some châteaux may be visited. Enquire locally, though none are oustanding. Note the twin-towered **Château Bayerville**, the Renaissance **Château Lambert** and the Chinese style **château at Cos**. Despite its famous name, the village of **Pauillac** (16km from ferry) is disappointing.

Take the pretty road through Lespare, after which the countryside becomes a scrubby breckland. From here on, the scenery is remarkably different, with thick woods, lakes and of course, the sea. The land ends at **Soulac-sur-mer** (65km from ferry), a 19C seaside town of Roman origin, retaining a prettily- painted gentility. (Tourist Office, 95 Rue de la Plage, 33780. Tel 56 09 86 61, fax 56 73 63 76.) It also houses a splendid Romanesque **abbey church** quite literally dug out from the sand. By 1757 the 11C church had become buried in the encroaching dunes which still figure prominently all around. At one time they almost reached the roof. The exterior is much restored, though the east apse looks intact. The transepts are lost. The interior is tall but note that the floor is more than 2m higher than the original, explaining the curious floor-level windows in the side apses. The nave and aisles are barrel vaulted all at one height. The capitals are interesting, particularly along the south arcade, which has monsters chewing foliage, and men doing odd things between the legs of fantastic animals. The north arcade contains an integral stair turret, perhaps from a lost screen.

The 101 going south is the Route des Lacs and follows the coast at a discreet distance (naturist beaches). The woodlands hereabouts are beautiful, especially in the late afternoon. At Carcans (53km), a right (D207) leads to **Lac Hourtin Carcans** (8km), whose sedge filled shallows are rich in water-lilies and plants. The area is popular for boating and wind surfing. A little beyond lies the sea (4.5km) and an enormous beach.

Return to Bordeaux via the D207, D1, N215. The round trip including detours, is 260km.

Blaye

3

St-Émilion

This route begins unpromisingly with the Libourne road from Bordeaux but once past this initial obstacle, the rest is rural and sometimes idyllic. It forms a good introduction to the affordable wine country and has plentiful sites and attractions.

Leave Bordeaux on the N10 then N89 for Libourne (31km).

Libourne (Hotels/Rest.) was a *bastide* town founded in 1269 by the Kentishman Richard de Leybourne. (Tourist Office, Place Abel Surchamp 33500. Tel 57 51 15 04.) It has a typical grid plan, a market square preserving a number of characteristically arcaded buildings and a severe traffic problem. A half-finished bypass may one day ease this. For those wishing a quieter centre than Bordeaux, Libourne is well situated and served by a main station on the Paris–Bordeaux railway. Trains also go to St-Émilion, Bergerac, Angoulême and Périgueux. From the station at Guitres, 16km north of Libourne, a period railway runs through the pretty valley of the Isle.

Libourne stands on the confluence of the Isle and the Dordogne, which should have assured its success as a port. Yet the town had several false starts, the Romans settling just south at Condat, the town vanishing with the Empire. Charlemagne had another go, this time on the present site but that too languished. It was the English who made Libourne.

The central *bastide* square is now mostly 16C and later. The town hall is part-15C but very restored. In the east corner, Rue Victor Hugo begins with some attractive 18C houses and Rue Fonneuve has a fine intersection with Rue des Chars, 18C on the right, 16C to the left, and late 18C on the opposite corners. Rue des Chars leads (right) to the river l'Isle and the Grand Port, the only surviving gate and dating mostly from 1358. Only one tower is carried up with a conical roof. The river banks could be attractive. Behind the gate is a medieval shop. Rue Victor Hugo returns to the square past more attractive buildings. The big church to the south is mostly 19C but impressive. (Market Tues, Fri, Sun am.) South of the town, beyond the railway, is a little chapel of **Condat**, said to have been founded by Eleanor of Aquitaine. It is Gothic, probably 15C, and usually locked.

Fronsac, 3km north west of Libourne on the D670 is one of the most famous vineyards of Bordeaux. The dishevelled church once had a Romanesque rib-vaulted chancel (key at rear, pretty overgrown garden). After a 16C modernisation and extension, the church seems to have fallen on hard times. Its present appearance owes much to the 18C. There is a good pulpit and a number of Merovingian tombs in the entrance plus a late-Antique marble capital employed as a flower-stand. The great château, founded in 769 by Pepin the Short, fell foul of Richelieu and was demolished in 1633 (the Cardinal took the title Duc de Fronsac) but the hill-top site still commands magnificent views and the *dégustation* is superb.

4km east of Libourne is **Pomerol**, home of another famous Claret, and 12km further east **ST-ÉMILION** (Hotels/Rest), perhaps the best known name in the region and certainly the most interesting town (tourist office, Place Créneaux, 33330. Tel 57 24 72 03). The town is best reached fom the Libourne east radial road, then the D243. The area was well-known for its wine in the Roman period, the poet Ausone owned vineyards here, but the town began as a pilgrim centre around the cave dwelling of its name saint. St-Émilion lies off the main road in attractive rolling countryside dotted with vineyards and *petit châteaux*. The town is approached suddenly and it is best to park immediately at the Porte Bourgogne. Parking is also possible at the northern approach to the town, still the D122, at the Porte Bourgeoise. This has the added advantage of being at the top of the hill.

St-Émilion is steep, full of picturesque corners and packed with tourists. Unlike many famous wine towns, here there is plenty to see. The two dominant monuments are the hill-top church and the castle, both commanding good, complimentary views of the town. The other monuments are best seen on an official tour, especially as many are kept locked and need to be opened up. (Enquire at the tourist office at the top of the town, south of the church.)

The walk from the southern parking area takes you straight into the medieval town on the Rue Porte Bouqueyre, passing stone houses and shops of many periods, often with vaulted cellars open to the street. To the left is the **château**, a real castle this, not a house. It is approached via a rather slippery rockface and through a number of natural-looking caves.

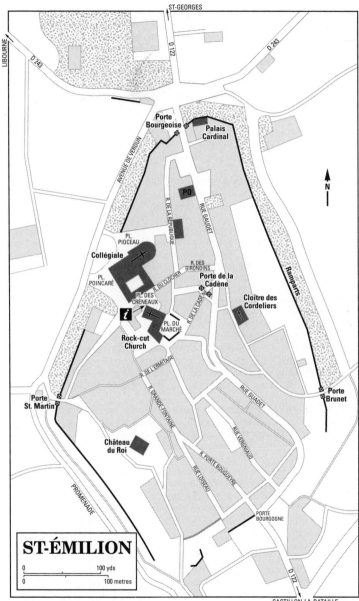

ST-GEORGES

LIBOURNE

D 243

D 122

D 243

Porte Bourgeoise

Palais Cardinal

AVENUE DE VERDUN

PO

R. DE LA RÉPUBLIQUE

RUE GAUDET

PL. PIOCEAU

Collégiale

PL. POINCARÉ

R. DU CLOCHER

R. DES GIRONDINS

Porte de la Cadène

Ramparts

PL. DES CRÉNEAUX

R. DE LA CADÈNE

Cloître des Cordeliers

PL. DU MARCHÉ

Rock-cut Church

R. DE L'ERMITAGE

R. GRANDE-FONTAINE

RUE GUADET

Porte St. Martin

Porte Brunet

Château du Roi

RUE VERNHAUD

R. PORTE BOUQUEYRE

RUE LOISEAU

PROMENADE

PORTE BOURGOGNE

N

ST-ÉMILION

| 0 | | 100 yds |
| 0 | | 100 metres |

D 122

CASTILLON-LA-BATAILLE

Much of the stone for the building above you was quarried from the rock below. The 13C building was begun by Louis VIII, who seemed very fond of stairs. The central keep is extremely slim and has more buttresses than wall. The first floor chamber retains paint fragments suggesting curtains. The views of the dusty brown village tumbling off the rock are memorable.

The main street continues past the castle as Rue Grande-Fontaine, then turns right into Rue de l'Hermitage and enters a little staggered square before the rock-cut churches. (These can only be visited with a guide.) The arrangement is almost theatrical. To the left is the little 13C hermitage built over the saint's cave dwelling, next, a Gothic portal leading straight into the rock face, then various Flamboyant windows again cut into the rock while the rest of the square is made up of cafés, shops and twisting street entries. Dominating the lot is the giant belfry, soaring above the cliff-face and threatening collapse.

Continuing the climb up Rue de la Cadène, notice the **Porte Cadène** with its associated late-medieval timber-framed house all jettied, criss-crossed and dotted with sculpture. At the top, notice too the large 15C stone house opposite on the Rue Guadet. Turn left into Rue Girondins, and you are at the tourist office; walking further round you reach **Collégiale**, the principal ecclesiastical building of the town. It is a domed church though neither wide nor vast. The west front is very damaged, a Virgin and Child can just be made out to the right of the door. The entry is two storeyed, the upper rib vaulted. The nave has two domed bays preceding a big transept, rebuilt in the 13/14C. The choir is 13C though the present apse represents a rebuild of the 15C. The Romanesque capitals throughout are curiously bald but seem original. The two-bay chapel against the north wall of the nave is a 15C addition, with complex rib-vaults and heraldic bossses. There are numerous fittings. The 16C choir stalls have misericords. Paintings survive from several medieval periods, on the west wall (a Crucifixion) and in the south transept, and there are also painted consecration crosses. The south nave wall shows several overlaid painted schemes including figured scenes, roundels and curtains. The wooden door in the south transept is ancient.

To the south of the church is a **cloister** (apply Tourist Office). The 14C arches rest on double columns though sections of Romanesque work survive along the east walk (chapter house door.) The two traceried arches adjoining were probably book cupboards. Note the canopied tombs along the south walk.

South of the cloister, the free-standing bell tower zips skywards, the airy openwork middle storey merrily ignored by the rocketing stair turret.

Opposite the west front, notice the stretch of machicolated **town wall** now severed by the road. It once sliced the north west angle of the church.

Passing round the north side of the church, the north door of the *collégiale* contains what looks like a damaged Christ in Majesty. Further on, the Rue de la République ends at Porte Bourgeoise, and another exposed section of the town wall (right) into which was built the Palais du Cardinal, a 13C mansion with twin-light upper windows, now very ruined. On the other side, the remarkable series of arches and windows standing in a field is the remains of the 14C Dominican church, abandoned in the Hundred Years War.

The **guided walk** about the town descends from the Tourist Office through steep and often slippery streets until the rock-cut churches are regained.

The visit begins with the hermitage, passing by the late 12C Gothic **chapel** which is in danger of dereliction. The interior may be viewed from the west end, the apse vault is effective. St. Émilion, died 767, was a wandering Breton monk who settled in a cave in the abandoned ruins of a Roman settlement. He attracted a number of followers and a monastery evolved. He spent much of his life in a cave under the present church. Steep stairs lead to a small rock-cut chamber in two parts. An arch opposite the entry is said to contain his bed, while to the left is a small spring. The second area was an oratory and preserves a primitive altar and a niche containing a modern work. The far wall reveals a blocked arch, formerly the pilgrim's entrance.

Next comes the most curious of all the sites. A simple door leads into a funnel-shaped chamber, rising through the rock in the form of a spout. This is domed within the natural rock, the upward extension surrounded by a spiral stair. Note the curious rock-cut bearded half-figures 'supporting' the roof. The chamber served as the entry to an extensive catacombs. To the left is the most interesting area with multiple tombs, and an abandoned architectural scheme. Zig-zag piers and rib-vaults were cut directly from the rock face, and at one point, a complete 13C clustered pier supports the natural roof. It would appear that the catacombs occupied what was originally a quarry.

The main route from the catacomb entry leads in a roundabout way to the most famous curiosity of St-Émilion, the **rock-cut church**, begun in the 8C and completed in the 12C. It has its own street door, though this is not used by the tour. The church is basilican, that is, it has a 'nave' and flanking 'aisles'. Needless to say there are no upper or side windows, lighting being achieved entirely from windows cut into the west face, hence the Flamboyant openings fronting the little square. The 'barrel vaults' are supported on giant cross-plan piers but otherwise the interior is generally featureless. Deep in the gloomy interior, it is sometimes possible to make out crude carvings in the rock vault including angels and signs of the Zodiac. Tragically, the decision to erect the *collégiale* belfry on the rock edge immediately over the underground church was not wise, the whole edifice threatening to telescope down through the vaults. Only this excuses the unfortunate scaffolding contraption that permanently disfigures this most intriguing interior.

The ruins of **Des Cordliers** in the Rue Porte Brunet are also worth seeing (note the early medieval house façade diagonally opposite entry). The monastic ruins are well kept and house a café specialising in a *méthode Champenois* wine. The apsidal church is mostly 15C while other sections include bits of the cloister. Beneath, the cave is housed in a tunnel said to be in excess of 1km long. It may be visited (fee).

Market day is Sunday morning; festivals in May, June and September.

At **Petit-Palais**, 14.5km north of St-Émilion, there is a small Romanesque church, said to be papal. It has an elaborately arcaded west front in the manner of the Santoigne. The interior (south side door) is very pointed and gives the impression that it once had broken barrel vaults. Now, it has late-Gothic ribs. Fancy capitals line the north wall arcade.

The D670 leads south from St-Émilion over rolling vineyards towards the Dordogne, where there is a pretty crossing at St-Jean de Blaignac (11km).

Beyond, is **Rauzon** (D670/D23, 7km), a tiny town dominated by the great ruined early-14C **Château des Duras** (here is also the Tourist Office 33420. Tel 57 84 13 04). It was still in English hands in 1437 when the young Henry VI granted it to Bernard Angevin.

On close inspection, the château seems set in a large hole. A big round tower flanks a gutted residence block, resplendent with long sharply cut arrow slits. The living quarters have massive buttresses and four-square windows high up. The circuit walls have long exposed rubble strips where the dressed stone buttresses have been robbed. It is worth walking around the moat to see the raw rock face, the *garde-robe* exits and the views. The *garde-robe* chutes seem too wide for safety. An old bridge gives access to a ruined bailey. The **interior** is collapsed but appealing. The ivy-clad ruins include some barrel-vaulted rooms.

On the opposite side of the valley, the **church** enjoys a magnificent view of the castle, especially from the little path from the east end which is truly rural. The 13C church was aisleless but was widened late in the Middle Ages. The west loggia is 16C. Above, the typical bell-cote occupies the width of the nave gable. The west door is 13C, flanked by arches with a later door to right. A widening towards the south explains the odd appearance of the interior. The 13C building was a single space and barrel-vaulted. The south wall was then pierced, the remaining wall stumps being shaped into lumpy piers, all this without disturbing the main vault which now appears perilously perched on corbels. The new aisle has tierceron vaults with heraldic bosses and some crude figures of St. Sebastian, bishops and saints.

Return to the D670, then the D127 for **Blasimon** (8km; Tourist Office, Hôtel de Ville, 33540. Tel 56 71 52 12). The **abbey** of Blasimon is one of Aquitaine's secret delights. Set in a gentle, secluded valley, the church and monastic ruins form a memorable picturesque grouping (if locked, key at the *mairie* in the village above). The abbey belonged to Sauve Majeur and was burnt by the Huguenots in 1587. The claustral buildings are very ruined but the cloister and chapter house range are clear enough, as is the abrupt turret standing at the south-west angle. Big buttresses have been added to the church. The joy of the site is its waterlogged state, the shallow pools with plants and wild-life may be bad for the buildings but are unforgettable. The church is approached down a shady avenue. It is surprisingly complicated.

The north exterior wall should be inspected first. The eastern end reveals the low rubble wall of the earliest church. In the 12C this was extended west with a new building, just over two bays long plus a west front. In the 13C the old church was raised and vaulted. There are no aisles. The west front is famous for its curious sculpture. The façade is divided vertically by half-columns, with a single west window. All the details are High Romanesque. The west door has splendid sculpture, scenes of battles, confronting beasts and luxuriant foliage. Most famous are the elongated knight and lady, legs crossed and curving round the arch. The interior has four bays divided by big wall piers. The saucer-shaped rib vaults are heavily restored. All the internal sculpture is post 1200. The first bay west has a fine Romanesque window opening, beautifully detailed and preserved. Not surprisingly, the other windows are somewhat erratically placed.

From the abbey, the hilltop village of Blasimon, founded c 1320 is quickly reached. A detour from here is a pleasant rural ride to **Mauriac** (D127/D127E4, 5km), another remote gem of the region. The setting is

The church at Mauriac

lovely; just when you have given up all hopes of finding it, there it stands on a leafy knoll, the church and farm making an attractive group. The church key usually sticks out from the lock. The Romanesque church is almost perfectly cruciform, one bay projecting each side of a crossing. Over the east window, a curious roof structure that appears to end in a double *garde-robe* chute which could be defensive. The interior is impressive with barrel vaults in all directions and windows in the gable ends. The crossing is covered by an irregular dome supported by piers with extensive sculpture, not of high quality but fun: see Adam and Eve covering their nakedness on the north east pier. The south transept chapel has rustic wall paintings of the apostles, 16C, and a *papier mâché* Lourdes to save you the journey.

Pick up the D232 beyond Mauriac church, note the amazingly grand *mairie*, and head south for the D672 and **Sauveterre** (8.5km), which is entered through a fractured arch. (Tourist Office, 1 Rue Saint Romain, 33540. Tel 56 71 53 45, fax 56 71 59 39.) Of all the towns called Sauveterre in Aquitaine, this is the one for Entre-Deux-Mers. It is also a real town with real shops. Sauveterre is a *bastide* town, founded 1281, diamond-plan with the gates at the points. The centre has the usual square retaining some of the original arcaded buildings. (Market on Tuesdays.) Note especially the timbered ceilings within the arcades of the Hôtel de Ville and the town gates spotted in the distance. The lane beside the Hôtel, Rue Lafon, has timber-framed buildings all wonky, with criss-cross timbers and rare, unglazed shuttered openings. On the corner is the Tourist Office, occupying a well restored 13C building. The vaulted crypt may be visited, with its delivery chutes from the street. There is a small display of distilling. The office holds the key to another medieval crypt in the square where the local white may be tasted (usually groups only but try asking). The little 13C church needs scant attention. Another gate, tall and pencil-thin, leads out on the D671 towards Sauve Majeur, 22km.

The great hilltop abbey ruins of **Sauve Majeur** dominate the little village and can be seen for miles around. As a ruin it is on a par with those of Yorkshire. The abbey was founded in 1079 by the Duke of Aquitaine, the Pope and the saintly Gérard, whose relics are in the parish church. It was well endowed and had daughter houses spread from England to Spain. It was known as la Grande Sauve and had at its height some 300 monks. Standing on the pilgrim route to Santiago, it received many important visitors, including Eleanor of Aquitaine.

The former Benedictine abbey is entered through a late building, housing a display of photographs and finds: note the elaborate columns and the carved owl. The **church** has three parallel apses, a transept and aisled nave. The surviving tower is curiously placed over the south aisle at roughly the mid-point of the nave. The **east apse** exterior is heavily decorated with Romanesque capitals and a dwarf arcade over the windows. The side apses have sculpted corbels including acrobats. The interior of the chancel has odd, dumpy piers between the sanctuary and the aisles, decorated with bunches of grapes (south) and fighting centaurs (north). The side aisles are barrel-vaulted and end with semi-domes. The main apse is very dramatic, mostly standing but the retaining arch has been seriously fractured. The chancel clerestory windows have more sculpture. The chancel fittings were late Gothic, see the aumbry cupboard with remains of painted decoration. Dotted about the church are sculptured roundels containing apostles. There is also a rare form of consecration cross.

The **north transept** has particularly good Romanesque sculpture: Adam and Eve, lions biting men by the legs, Ulysses and the Sirens and men generally tangled in foliage. The winged monsters resembling chickens are said to be basiliscs. The rest of the church is generally ruined, save for the majestic tower, which may be climbed. Note in the preceding bay east, Romanesque capitals depicting Abraham and Isaac and the St. John the Baptist saga. The vault here was groined, that is pre-c 1130. Beyond the tower, the aisle has a later rib vault.

The interior of the **tower** has a fine stellar vault with a central bell-opening. The tower becomes octagonal and has flying buttresses supporting the upper stage. The views from the top (steep climb) are rewarding. The west front had a narthex Cistercian style, now ruined. The sculpture includes a very Islamic basket capital and an angel. This end of the church clearly fell in the late Middle Ages, much of the structure is a late-Gothic rebuild.

The claustral buildings are less well preserved. Two book cupboards survive against the south transept, then a little sacristy followed by the chapter house in five aisles and a tiled floor. To the south stands a section of the refectory, formerly vaulted. The plate tracery windows suggest a date of c 1200.

On the far hill stands the **parish church**, oddly sited within a triangular churchyard with medieval crosses at the angles representing the Trinity. The church is Romanesque and later. Notice especially the sculpted figures of SS. Peter, James, Michael and the Virgin and Child flanking the east windows; also St. Peter over the main south door. The dark interior has a painted chancel, very restored, with scenes of the Magi and St. Martin. There is more painting, this time 15/16C with St. Michael in the second bay on the north side. The late-Gothic twisted vault supports are unusual. At the west end north aisle is a 14C altar tomb of Gérard, founder of la Grande Sauve, topped with the (unrelated) figure of an abbot. The sculptures show scenes from Gérard's life. On the west wall is a painting of the Crucifixion.

The D671 returns to Bordeaux via **Créon** (3km), another *bastide* town with a central uncommercialised square. (Tourist Office, 7 Bis Rue Docteur Fauché, 33670. Tel 56 68 54 41, fax 56 68 54 46.) It was founded in 1315 by Amaury III de Craon et de Sable, Lord of Ste-Maure and of Marcillac, Hereditary Seneschal of Maine and Poitou. The central square has arcades on three sides (Market Wednesdays), while the late-Gothic church (porch dated 1538) has a stellar vaulted apse and a 13C stone Virgin and Child in the north chapel. Return to Bordeaux via the D671 and D936, 24km.

4

Périgueux

PÉRIGUEUX (Hotels/Rest.) is one of the most interesting and attractive towns in Aquitaine, and a good centre for touring the Périgord and Dordogne. (Tourist Office, 1 Avenue Aquitaine, tel 53 53 10 63 and more conveniently at Place Francheville, 24000, tel 53 53 10 63, fax 53 09 02 50. Also, the Département of Dordogne, 16 Rue Président Wilson, tel 53 53 44 35, fax 53 69 51 41.) Trains to Bordeaux via Libourne, 75 minutes to Limoges, 80 minutes, to Agen, 150 minutes, to Bergerac, 90 minutes, to Les Ezies and Le Bugue, 90 minutes.

Périgueux is famous for its food and cooking. A Roman town of some stature, it contains the region's principal standing remains from that period. The town is in two distinct sections divided by a modern shopping zone. One area, dominated by St-Etienne de la Cité, represents the Roman and early-medieval town and contains all the main Roman remains. The other, more obviously medieval, surrounds the important Romanesque abbey of St-Front, now the cathedral. If you are staying in Périgueux then the two parts may be seen in any order. But if you are spending only one day in the town then parking is most convenient at Place Francheville, half-way between the two. If you come by train, take a taxi to St-Etienne and then walk.

ST-ETIENNE DE LA CITE was formerly the cathedral of Périgueux. It was severely damaged in the French Wars of Religion, and the see transferred to St-Front in 1669. The building has been rather dryly restored, and some parts have disappeared. It stands on a dreadful traffic junction, and its size and grandeur can only be judged from the south. The building consists now of only two box-like bays; the third to the west is in ruins, a fourth quite lost. The mid-12C east bay is the larger and has a red tiled roof surrounding the raised dome. The tall wall arcades framing the windows have a curiously modern look, like some Louis Sullivan Chicago warehouse. The next bay is smaller and earlier, and gives the impression that it would happily slip inside the first like a Chinese box. It dates from the late 11C and curiously recalls the early mosques of Turkey. We now come to the ruined third bay and the present entrance. Standing before the west end, notice the remains of the side walls of the lost bay with evidence of internal wall arcades, and sections of the lost dome bulging from the corners. The whole entry wall is a 17C infill of a previous internal open arch.

Entering the church you see the significance of the building. It is vaulted in single spaces by giant Romanesque domes. Indeed, St-Etienne may well be the forerunner of all the 60 or so domed churches in south west France, and the influence of the eastern Mediterranean world is immediately obvious. The **interior** is also gloomy, evidence that such domed designs though suitable for the intense light of Cyprus or Anatolia, were not so good for Aquitaine. The difference in date between the two surviving domed bays is also very obvious. The earlier west bay is crude in construction and finish and has little or no decoration. The lateral wall walks appear impracticable. The dome is carried on pointed arches and proper Classical pendentives (spherical triangular angles). The later east bay is more elegant and light, with strong articulation of parts and larger windows. The dome is amongst the largest in the group, 15m in diameter (St-Front is 13m). Looking back, the junction between the two phases is all too evident. The 11C church ended with an east apse which opened from the lower arch of this junction. The foundation of the apse can be seen in the modern crypt beneath the altar. Few fittings survived the religious turmoil of the 16C. On the north side is the arcaded tomb of Bishop Jean d'Asside, died 1168, the probable builder of the new east end. Next door is an inscription naming the sculptor, one Constantine de Jaurnac. Opposite is a big 17C Baroque altarpiece in wood, with SS. Peter and Paul and scenes of St. Front: see him casting the devil from the Tour Vésone. It came from elsewhere.

From St-Etienne, a **circular walk** will take in the Roman and other sites of the area. (Access to the Roman villa excavations is via an official town walk with a guide, ask in the tourist office at Place Francheville.)

Begin south of the church on the Rue Romaine and pass sections of the Roman **town wall**. On reaching the railway, the great Roman **Tour Vésone** is most obvious. It is reached by a left, then over the railway, then a little gate leads into the surrounding park.

The Tour Vésone is a massive cylinder of rubble and (surely) concrete. It is very thin-walled, immensely tall and dramatically torn-down at one point. It stands on the remains of a podium, also circular. What precise form the original structure took is unclear but it was certainly a temple, centrally planned, that is, a circular sanctuary probably surrounded by a lower colonnaded structure. The lower sections of the surviving drum were inside the enclosing structure, while the upper part was exposed and had its own roof. The entrance was via a platform and stair near the lost section, and the door must have provided an easy point of destruction. While centralised temples were common in Roman Gaul, this one must have been very strange. The large blocks visible about one third of the way up may be remains of through-stones forming part of the connection between the outer and inner structures. Otherwise the tower is featureless save for a brick band, some subtle changes of material and construction marking the phases of its building and the little brick-arched openings near the present top, said to be windows though they appear blocked. Red plaster survives

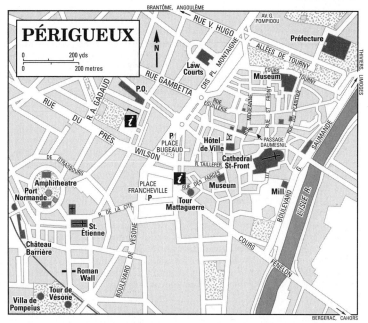

in patches both inside and out. The loss of much of the surface some way up the drum represents the robbing of the cut blocks at what was then the rubble strewn ground level. The temple, of unknown dedication, was apparently abandoned c 270, when defensive walls were hastily built against barbarian attack, leaving the Tour Vésone outside. Material from the site was probably used in the town walls.

Leave the garden by the back gate nearest the railway and after 100m the net fencing left encloses a major domestic site, the **Villa de Pompeïus** (visit with guide). The site is confusing and as yet unexplained. The villa has three phases of building and expansion, the first from Augustus, another around c 100 and yet another a century later. The house was abandoned c 270 but possibly re-occupied later. The earliest work furthest from the road preserves a 'swimming pool' with a typical black and white mosaic floor. From the second phase comes the peristyle courtyard, with Doric columns, some re-erected. The central round basin comes from the third period. The flanking chambers have yielded considerable areas of painted fragments, currently stored in the city museum but destined for a museum on site. Other areas of colour remain in situ. The rooms include a complete bathhouse complex and a triclinium (dining room) over a hypocaust.

Continuing on from the Roman site, a small bridge on the right crosses the railway once more. From here, a remarkable view of the Roman **town walls**, complete with semicircular bastions now sporting a variety of tops. The railway acts almost as a moat. The walls contain much re-used material. To the left the **Château Barrière**, Roman, Romanesque and medieval, is a real jumble of bits. To see this at closer range, cross the railway and turn left along Rue de Turenne. The château is really two buildings built over sections of the Roman wall. The main structure is c 1480, with a pretty Gothic stair turret and entry door. The base of the wall is dense with Roman fragments. The second building (right) is 19C Romanesque, perhaps real underneath. There follows a single Roman arch, the **Porte Normande**. Passing through, note again the Roman fragments stuffed into the wall. A new footbridge to the school beyond affords good views of the whole ensemble.

Passing back through the gate, a little passage across the road leads left into the arena gardens (another good place to park). The gardens follow exactly the outline of the Roman **Amphitheatre**, and several chunks of the substructure survive. Turn left and pass around the outside of the railings and it is possible to make out arches from the inner arcades, vomitoria, and stairs ramping up. Though ruined and fragmentary, its condition and surroundings are impressive. As you circle the arena, St-Etienne appears to the left.

The area of St-Etienne can hardly be described as picturesque and the Place Francheville has been wrecked by an underground car-park and modern bus station of abhorrent design. However, the **Quartier St-Front** more than compensates for them. An area of twisting streets and steep alleys extends from the riverside all around the cathedral and on up to the higher ground north of the shopping centre. It is rapidly becoming gentrified.

If you start from the Tourist Office on the edge of **Place Francheville**, next door, is the massive bulk of the **Tour Mattaguerre**, a white, smooth, machicolated defensive structure of the 15C named after a notable prisoner. Note the gun loops. Ask at the Tourist Office about access. There is a good view from the top, especially of St-Etienne. The rather scruffy Rue de la Bride begins left of the tower but eventually becomes the rather more upmarket Rues des Farges. Many of the stone houses have small projecting turrets resembling *garde-robes*, but with no street exits (as with **No. 3**). If they were *garde-robes* then they must have internal chutes to basement level. The best known house in this area is the **Maison des Femmes de Foix**, No. 6 (right), with blocked arches on three levels, pointed below, round above, and with carved chevron decoration. As its name suggests, the house was once a convent, and still has a little bell turret. Opposite No. 8, an interesting alley was cut recently through a stone block, with huge corbels supporting something unseen upstairs. **No. 24/26** is a characteristic building from c 1600.

Rue des Farges gradually rises towards St-Front but a right turn at the small military museum will lead into Rue Aubergerie. The narrow alleys serve to emphasise the great height of medieval domestic buildings in France, unlike contemporary England. **No. 25** has four-square windows with traceried heads, **No. 23** has triangular top windows while No. 21 has an attractive stair. Straight ahead and blocking the view, No. 16 is the Hôtel d'Abzac Ladouze, a three storey 15C block with 13C arched windows which were walled up and replaced with more 'modern' four-square windows in the 16C. At the turning left into Rue St-Roch, there is a tall block with a defensive machicolated top, a common sight in Périgueux. Was it genuinely for defence or merely for show? Proceed up Rue St-Roch, with more *garde-robe* turrets and some rare timber-framed buildings, Périgueux is generally stony. High up on **No. 4**, (right) is a four-light Romanesque window with plain capitals and dog-tooth decoration. Now enter Rue du Calvaire (left), the street of penitents, heading for St-Front. The street gets extremely narrow, only about 4m wide in places, yet the buildings go on getting taller. On the right of this increasingly steep climb is a perfectly preserved medieval shop-front and on the left, **No. 3**, has a Renaissance doorway leading to an internal court. Some of the properties on the hill are gutted and will doubtless become executive flats.

The street ends with a pretty polygonal turret and opposite, the west front of **ST-FRONT**, the single most important church in the region (closed 12.00–14.30).

A former monastery and the cathedral since the 17C St-Front must count as one of the strangest buildings in France, more alien since a radical mid-19C restoration by Abadie. Seen from a distance above the stone houses and rust-coloured roofs, it could be some fantasy from an Edwardian World's Fair. Tent-like domes dotted with turrets and a wedding-cake tower are sandwiched between an odd assortment of gabled towers and an elongated east apse. The closer you get, the odder it seems. Much of the blame for the present state of St-Front is laid at the architect Abadie's door. His restoration was more truly a rebuilding. Perhaps we are too hard on the man. It is argued that if he had not taken the building in hand, it would not exist today (which is possibly true) and that in any case, his additions are not that bad (not true). Yet St-Front was always an oddity, and Abadie simply tipped it over into the bizarre. Veneto-Byzantine or Islamic, the lasting impression of St-Front is now Parisian. While restoring St-Front, Abadie was designing the Sacré Coeur, and it shows. While St-Front may have been the inspiration for the Parisian church, Sacré Coeur made its own peculiar contribution to St-Front, notably the white contours and the pepperpots. It is almost as though Sacré Coeur had been remodelled in blancmange, only to sag and spread in the southern sun. In order to think away the later additions we must rough up the smooth exterior, which looks almost shaved, and restore the original and quite shocking colour contrasts—domes of russet stone and red-brown roof tiles, then, sweep away the pepperpots, the long apse and the stripy décor. Amazingly, the tower represents much of what existed previously.

The monastic church of St-Front was built originally to house the important relics of the local saint for the benefit of pilgrims on the famous route to Santiago. Even before Abadie, the church had a complex history and appearance. Two Romanesque churches of different dates interconnect, more accurately collide, to form the present ensemble. The west front with twin pylon towers flanking the single arch, resembling some provincial Roman military gate, now leads into an open court whereas it was built as the entrance to the earlier church, begun c 1047 and completed by 1077. At that time the nave occupied the present open court and was preceded by a tower or porch (lost). The substructure of the present tower formed a link into a lost chancel further east. This chancel contained a famous shrine, built in 1077 by Guinamundus, monk of La Chaise-Dieu, and described by Aymery Picaud, author of the well-known *Pilgrim's Guide to Santiago*. Around 1120 a completely new scheme was begun east of the old church. A great five-domed Greek-cross plan structure was erected, the western-most dome standing on the site of the earlier chancel. This is the church seen today. The shrine was left in situ, the new church having a reverse orientation. At the same time, the old nave was prepared to receive a dome, thought this was mysteriously abandoned. By the 19C the old nave was an open court, and Abadie corrected the odd orientation by adding an east apse in a pseudo-Romanesque style and moving the altar to the more usual position. The shrine had long since disappeared.

The **main entrance** is a loggia-porch against the north transept, though the west door is commonly open. The west front shows considerable evidence of both burning and restoration. Note the Romanesque arch over the Gothic door. Before entering, a walk along the north exterior flank is recommended, though a complete circuit is difficult. From the west front, proceed north and then east to see the lateral façade of the earlier 11C church, now topped by a series of gables, and the projecting wing of the 11C transept. Passing the restored north transept of the second church, the 19C apse can be seen standing in a pleasant garden.

The church proper may now be inspected. Begin back at the west door. The present atrium, the original 11C nave, contains the large 12C corner piers added to take a dome (unfinished). They now carry little towers. The lateral walls indicate that this first church had wall arcades in the manner of St-Etienne. This work now crashes into the west tower substructure, confirming it as later. The two bays beneath the tower are covered by domes on squinches—mostly original. The inner bay has a doorway with columns and frothy Corinthianesque capitals, again unrestored. Look either side beneath the tower and see the 11C masonry of the earlier outer walls.

On entering the church, the initial impression is of cool spaciousness. The severely defined spaces explain the plan better than words. There is one dome in the centre, and one in each direction. The domes stand on curious piers, both detached from the walls and pierced with through arches and little windows. It is the architecture of 19C waterworks. The detachment of the piers allows for narrow aisles yet the church is not truly basilican as the lighting comes from the lateral and end walls. All the surfaces are now smooth and polished, as if waiting for the medieval decorators to move in. We must imagine them covered with colour, if not gold mosaics then real and fake marble, fresco, patterns and stained glass. The interior would be darkly luminous and rich, not stark and clean. Still, the view from any direction is undeniably impressive, the rhythmic domes creating a visual harmony. Yes, the 19C glass is ghastly and the huge metal light-fittings should be thrown out, preferably through the windows. Standing beneath the little west gallery you are on the site of the medieval High altar and shrine. Presumably, in the 12C church, the people stood beneath the crossing looking west but it is difficult to imagine where the monks sat. The lateral wall arcades are immensely tall, and could hardly have been intended as practical walkways. Surely by c 1120 they were already mere convention. The domes themselves are surprisingly small, only 13m in diameter, and are lit by windows on the skew—facing north east, south east etc. The transepts have apsidal chapels, the northern one with a two-tier design, the lower trabeated, that is post and lintel, while other features include triangular arches. If these are original motifs and not by Abadie, they might well reflect local Roman designs. The south transept is different and avoids the awful gloomy green light. The apse chapel is flanked by a tiny alcove, containing a medieval painting possibly of God the Father. Moving to the 19C apse, the interior of which resembles some plush 19C Parisian bank, note the vast Baroque wooden altarpiece. Could

St-Front, Périgueux

you miss it? It depicts the Assumption plus a female donor (kneeling). Turn round and you see the view of St-Front as intended, though missing the altar and shrine. The present chancel bay retains wall paintings on the north and south sides, depicting the life of St. Front. The pulpit is a wonderful piece with magnificent turned balusters, c 1680. There are no other fittings of note.

On the south side of the entrance atrium is a door to the little cloister. The north and east walks have round arches, and the rest are pointed. The cloister contains sculpture fragments from the church replaced by Abadie, casts of other capitals and the pineapple that once topped the west tower. The chapter house survives along the east walk, with three aisles and a permanently locked door. The charming gardens provide roof-top views of the church and the tower, which is basically original and very Classical.

Leaving the church via the west door, turn left to the the south terrace and garden; then descend the stairs fronting the restored south transept. At the foot (left) is a massive stone structure with towers and turrets. Cross the car park towards the river and to the left you find the **Vieux Moulin**, a timber-framed, tiled-roof mill balanced upon a length of the old abbey wall. It is now separated from the river by a busy road.

Walk north along the river to the bridge, which gives a good view of St-Front and beyond it of a group of fine houses again built into and on top of the abbey wall. On the corner, the first house is the **Maison de Lur** (left), 17C with an L-plan, four-square windows, dormers and a tall roofline. The middle house, **Maison des Consuls**, is again stone, but this time late-medieval, four storeys with a machicolated wall-walk on the third carrying a timbered loggia beneath the roof. The battlements are decorated with a variety of tracery designs while the russet-tiled roof is broken by fancy dormer windows. The last (right) block, the **Maison Lambert**, is c 1600 and ambitious, with four storeys, an L-plan open to the street, fine dormer designs and a most unusual loggia traversing the garden.

For the rear of this block, continue north and cross the road, then work your way back along the **Rue Porte de Graule**. This is a most characteristic lane with hugely overhanging roofscapes and no gutters which should be avoided on a rainy day. The multiplicity of dormers cuts some of the roof into impracticable bits which at times look quite comic. No. 7 is late-medieval and stone but with another variant, a timber-framed top. The rear of the major riverside block appears on the left. The first house you come to is the last one described above. Somewhat derelict—a shutter hangs from one window—all the detailing is early-Renaissance though much of it is blocked up. The middle building has a rear court cut off from the street by another machicolated wall-walk. The façade details are all late Gothic except for a Renaissance doorway at the base of the stair turret. Note the shop opposite, the Malicious Cheese. Everywhere, small notices give interesting details and routes, though unfortunately many of the indicating arrows have dropped off.

Return to the start of the Rue Porte de Graule, turn left, and ascend the steep staircase of Rue de l'Abreuvoir to the Rue Barbecane, whose concrete garages can be ignored by turning left to reach Rue Plantier, the first crossing. This whole street is historic and attractive, though without any obvious stars. Taking a right and then left will bring you to the **Musée du Périgord**, with an interesting Roman collection. The prehistory rooms include decorated artefacts and the 15,000-year-old skull of Chancelade Man. The Roman finds include altars, sculpture, bronzes, glassware, mosaics and painted decoration. This will form the basis of a new museum near the Tour Vésone. The medieval collection includes Limoges enamels while the art gallery houses the **Rabastens Diptych**, 1286.

Returning along Rue Plantier, and past Rue Barbecane, a tall crocketted building on the left, No. 24, was the Mint, while further along opposite No. 14, are two medieval shop-fronts. A turning right into Rue de la Constitution is most rewarding for it contains the **Logis St-Front**, a splendid late-medieval town house typifying many in Périgueux. Set back in a yard, the building is L-plan with a stair turret in the angle. The windows are predominantly four-square, and some, like the first in the polygonal turret, have ogee heads echoing the dominant form of the main door. There is a well in the corner. The Rue de la Constitution continues with interesting side streets until No. 3, late Gothic with a fine doorway.

Emerging on the busy Rue St-Front, cross and enter Rue de la Miséricorde. Almost immediately an archway left leads through an entry to the **Gallery de Général Daumesnil**. All around are tall reconditioned medieval buildings forming little courts and alleys. To the right is a four storey building with blocked windows of many periods, some 13C. Continue right, then left and right again and enter the last court, where, high up to the left, is a blocked four-light window with columns, from c 1200. Other buildings include a five-storey late Gothic block to the right with stair turret and a wooden loggia perched on high. Exit across the court and into the **Rue Limogeanne**.

Immediately opposite is **No. 3**, a splendid pile decorated with the Salamander of Francis I, making it post-1515. The block is inventively arranged about a tiny courtyard. The façades are richly embellished, the four-square windows with Renaissance detail and a fine Florentine doorcase. The building now houses the regional department of architecture and can usually be visited. The spiral stair turret divides the court unequally. The ascent is impressive, wide enough for a horse. The first floor lobby has a flat vault with terracotta bosses. The rooms which are accessible have been restored, their wooden ceilings showing obvious signs of removed plaster. Leave the house and turn left to view the façade of No. 5 next door, the **Estignard Mansion**, more fully Renaissance with a three storey panelled façade, Ionic pilasters, other capitals with strange heads, big, flashy dormers and a massive joggled lintel over the entry. One end of the block bulges unnervingly.

Opposite, the end of Rue de la Miséricorde offers interesting views. Further along on the right, No. 12, is the **Hôtel de Meredieu**, a pretty late Gothic building with a little court, 16C. Turn left at a little inset square and pass along Rue Eguillerie, where the first building left has an intact medieval shop-front with a cellar chute above the pavement. The short street ends enticingly with the side façade of the **Maison du Patissier**, 1518, appropriately a confection of Renaissance details including dogs and ivy. It once belonged to the Talleyrand family. The angle into the adjoining square recalls the prow of some ancient ship. Facing the Place St-Louis, the house is more sober, with a little barbizan tower and up to the left a blocked 13C window. The square is surprisingly modest, with a number of attractive side streets.

On the corner of Rue Solomon, is a 16C house, while at the start of **Rue Sagesse**, No. 12 has a handsome 17C door with a baluster window above. On entering the Rue Sagesse, the tiny alley to the left leads into a stone court. Further along, a whole series of medieval shop-fronts is on the left, while opposite a hideous glass door gives access to the star house of the town, the mid-16C **Maison Lajoubertie** (for access ask at the Tourist Office).

It preserves a hefty Renaissance staircase, with bulbous columns and ceiling decoration depicting Venus. It dates to the reign of Henry II. The initials 'S' and 'H' may refer to the local families of Solminihac and d'Hautfois.

You then arrive at an elongated square, Place du Coderc, with the market buildings to your right. Proceeding left of the market hall, you reach the **Hôtel de Ville**, set in another square, the Place Hôtel de Ville. Here, No. 7 (right), the 15C **Logis Gilles-Lagrange**, has a very dramatic stair turret, sprouting a second before it is done. The block is very tall with a machicolated wall walk along the top. Opposite the Hôtel is another 15C building. Turning back to view the Hôtel, a 17/18C building, formerly the Hôtel de Lagrange-Chancel, note the excellent view of St-Front to the right. Follow this view to inspect the rear of the Hôtel, noting the extensive blocked traceried windows of a much earlier house. Leaving this small place, turn left along the Rue Limogeanne and then right to enter Rue de la Clarté, where No. 7 (left) was the house of the Napoleonic Général Daumesnil, who is remembered chiefly for his defence in the siege of Vincennes in 1814. When asked to surrender by the allies, he remarked that he would give up the fortress only when the allies returned his missing leg. Opposite, No. 6, the Hôtel Biron has a court with a circular stair, a Renaissance door and renewed wooden galleries. You now arrive back at St-Front.

In the suburbs, the **Abbey of Chancelade** is worth a detour. Take the D939 north west from the centre and, after 5km turn left on the D710. Almost immediately, a signpost on the right points to Chancelade. Pass through the village and follow the D2 and signs for the abbey, squeezing between two buildings, then take a sharp left and descend to the site. Chancelade is an amazing survival, and it is hard to believe that such a place can still exist so close to civilisation. It was founded in 1129 as an Augustinian house. The shady area before the little church offers a splendid view of the buildings over a tiny stream and washing place. To the left, is a tiny Romanesque **Capella Porta**, sadly locked. The whole south side of the main church is exposed. The long aisleless nave has a series of wall-arches, above which Gothic windows are set rather randomly. The central tower looks unfinished, with big early Gothic openings half-way up, and odd angle blocks supporting a low roof. Whatever else it is, it is certainly defensive. The west front forms a picturesque group with the adjoining monastic range. The early-Gothic entry façade has a large pointed doorway with lots of mouldings, and an arcaded upper section with a single window. Above, is a distinctly Italianate gable.

The interior begins with a view from a high inner west platform. The narrow nave has 12C wall arcades within, while the upper window wall looks, and is, later. In fact the church was extensively restored after 1629 but still in Gothic style, and the windows and vault are from this period. The crossing is earlier, with a Romanesque dome on pendentives. The transepts are mismatched in size. The chancel had wall arcades along the sides, but these have been partially destroyed. The fragments contain wall paintings showing St. Christopher and Becket to the south (Chancelade was one of the earliest churches in Europe to dedicate an altar to Becket, murdered in 1170). The east end is square.

The remaining buildings of the abbey are set in a beautiful semi-wild garden. They are entered from the gatehouse near the west door. (Usually open in July and August, at other times enquire.) The outer court has stables and a medieval mill, mostly clothed in 18C guise. Fragments of the cloister c 1200 (renewed) survive north of the nave, while adjoining the church is a fine late-Gothic building with stair turret and doorway. The north side of the nave shows considerable 18C damage, inflicted when the medieval cloister was demolished. On the east wall of the transept, painting fragments on the exterior indicate the former presence of a chapel. The field beyond is perfect, the grass strewn with wild flowers and odd architectural fragments. To the left stands a large loggia-like building, clearly of the 17C but now derelict. This was built as an abbot's house. Returning along the far side of the cloister, look over the terrace wall and see the tiny mill stream. A museum of sacred art has been established in one room of the former abbey.

The D2 continues past the abbey, and after 3km, a left turns for **Merlande** (2km). The little Romanesque monastery here was a dependency of Chancelade, and had two domes. One was destroyed in 1170 and replaced with a barrel vault. The interior has good capitals. The abbey was fortified in the Wars of Religion and finally sacked at the Revolution.

5

Bourdeilles, Brantôme, Puyguilhem, Villars

Round trip, not including Jumilhac, 143km. For Jumilhac, add 38km. Bus Périgueux to Bourdeilles and back, Wednesday.

Leaving Périgueux on the D939, turn left on the 710 at Chancelade, and at Tocane St-Apre a right crosses the River Dronne for Montagrier (26km) and Grande Brassac (2km). The church at **Montagrier**, set high on the hill, has commanding views of the rolling countryside. The little Romanesque building, much restored, has a trilobe plan with additional apses on the east face of the transepts, like the choir chapels of Norwich. The D103/D1 road up to **Grande Brassac** is lonely but most attractive, as is the tiny village. Here you can play 'spot the person'. The tiny church is the principal attraction, perched on a ledge, it is fortified and has an odd collection of exterior sculpture. The fortification extends around the building, though now roofed over, and includes the tower. The sculpture over the main (north) door is an amalgam of bits and pieces of various dates, some retaining traces of paint. The figures include Christ with the Virgin and John, the Adoration of the Magi, and St. Peter. The Romanesque and Gothic interior is domed, and has a west gallery.

Leave the village the way you entered via the D1 and descend to **Lisle** (5km), an idyllic spot with a crossing of the river Dronne. The little village centres around a Doric market hall and a curious church—be warned, once inside it is very difficult to relocate the door. Amongst the fittings is an extraordinarily windswept Madonna. The alleys behind and north of the church are, to say the least, unspoilt.

The D78 continues to **Bourdeilles** (8km; Tourist Office, 24310 Bour-deilles), a splendid sight when seen from any angle. Bourdeilles has both a medieval castle and a Renaissance château standing cheek by jowl and dominating the little town. Bourdeilles was one of the four major baronies of Périgord. The castle, first mentioned in 1183, is built along a narrow cliff edge over the Dronne. In 1259, St. Louis ceded the Périgord and Bourdeilles to Henry III of England, against considerable local opposition. The present buildings, dating from after 1283, were erected by Géraud de Maumont. In 1307, Bourdeilles was seized by Philippe-le-Bel, but fell to the English again in 1369. Recaptured in 1377, it passed to the Count of Périgord in 1400. In 1481 it was sold for 4000 gold écus to François de Bourdeilles, descendant of the original owners. It became state property in 1960.

The **castle** consists basically of an outer bailey, a long hall range with plate tracery windows (old-fashioned these) and a heavy timbered ceiling, plus an octagonal tower containing fine star-pattern vaults at each stage, a *garde-robe* near the top and a wonderful view from the roof. While admiring the red-roofed town, the little church and the hilly surroundings dotted with 17/18C châteaux, be careful not to fall down the unprotected stair well. The medieval walls are machicolated along the river front.

The **château** next door, begun in 1598 by Jacquette de Montbron, wife of André de Bourdeilles, was clearly intended as a replacement though apparently it was never completed, anticipating a visit from Catherine de Medici that apparently failed to occur. It is a very severe design with a U-plan facing away from the river and with projecting stair turrets and angle pavilions. What exists represents only a wing of the intended design. The three storey façades have plain four-square windows and fancy battlements alternating with triangular and segmental pediments. The corner pavilion by the stair turret has applied orders in sequence and trailing sculptural details. Inside (guided tour in French), the built section consists of a long central gallery on each floor with rooms branching off it. Most of the fittings are imported, including Spanish pieces, a Burgundian wood-carved **Education of Jesus**, a late Gothic chest and a 16C **Dormition of the Virgin**. In one ground floor room lies a huge sculptured **Entombment of Christ**, said to be Burgundian and housed at Montge Priory and the tomb of Jean de Chabannes, chamberlain of Charles VIII died 1498. They are a curious Gothic and Renaissance mix. The angle pavilion has decorated ceilings. The first floor repeats the floor plan below. The rooms are gloomy and heavy, though some have splendid fireplaces, tapestries, fake marbling and painted ceilings, and the furniture is rarely less than interesting. The **Gold Room** has fireplaces by Ambroise Le Noble (Fontainebleau School), a finely painted ceiling and a tapestry after Laurent Guyot depicting Francis I hunting with falcons. The top floor features the bed of Charles V among a collection formerly belonging to Alexander of Yugoslavia. The gardens include a terrace high above the river, and a formal parterre.

The little street to the (dull) Romanesque church contains the **Château de Seneschaux**, an attractive 17C combination of Renaissance and Gothic. The petrol station in the parallel street must have the oldest petrol pump in the world.

Leave Bourdeilles by the D106 crossing the river. Immediately park before the *mairie* (right) and admire the view, the river and the bridge. From here, the energetic can take country walks through the peaceful valley, see the board near the parking lot for details, routes, and times. The road to

Brantôme

Brantôme on the north side of the river is very attractive, with meadows, woods and overhanging rock faces.

You arrive at **Brantôme** in 10.5km. (Tourist Office, Pavillon Renaissance, 24310. Tel 53 05 80 52, fax 53 05 73 19.) It is a picturesque and bustling town with an enviable riverside setting; indeed, the town proper sits on an island in the Dronne. Park south of the town on the Quai Bertin, whence a pretty walk leads you through the old monastic fields and affords good views of the river, town and abbey. Passing the Renaissance garden pavilion, one arm of the river is crossed by a weir reaching another pavilion, once the angle tower of the monastic walls. Now it houses the Information Office.

The **abbey** provides the main interest in Brantôme, not only buildings of note but curious natural and artificial caves, some with huge and crude rock sculptures. The entrance to the abbey is via a late-Gothic cloister fragment and beneath an amazing 18C stair. Upstairs, the huge room which looks like a dormitory has an exposed timber roof. Tours of the abbey include the church and belfry, while the caves are visited independently. The monastic plan is chaotic due to the narrowness of the site squeezed as it is between the river and the rock-face, and to the inclusion in the layout of the rambling assortment of cave-chapels. The site began as a hermitage and several early cave habitations are shown. Charlemagne is credited with the founding of a monastery, to which he donated the relics of St. Sicaire, one of the children killed by Herod during the Massacre of the Innocents. A monastery was mentioned here in 817.

To the west of the hermitages, several **caves** were enlarged by quarrying, and some contain a variety of sculpted scenes. Each cave has a large display board in English and French. Cave 5 (they are numbered) has a large Last Judgement. God is fairly obvious but little else, though there do seem to be heads popping out from boxes. To the right is a crude Crucifixion. It looks 17C. To the west a sacred spring has been framed by rock-cut arcading, and then a mill, a pigeon house singularly devoid of birds, and tanks for fish farming (there are no fish either). Returning to the entry you pass the forbidding exterior of the 18C block. The main monastic **church** seems almost detached from everything else; the cloister lay at its west door, the chapter house led off from the north walk, and the dormitory lay to the west. The cloister and chapter house are c 1500, the latter with a central column but no capital. The square-ended church is earlier but very restored. It has three bays, the first two Romanesque, the easternmost, early Gothic. The windows are heavily moulded outside. The interior is tall and damp. The little chapel beside the west door has the best original sculpture; all the rest is restored. The east bay circular vault boss is unusual. The belfry tower, which may be climbed as part of the tour, is late Romanesque, the single gable on each face and stone spire recall the south tower of Chartres.

Leaving Brantôme on the D78, signs implore you to visit the Château of Puyguilhem. You would be foolish not to. Puyguilhem stands in one of the most romantic, tucked away sites in Aquitaine. That it is also a fine piece of early-Renaissance architecture is a bonus. At les Roches (3km) take the D83 to **Champagnec-de-Belair** (3km), with its attractive church (fancy south door), peace, quiet and good local restaurant. After another 3km, pick up the D3 to **Villars** (3km). Here, apart from the curious spread of the village, there are interesting **caves with prehistoric paintings**, some 17,000 years old. (Open Palm Sunday–14 June and 15 September–31 October, pm only, summer am/pm, July and August all day.) The caves have translucent formations, and the paintings include scenes with bison. To reach them, take the D83 from the village (signposted, 3km). The visits are guided. The underground route is relatively easy with few low moments. The natural formations are impressive, with vast overhanging groups of pinkish stalactites, a flowing calcite wall and almost 12km of galleries, not all visited! Some of the chambers are littered with the debris of the volcanic disturbance in the Auvergne 7000 years ago. The paintings are of considerable interest and are amongst the few that can be dated with any degree of confidence given that some are trapped beneath a transparent calcite deposit, the growth of which can be measured. The calcite overlay has turned the black pigment blue. The most famous painting is the so-called blue horse. There are also bison and horses, half-painted, half-carved from the rock.

Puyguilhem (open am/pm) is less than 1km from Villars along a hillside road. Park and walk until the **château** comes in view. The house has a fairytale charm, complete with pointed conical roofs and spiral stairs. It straddles an exposed rock ledge, now formed into a terrace. A walk down through the meadows is recommended, for the views of the château and the clouds of butterflies, in season, Small Blues. Puyguilhem was built in the early 16C by Mondot de le Marthonie, president of both the Bordeaux

The Château of Puyguilhem

and Parisian *parlements*, who purchased the estate from the Lord of Condat. Marthonie was the chief minister of France during the regency of Louise of Savoy, mother of Francis I, but he died before the house was finished—poisoned, so it is said. The place actually takes its name from a troubadour from the 12C court of the Count of Toulouse.

The present house has 14C cellars (not shown) while the building above dates from 1517–30. The main façade consists of two unequal towers, that on the right, dumpy, machicolated and with a witch's hat of a roof broken by an intruded Renaissance dormer, while the left tower is octagonal, taller, slimmer and with an elegant parapet and dormers. The tower roofs are slate-blue, the intervening roof russet-tiled. The windows of the central block huddle towards both ends as if they are no longer on speaking terms. They are all four-square and rather plain. Decoration is reserved for the stair turret and for the flouncy dormers and chimneys, embellished with shell motifs and miniature turrets. The staggered windows of both end blocks make it clear there are two stairs. On closer inspection, the fatter right tower is late-medieval in style, its battlements roofed over when the dormers were built. But is it actually 14C? The left tower is certainly 16C. Gun loops protect the entries. The left doorway has fancy strapwork designs forming the basis for a three-storey arrangement. The parapets carry the inscrutable initials 'QBFMK IVOCTAV'. A date of 1524 appears on the stair turret squeezed up against the right tower. Walking round the house anti-clockwise, the rear projects straight into a wooded park of great beauty. The back of the house is far more domestic, though the fancy dormers continue. A short path leads down to an 18C pigeon house. The west side of the château overlooking the valley shows signs of an intended extension, quite how is not clear.

The visit to the interior includes rooms on all floors and in both towers. They are generally unfurnished but normally contain an exhibition. The entry vestibule at the foot of the left stair has a flat rib-vault supported by various animal corbels. The rooms are surprisingly small, and have thick, moulded ceiling timbers and attractive fireplaces. The stair leads to a vestibule with a coffered ceiling. The main hall is on the first floor, the fireplace here decorated with the Labours of Hercules. The top of the stair gives access to the attics, where the original roof timbers are exposed. The structure has double 'A' frames with axial criss-cross support. The parapet walk has good views of the countryside and of the adjoining roofscape.

The D98 from Villars heads for St-Jean-de-Côle in 8km. Alternatively, a recommended detour to view the Château at Chapelle-Faucher may be made by retracing the route on the D3 towards Brantôme, then 3km from Villars, stay on the D3 for 5km to **Chapelle-Faucher**. This agricultural village boasts a dotty château with a dramatic setting, but that is yet to come. The village **church** has a domed crossing and apse with vigorous Romanesque carving, and a 17C(?) nave, strangely vaulted. The rustic and partly arcaded exterior is disfigured by a hideous Virgin and headless child. The church is set amid farmyards. The **château**, begun by Etienne de Farges, is unpretentious towards the village, with just a low wall and gatehouse (visit July/August). It suffered two great sieges, the first in 1569, the second during the *Fronde*. The buildings date from most centuries starting with the 15C. The main block set in a courtyard has a huge round tower and a polygonal stair-turret, and a machicolated roofline broken by Flamboyant dormers. There is a fine main hall, though large sections of the other roofs were lost in a 20C fire. Note the elegant, vaulted 17C stables. Leaving the village and proceeding south, there is an impressive view back from the valley floor of the vast fat towers and the frilly skyline of battle-ments, bartizans and dormers.

Continue for 1km and the D78, then turn left. At 3.5km is **St-Pierre de Côle** and the start of a pretty valley route towards Thiviers. St-Pierre has an odd church with exterior sculpture on the west front but precious little else. 2km south-east, at **Lempzours**, is a three-cell Romanesque church with domes. The setting is charming and if the church is locked, try the nearby house on the north side. The east end has good if naïve sculpture including a man playing the violin. The interior is rustically simple. Of the domes, two survive, the other has fallen.

Back at St-Pierre-de-Côle, the crossroads where you entered the village leads over the River Côle, then after a right up the hill (marked les Piles) you find a little road leading to another turning right (Bruzac 300m) and the ruins of **Château Bruzac**. The hilltop site has been fortified since the 12C when it was owned by the Flamenc family. It then changed hands at least ten times and by the 18C, was owned by the Bonevals. The early castle, seized by the French hero Du Guesclin in 1371, was demolished after another siege in 1387. The three storey shell of the 15C castle stands beyond a chaotic farmyard full of ducks. The drawbridge slots are very clear, the bridge once spanning the rock-cut moat. There are two blocks, an upper and lower château, the upper with an L-plan, the lower, a great round tower. There are also remains of a 15C chapel, the door sporting the arms of Beynac and Marqueyssac. Note the fine finish of the stonework, particularly the chimneys. The ensemble and setting are irresistible but visitors are requested not to disturb the 300 ducks, not to climb the fallen fencing and on no account enter the unstable ruins. For those with less time, the valley road leaving St-Pierre has a fine distant view of the castle.

From the château, return to the hilltop road, turn right and proceed until a give way, turn right and descend, crossing the beautiful river by a narrow bridge and find the main road. Turn left for **St-Jean-de-Côle**, 2.5km (6.5km direct from St-Pierre). In any contest for pretty villages, St-Jean-de-Côle would leave all others behind. It is set back from the main D78 and is first spied across meadows and fields, giving little hint of what is to come. It seems almost a crime to drive in, and being tiny, it is possible to park on the perimeter and to walk down any of the picturesque lanes towards the château. Some of the houses are timber-framed, not common in the Périgord, all are flower-decked in season and dis-arranged in wonderfully higgledy-piggledy fashion. Few of the lanes are metalled, adding to a sense of timelessness. A little square with an Information Office also contains a hotel/café, the château entrance, a market cross and the most amazing church.

The **château** calls for attention first (visit July/August). It is known as La Marthonie, after the family of the same name, builders of Puyguilhem, who also owned this property in the reign of Francis I. Two 14C towers survive from the earlier castle, which was burnt in the Hundred Years War. The rebuilt château withstood a further siege by Coligny and his Huguenot forces in 1569, and passed to the Beaumont family about 1760. The erratic ensemble and the gardens exude charm. The main buildings are 15/16C, and the square, battlemented towers have added pyramidal red-tiled roofs. The elegant loggia is *tempo* Louis XIV. Inside is a splendid 17C(?) stair resting on a sequence of arches. The house contains a parchment and poster museum.

Adjoining the rustic market cross there rises the huge stone bulk of the **church**. Hard to accept as medieval, it is one of Aquitaine's great curiosities. The church formerly housed an Augustinian priory, sections of the cloister survive (private, see below). What we now see is merely the easternmost bay of a 12C aisleless, domed structure, but one most oddly planned. The exterior is not revealing but inside it makes a little more sense. The first thing to grasp is that the main dome collapsed in 1860 and has been replaced by a wooden roof. The 12m dome covered a square space, yet on three of the sides there project triangular bays that in turn sprout deep apses. With no free-standing supports, all the spaces flow into a confusing sprawl. Were the dome still present, it would pull the thing together. The west wall shows the blocking where once the church continued with at least one more domed bay, but this time without the flanking apses. To imagine St-Jean complete, one must see Souillac. The dark interior all but conceals some Romanesque capitals and 17C woodwork in the apse but otherwise has no fittings of note.

Leaving by the south door (there is some damaged Romanesque sculpture of the Annunciation etc up to the right), proceed west to stand in the lost nave. The springing of the next dome is obvious. The little yard leads into a gravelled main street, with attractive houses leading to a ford, a medieval bridge and a mill. It looks like another film set waiting for the cry of 'Action!' From the opposite bank, you get a sneak view into the remains of the priory and its 18C cloister block. A small museum nearby is dedicated to rural life and arts. The lane leading nowhere on the far side of the through road has yet more attractive buildings, including a fine, rambling, timbered block.

The D707 brings you to **Thiviers** (7km), a bustling market town with good food shops. The centre is dominated by the church and by cars. The church is very restored; it had domes but they are now gone. The square chancel and crossing have Romanesque capitals which have been badly interfered with. The nave piers lean so far out as to suggest that the domes collapsed. The present vault looks 17C. There is some 16C and 17C sculpture. The terrace surrounding the church has good views and looks down directly upon a picturesque mansion with round, machicolated corner towers and pointy roofs. The middle block could be 19C. To the left is another fine stone house. The narrow streets north west of the church are photogenic.

A detour of 38km north east of Thiviers brings you to the **Château of Jumilhac**, a vast fortress palace dating from the 13C and much reorganised after 1579. Rooms of several periods are shown, and some have floors of coloured cobblestones called *pisé*. The cellars contain a Gold Museum.

The N21 south from Thiviers reaches Sorges in 14km. **Sorges** is best known for truffles, and a museum dedicated to this Périgord obsession can be found in the village. (Tourist Office, 24800 Sorges.) **Truffle walks** are signposted, enquire at the Tourist Office or in the Truffle Museum. The small double-aisled **church** has an almost conical dome over the crossing, plus some crude Romanesque carvings. There is a notable Renaissance doorway.

The rural D106 south-west from Sorges (follow signs for Agonac) leads to **Jaillac** and its little château (5km). A signpost left points down a track to the house, usually open July/August. The tiny house is four-square in plan around a courtyard which you enter through a toytown gate. The corner turrets project from the walls, yet the whole thing is in miniature. Such small

St-Jean-de-Côle

châteaux cannot often be visited. Opposite the turning to the house, woodland walks are signposted. The road continues to **Agonac** (5km), locally famous for its fortified church, south of the village on the D3E. It might be said that the church is famous for being locked (enquire at an Office du Tourisme in advance, it is worth seeing). The nave is barrel-vaulted with wall piers standing proud of the aisle walls in the manner of St-Front. The space under the tower has a big dome, while the square-domed chancel shows extensive remains of wall paintings.

Another 7.5km brings you to Château-l'Evêque and the main D939 to Périgueux. **Château-l'Évêque** is named after its episcopal residence, enlarged and altered since its initial construction in the 14C by Adhémar de Neuville. The former palace of the bishops of Périgueux (currently a hotel), it was sacked by the Huguenots, and the bishop assassinated in 1575. It has sheer walls, asymmetrical arrangements of machicolated towers and a picturesque red-tiled roofscape. The interiors include an oratory with a decorated ceiling, and one of the chimneys carries a date of 1520. There is also a rose garden. The nearby church witnessed the ordination of St.Vincent de Paul in 1600. The D939 returns to Périgueux in 11km.

6

Périgueux to the Vézère, Les Eyzies and the Valley of the Caves

The final destination of this route will depend where in the Dordogne you have chosen to stay. From Périgueux, it is 130km to Les Eyzies, and 115.5km to Sarlat. The beautiful valley of the Vézère has both Les Eyzies and le Bugue, while close by, Sarlat offers a number of hotels.

Leave Périgueux on the N21 going east. The suburbs are dismal until the area of Antonne-et-Trigonant (6km) and the River Isle. To the right near the airport, is the Château Rognac, an attractive 16C house standing in the river. Partly ruined, it features one big battlemented tower and an interesting roofscape. The adjoining mill is picturesque. Just beyond Antonne, a sign right to **Les Bories**, one of the most surprising houses in the area. Set in a blasted landscape that must once have been idyllic, the fairytale building is stranded on an island site (open 1 July–30 September, am/pm). The north façade is hugely impressive and unexpectedly white. The three-storey central block with four-square windows is flanked by robust round towers with machicolated battlements, now covered by immense pointed roofs. Nothing relieves its austerity, not even dormers. The south entrance façade is much jollier, with a staggered plan, little bartizan towers popping out from the corners, and a big, square, stair tower which is one of the interior's main attractions (ring the hanging bell for entry).

The house was built after 1497 by the mayor of Périgueux, Forton de St-Astier, for his son Jean, who had recently married Jeanne d'Hautefort. In 1651, during the *fronde*, Les Bories was pillaged by the supporters of the Prince of Condé, the St-Astiers remaining loyal to Louis XIV. The family died out in 1892. Since then, the house has belonged to the comte de Paris, the duc de Monpensier and the baron de Nervaux-Loys. Presently, the interior has a faded charm and the whole guided visit has great character.

The **tour** includes the superb stair, an amazing creation which is almost a building in itself. It encloses a tower-like structure, housing a tiny chapel at its summit. Most romantic of all is the vaulted kitchen, a perfect period piece with huge fireplaces and cupboards hung with pots and pans. It is surely the first scene of Cinderella. The *grande salle* has a Renaissance fireplace, Flemish tapestries, portraits and other family items. The cellars are appropriately sinister.

Turning back on the N21 towards Antonne, a left on the D6 then D5 will lead to le Change (8km) and the valley of the Auvézère, our route to Hautefort. Almost immediately, you arrive at **Escoire** with its sedate 18C château, which has a semicircular middle. The road from here is unspoilt Périgord, with gentle hills, tumbling streams and quiet villages. **Le Change** has just such a setting featuring a tiny bridge, weirs and a mill, a humble church (note the east tower) and a café. It also has some small château-like houses with towers, machicolations and the obligatory pointy roofs. The little D5E leaving le Change stays south of the river and affords the better views, though at Cubjac (6km), you cross the Auvézère once more and rejoin the main D5.

The road winds on through villages with names like St-Pantaly-d'Ans, until you reach **Tourtoirac** (13.5km Hotel/Rest.) where you have to do a bit of detective work. Tourtoirac has the remains of an 11C Benedictine monastery but it takes some tracking down.

The **church** is easy enough to find, at least the mutilated remains of the nave. For the rest, park at the *mairie* behind the church and wander into the garden surrounding a tower. This is the crossing of the Romanesque church, and the bulge facing north is an apsidal transept. Next door is a modern house retaining sections of the chapter house, while scattered around the riverside garden are an ancient forge and a vaulted room called the Prior's chapel (note the pottery vases embedded in the vault, possibly for acoustics). The whole thing is delightfully odd. Access to the Romanesque sections of the church is unpredictable. Sometimes the north transept door is open, if not, go round to the west front, beneath the remains of a big west tower, walk up to the altar and try the left-hand door. It leads into a tall and extraordinary space, featuring an octagonal dome over the crossing, apses north and south with wall arcading, crude capitals and scant remnants of wall paintings, all horribly overgrown with mould and moss.

A plaque on a house south of the church recalls the memory of Arélie-Antoine I, King of Aurucania, exiled to Tourtoirac and buried in its cemetery. It is a complicated story of a Périgueux lawyer, who sailed for South America in 1860, only to find himself hailed as liberator of the Indians on the Chile/Argentine frontier. He proclaimed himself king and his country, Aurucania. Contemptuously thrown out by the Chileans, he returned in 1869, this time to Patagonia, only to be thrown out by the Argentinians. Two further attempts to recover his throne failed, and he eventually retired here. He died in 1878.

From Tourtoirac, the D5 leads for Hautefort in 9.5km, though it becomes the D62 after 4km, crosses the D704 after another 3km and is called the D62E1 for the last 2.5km. Just follow the signs.

The **Château of Hautefort** is a big Renaissance pile dominating the hill village (open 1 March–15 November, am/pm. Other times, Sunday pm and public holidays. Tourist Office, 24390 Hautefort). Seen from afar, it impresses with its fat round towers, variety of windows and odd blue-grey roofscape. The site was first fortified in the 9C. In the 12C it passed to Bertrand de Born, a famous troubadour mentioned by Dante. He was overthrown by his brother in 1186 and the castle destroyed. Hautefort was also the home of Marie de Hautefort, favourite of Louis XIII. The present house was designed by Nicolas Rambourg and dates from c 1630–70, though there are later additions. It was built for Jacques François de Hautfort, the second Marquis, whose family remained in possession until 1818. They must have been out when the Revolutionaries came to call. Passing through the female line to the family of Damas, it was sold in 1890. Subsequent owners stripped many of the original furnishings and sold off much of the estate. The current owner, the Baroness de Bastard, has restored much of the former glory, though a disastrous fire in 1968 gutted the whole centre block. What you now see are very much the periphery sections and of course the splendid grounds.

You approach the house over massive 17C outworks. A walk around the exterior of the house is enjoyable and usually necessary while awaiting the tour. The **yew walk** is a marvel, while the back of the house, standing on a high terrace with clipped box hedges, is 13 bays wide and not quite flat, as the ends kink a bit. The **tour** begins at the main gate, a modest affair with evidence of earlier structures and a date of 1588. Within, the great court commands a fine view.

The house has a great central block with two storeys raised on an Italianate open loggia, four- and six-square windows. The side blocks are consistently three-storeyed while the end pavilions are raised upon basements. The style is very severe apart from the dormers and big, pumpkin roofs. The lower side wings end in round towers, the one near the entrance being 15C. Both have wonderful pepperpot roofs and resemble some giant cruet set. You then see the 17C basement passages, the circular chapel with its *trompe l'oeil* ceiling and altarpiece, the latter made for the coronation of Charles X in Reims, 1830. The pulpit is made up from late Gothic and possibly Flemish carved panels, c 1500(?). The loggia is attractively shown, while the great stair can only be glimpsed—it was all but destroyed in 1968. The Damas room, which is really a lobby, contains Aubusson tapestries, a Louis XV cupboard and offers fine views. Note through the glass door, a wonderfully designed back stair. At the opposite end, the weaving room has Brussels tapestries (16C), some good 17C pieces and a stunning 17C Turkish vase. From here, glimpses are permitted of two rooms in use, a bedroom and a dining room, both survivors of the recent fire. They feature wood panelling, embossed Cordoba leather panels, elaborate fireplaces and some good furniture. The rest of the tour concerns the older tower, with rooms containing early 17C furniture, a pair of huge bellows plus local and family memorabilia. The machicolated walkway can be seen, and the famous 17C roof, which stands both on and over the earlier battlements.

Down in the village is a huge 17C cruciform hospital block with a central dome. Its chapel is sometimes open.

The D62 from Hautefort winds for 6km to **Badefols-d'Ans** (Hotel/Rest.), a small town dominated by a dumpy château in classic Périgord style (unfortunately private). The tiny town centre is built on slopes, with little alleys, a triangular place and a simple church. From here the D71 heads east for Coubjours (6km) and in another 4km reaches St-Robert (the road becomes the D5 at the last minute. **St-Robert** (Hotel/Rest.) just 2km over the border into Corrèze is a hilltop village with an erratic square (market Wednesday am), a grandiose church and huge views. Drive up to the church and park. This is a real village, with no concessions to tourists though there is an Office du Tourisme (to the left of the church).

The rather abrupt **church** is but a fragment of a bigger Romanesque monastery, only the choir and transept survives. It is late 11C/early 12C with additions of the 14C when it was fortified against the English. The best view in every sense is from the little gardens from the east. The vista looking south and east is staggering, revealing a vast sway of rural France. The church has an apse, ambulatory and radiating chapel plan, the axial chapel curiously embedded within a later tower.

The interior is big in a little way. The plan imposes a certain grandness but the actual dimensions are small—the aisles are little more than 2m wide. The choir rests on tall columns with oversize foliate capitals. Above this, small holes punched through the wall serve as a triforium, while the clerestory is enclosed within an arcade. The whole is barrel vaulted with a half-dome over the apse. The ambulatory has historiated capitals—men pulling their beards and animals fighting. The crossing shows remains of a squinched dome with a foiled opening in the centre. The tall, barrel-vaulted transepts survive with east apsidal chapels, and the evidence for the lost nave is clear. High up, there are more historiated capitals and an interesting crucifix on the north wall of the crossing.

A short and pleasant walk can be made by passing between the church and the tourist office, down a rustic lane, past a small chapel to a gate, once part of the town or abbey fortifications. A left down the next small alley leads to another gate, where, having passed through, a left leads back up to the small square. This is real France.

From here, the route takes the D51 south from the village towards Louignac and on to the major N89 at la Villedieu (18.5km). This delightful back road passes up and down though woods, valleys, over streams and waterfalls, and past picturesquely derelict railway bridges. At the main road, a left turn brings you back to reality. Head for **Terrasson-la-Villedieu** 2.5km, (Hotel/Rest.) and turn right over the Vézère and head up into the old town. Park on the steeply raked market square (market on Thursdays). Famous for walnuts and truffles, the name of the town gives away its major feature, terraces. This means quite a climb. Walk up to the church and see the view of the surrounding valley. The **church** is quite showy, with a west rose window and Flamboyant door. Try the north door for entry. The interior is a little gloomy with an apsed chancel and shallow transepts dating from the 14/15C. The nave is slightly later and has no vault capitals. The vaults are rather pretty. There is a pair of damaged figures from a late-medieval tomb, in the north transept.

Facing the church, or rather beneath it, is another small square with some interesting stone and timber-framed houses, 15/16C. A recent fire has damaged quite a few of them. The little lane with steps leads to the waterside. On the attractive riverfront, note the two bridges, one medieval, and the fair-sized dock on the far bank.

From Terrasson, take the little road along the south bank of the Vézère towards Condat (6km), then turn left on the main D62 going south. After another 6km, a right in the village of Coly, leads up a gentle country road to **St-Amand-de-Coly** (3km Hotel/Rest).

St-Amand is another 'special' place that would have been best kept secret but now it is too late, for it is being 'discovered'. It has every reason to be. It is a pretty place with no great stars. But it is dominated by a monster **church** that rears up from the hillside like the gateway to hell. That is not how the Augustinians thought of it when they built this splendid pile in the late-12C, but it certainly looks forbidding today. Said once to have housed 200 monks (which is unlikely), most of the monastic buildings have disappeared. Just a few walls and the general site south of the church remain. The church building exhibits two main phases of work, the original campaign towards 1200, which is extremely plain, and the additions of the 14C necessitated by the Hundred Years War. Approach via the west door and appreciate the height and defensive possibilities of the west tower. This is a 14C addition over the building, defending it against all-comers, not just the English but the local warring factions that proliferated throughout the late Middle Ages in south west France. Stray Romanesque capitals have been shoved into the west wall. The exterior is best seen from the higher ground to the south. The church is cruciform and very plain. Only the transept east chapels have any enrichment but there are still no carved capitals. Note the remains of further defensive positions on the transepts and the curious half-finished look to the roof-lines. The aisleless interior is sheer and cool, and dominated by its pointed barrel vaults. A wall walk is placed high up within the interior. Classically, they are defensive, e.g. defenders fired down into the church. But it looks as though they would have been equally exposed. The choir is raised high on steps reflecting the hillside site. The two-bay choir interior is rather blank (west), then rather fancy (east) with a simple but attractive arrangement of windows. The diagonal placing of the vault supports suggests north French influence.

The transept is big, with polygonal east chapels, and deep wall arcades. There is one historiated capital in the south transept. The nave is austere with simple windows high up. The west window is beneath the later tower which is propped over the west wall and on the added exterior buttresses. There are few fittings of note, but some painting fragments in the north transept.

From St-Amand, your route on into the Dordogne depends upon your destination. If it is Les Eyzies, then take the tiny unnumbered road south west for 3km, reaching the D704. A turning right will lead to Montignac in 6km, passing the short road (left) up to **Château de la Grand Folie**, a confection of angled towers and Renaissance bits, all clustered about what is essentially a farmhouse. From Montignac, Les Eyzies is 26km via the D706. If you are heading for Sarlat, then another tiny and extremely attractive road leads south east from St-Amand for 3km and picks up the quiet D64, passing St-Genies (see below) in 4.5km and joining the D60 in another 4km. Here, a right and then left, takes you on to the main D704 going to, to reach Sarlat in a further 9km.

7

Les Eyzies/le Bugue

The little towns of Les Eyzies de Tayac and le Bugue make convenient centres for the Dordogne, with numerous hotels and restaurants and good road connections. Though best reached by car, a train service operates from Périgueux (90 minutes). Both towns are situated on the banks of the Vézère, le Bugue with a splendid waterfront. Le Bugue is also the most obviously characterful, and has a lively Saturday street market. Some of the larger hotels here can be very noisy. Les Eyzies is more of a family centre and feels a little suburban. However, if it is the caves you are after, Les Eyzies is much closer, indeed some are within walking distance.

Les Eyzies is set beneath cliffs at the confluence of the Vézère and the Beune. (Tourist Office, 25620 Les Eyzies.) Prehistoric cave dwellings have been found within the cliff face. The town is dominated by the château of the lords of Baynec, seemingly wedged into the cliff as if about to fall. The castle, dating from the 13C was extensively restored in the 16C and now houses the important National Museum of Prehistory. This is arranged in two buildings and includes displays of stone chipping techniques, wall paintings and domestic utensils, carved slabs up to 30,000 years old, weapons and implements of bone, teeth and stone and a display of flint technology. The second building contains reconstructed prehistoric tombs. The museum is something for a wet day.

Tayrac, originally a separate village, is about a 1km walk away passing the **Abri Pataud**, a prehistoric shelter, and the more famous **Abri de Cro-Magnon**. This second cave was discovered in 1868 and contained carved objects from the Aurignacian and Gravettian eras, some 30,000 years old or more. Cro-Magnon Man is named after three skeletons which were found here. A little further, is the Romanesque church of **Tayrac**, massively fortified with twin towers. The main doorway is multi-cusped and has Antique columns and capitals. The triple-aisled interior is wood-ceilinged.

Just out of the town centre of Les Eyzies, on the D47, is the famous **FONT-DE-GAUME**, containing perhaps the most important original prehistoric paintings still to be seen by the casual visitor. Having said that, strict control of numbers means there is a ticket system, indicating what time the visitor should return. As all the tickets sell within minutes of opening, it is wise to get there early. One policy would be either to get on to the first group, or get a ticket timed for later in the day and plan your other activities around that time. Certainly, the cave should be seen. The entrance is via the shop, passing through the side door at least five minutes before the allotted time. No announcement is made and no-one will come and get you. A short climb (440m) with fine views brings you to the metal door where you wait your turn. The caves are easy to walk through, though some parts are narrow and the light levels are necessarily low. Small children might be upset and crying children are instantly ejected. The paintings date mostly from the Magdalenian period, and include bison, horses, mammoth, and deer. Apparently the figures were scratched in outline and then painted. Some take clever advantage of the natural rock formations. The interesting commentary is usually in French and the visit takes about 30 minutes.

The D47 leading west from Les Eyzies crosses the Vézère and then follows the river to the Musée de la Spéléologie, or Potholing Museum. Devotees might find the exhibits more interesting than others, though the display, set in rock-cut chambers of an old fort, is curious. About 1km from the bridge is the **Grotte du Grand Roc**, another fine site and one popular with children, though not with the claustrophobic (open all day). A stair leads up the valley side, fine views, to a ticket office and shop. The guided tour leads though an endless wriggle of passages, some cut deep into the original floor level so that the formations are often waist-high. The remarkable interiors are dominated by stalactites and stalagmites of a variety of colours, resulting from different chemical deposits carried in the water. The yellow is iron oxide, the grey manganese and the white calcite. Some of the formations are quite eccentric and have attracted the usual whimsical identifications. Some actually project sideways while many resemble water-swept sea-weed. One small pool contains triangular calcium deposits. The lighting is perhaps a little too much like Santa's Grotto, and the wire netting unfortunate. The floor throughout is wet but the interior is not cold. The French commentary lasts about 30 minutes and an English pamphlet is available.

A turning left at the Vézère bridge is signposted for the **Grotte de St-**

Cirq, which is about 3km along the valley road, a right turn indicated about 400m from the site. This cave has animal engravings of the Magdalenian period (c 35,000–20,000 years old) and the famous Man of St. Cirq, a rare and remarkable human figure.

Another group of caves occurs in the beautiful Beune valley about 9km from Les Eyzies. The D47 towards Sarlat arrives at **Les Combarelles** (2km), a twisting passage some 250m long, the last half decorated with numerous Magdalenian drawings of bison, horses and men. Access is limited and the arrangements very unsatisfactory. Timed tickets must be bought back at Font de Gaume, and by the time you discover this, most have gone. The D47 branches left after another 2km on to the D48, where in another 5km the **ABRI DU CAP BLANC** is signposted. There is no problem with access here, except that the road and car park can be muddy. Steps and a path lead to the cave. This site contains important high relief carvings of the Magdalenian period, some 14,000 years ago. It includes the famous **frieze of horses**, though there are other figures, partly carved and partly exploiting the rock formation. Bison and reindeer feature—all were once painted. A grave was discovered at the foot of the frieze. A visitors centre should be ready for 1994.

A little further along the D48 brings the twin hilltop **Châteaux of Commargue and Laussel** into view, built to flank the Beune river. Commargue is the romantic ruin on the south side, with rust coloured walls and a turreted main tower. The castle dates from the 12C. Laussel owes its rather Germanic look to a 19C restoration, though the effect is pleasing. The château stands on an exposed rockface, its walls poetically overhung with greenery. It dates only from the 15C. Inside is a litle vaulted chapel.

8

The Valley of the Vézère and Lascaux

The D706 winds along the riverside from Les Eyzies past farms and villages. The route is liberally sprinkled with 'attractions', some of which are actually worth seeing and involve minor detours. However, those wishing to see **Lascaux II**, as the reconstruction is called, are advised to arrive on site well before opening time. Numbers are limited and the arrangements and management of the site lamentable. Crowds gather early, no queueing system is in operation and the ticket staff are distinctly off-hand. There is a great contrast with the ordered and well-mannered arrangement at Font-de-Gaume. At Lascaux you have to wait, perhaps for hours. Tickets are sold in sequence and returning later seems not to be an option. If you are really keen to see the imitation cave, you must settle in for a long, and often cold wait. Once all the day's allocation of tickets are sold, the office closes. Some tours are given in English. What you see eventually is an exact replica of the famous caves, now suffering from the effects of human contamination. The exhibition is kept at a low temperature.

Entering the bunker-like underground shelter, the visitor sees first a display of the history and reconstruction of the caves, with their 17,000 year old paintings. The main chamber is admittedly impressive unless you spot the emergency exits and the ferro-concrete shell housing. It is better than nothing. The recreated paintings depict bison, deer and galloping horses and scenes of hunting. One figure is half-bird, half-man. Some scenes are painted over others. The ticket also admits to Le Thot.

Assuming that Lascaux has been visited first, the following route will work back towards Les Eyzies and le Bugue. None of the distances is great (Les Eyzies to Lascaux is only 30km), though two detours are included if time permits. **Montignac** is a pleasant spot, with a pretty river crossing, gardens and a ruined castle (Market Wednesday and Saturday am).

From Montignac the little D65 on the east bank of the Vézère is most attractive and at 5km offers a dramatic view of **Château de Losse**, perched on an arched terrace over the river. Cross the river at Thonac (2km) and return to Losse, which is one of the most attractive of the smaller châteaux of Périgord. The château (open till late September) is immensely picturesque from all angles. It sits on a rock-cut terrace, surrounded on three sides by a dry moat, a remnant of the 13C castle.

The present château, completed in 1576, was built by Jean de Losse, Governor of Périgord. The guided visit lasts about 40 minutes. A bell rings. The gatehouse carries an inscription roughly translated as 'Man does what he may, Fate as she will'. The view from here is fine. The façades are rather simple if irregular, with two storeys, four-square windows, and machicolated and battlemented walkways beneath a great roof. The main block is L-plan. The rooms shown include a hall, with a near flat vault, good Louis XIII furnishings and the Portrait of a Man by Antonio Moro. Also open to the public are a small study with a wax portrait of Henry IV by Dupré, a curious room— actually a boxed-in carriage drive from yard to terrace—an austere stair with shell niches on the landings, and a large bedroom with a decorated fireplace wall. There are also fine tapestries, inlaid furniture and antique beds. The gardens and terrace are very peaceful.

A short distance north of Losse is **Le Thot** and the Centre for Prehistoric Art and Research (same ticket as Lascaux II). The museum attempts a broad view of its subject, while the park includes live examples of animals depicted by prehistoric man, reconstructions of early dwellings and life-size robots of extinct creatures. It is not supposed to be funny.

South again on the D706 and to **St-Léon-sur-Vézère** (5km). St-Léon is one of those 'too-good-to-be-true' villages, though its enormous charm and interest has yet to be destroyed. Park on the approach as the village is tiny. The narrow lanes and tumble of buildings have great character. The 14C **Château de la Salle** stands abruptly in a private garden well seen from the square. The ancient donjon rises sheer from the grass, with two strategically placed *garde-robes*. Next door is a small turreted house. The little **church**, formerly a priory, stands facing the river. The Romanesque east end is much photographed, with its three parallel apses, transept and central tower. The rest looks 17C. Inside, the nave is wood-roofed while the crossing is domed. Barrel vaults cover both chancel and transept arms. The apse has Romanesque capitals and painting fragments which are said to be Romanesque though they look 16C. There are more paint fragments in the transept chapels. Against the north west crossing pier, is a 16C carved Madonna and Child; on the west wall, a headless knight and child on a horse.

Along the riverside south of the church stands another small turreted house, the 16C **Château de Clérans**, straight out of Disney. The back lanes and alleys are virtually derelict. On the opposite bank (cross at Thonac) is **Castel-Merle**, a prehistoric site with small museum (necklaces) and cave sculptures. The site adjoins the pretty village of **Sergeac**, which contains a 15C stone cross on the approach road and a fortified Romanesque church. Back on the D706 going south, we approach **la Roque St-Christophe** (6km). The cliff-face rises some 80m above the river and is honeycombed with caves on five levels, carved out since the Upper Palaeolithic period. There is a wonderful view from the top. Across the river, **Le Moustier** gave its name to a Middle Palaeolithic culture.

From Le Moustier, the D6 travels north to **Plazac** (5kms) with its fortified Romanesque church, and on to **Rouffignac** (6.5km; Tourist Office, 24580 Rouffignac.) This village was entirely destroyed by the Germans in a reprisal against the French Resistance in 1944. Only the church remains, all the rest is modern. The church is late Gothic in the Flamboyant style, with twisted columns and fancy vaults. The west door, c 1530, is early Renaissance, and is decorated with female figures including mermaids. Rouffignac contains one of the largest collections of prehistoric cave art in France, thousands of depictions, some 40,000 years old. The caves, the **Grottes de Rouffignac**, are 5km to the south and are signposted (open Easter to November every day, then Sundays only).

North of the village on the D31 followed by a side road, is the **Château de l'Herm** (6km), a wonderfully romantic ruin (open 1 July–15 September, 10.00–19.00, closed Sundays, am). It was built in 1513 by Jean III de Calvimont, President of the *parlement* of Bordeaux and French Ambassador to Rome and later to Charles V. The subsequent family history is somewhat bloody. Jean's heir was murdered in the house while his granddaughter was slaughtered here on the orders of her husband. It was abandoned to the forest of Barade in 1714. In summer the ruins are all but hidden in greenery. The main block is flanked by massive towers, all topped with the remains of machicolations. Like Puyguilhem, the building straddles a stylistic divide; there is a fine late Gothic door, flanked by a startling buttress, while the spiral stair ends with a spreading late Gothic vault.

The return to Les Eyzies can be made either by retracing the route to la Roque St-Christophe (Rouffignac to Les Eyzies 21km) or by taking the D32 from near the Grottes de Rouffignac and joining the D47 (Grottes de Rouffignac to Les Eyzies 18km). If you take the former option, then **Tursac** (3.5km from St-Christophe) has a Romanesque church complete with a set of domes and the late medieval Château de Marzac. **La Madeleine** (cross bridge before Tursac for Lespinasse, then left) is a troglodyte village dating from the 10C. About 20 rock-cut dwellings can be seen plus a little late Gothic church. The Upper Palaeolithic site at the foot of the cliff gave its name to the Magdalenian culture.

St-Léon-sur-Vézère

9

The Dordogne Valley

This route explores some of the most famous villages and sites along the Dordogne, on a 63km round trip from Les Ézyies. The route may start either at Les Eyzies or le Bugue. From Les Eyzies, take the D706 to Campagne (7km) or from le Bugue, the D703 to the same village (4km) then the beautiful D35 to St-Cyprien (9km).

St-Cyprien is a typical Dordogne village climbing the steep hillside and dominated by a large church. (Tourist Office, 24220 St-Cyprien.) There is an exceptional Sunday morning market. The village streets are worth exploring, though many are steep. The little square fronting the Hôtel de Ville is especially attractive.

The big monastic (Augustinian) **church** takes a bit of finding. From the Hôtel de Ville, climb up to the Rue Betrand de Got, then turn right. The view from the church steps is particularly fine, see the early Renaissance house to the right. The church is medieval, the adjoining monastic buildings (private) Renaissance. They stand on a higher terrace north of the church. The church interior has been tampered with and is sadly lacking in architectural interest. It is aisleless, vaulted and wide. There is a lot of woodwork, some of it Baroque, especially in the chancel. A monastic chapel stands behind the 18C High altar. Fault lines within the plaster along the north wall suggest the 12C church had a window arrangement of twin lights plus an oculus above. Gothic windows and buttresses along the south exterior confirm that the early church was later rebuilt but the main interest lies outside and at the east end. The chancel and its monastic chapel form the base of a giant fortified tower structure, which could be 14C. The shallow strip buttresses rising sheer up the tower recall such Donjons as St-Émilion or St-Léon-sur-Vézère. On top sits a more normal belfry. The grouping is distinctly odd. A street left runs helter-skelter back to the centre. Above the town off the D48, stands the Château des Fages, a Renaissance building with decorated interiors and a fine chapel.

Leave St-Cyprien by following the signs for Bergerac until the bypass D703, then turn left for **Beynac** (10km). The road starts fast and dull but soon becomes bad and interesting. Beynac (Tourist Office, 24220 Beynac) must count as one of the most photographed places in France and one glimpse will tell you why. The village hugs the hillside and splashes straight into the water. The houses are russet and faun, and almost disgustingly picturesque. Above rears the great castle, the stuff of fairy tales. But like all children's stories, there is a dark side—tourists. Beynac is popular. Parking is difficult and expensive. Added to this, the castle is 3km by road from the village, doubling the parking problem. The very fit can climb a signposted route from one to the other, but strictly the very fit, for whom the rewards are great. The village is charming and mostly real, the castle evocative and the views stunning.

The **castle** of Beynac commands the river valley from a great height. It dates from the 13C and was occasionally in English hands—it was captured

The castle at Beynac

by Richard I in 1189, again by Simon de Montfort in the 13C and then ceded
to Edward III in the Treaty of Brétigny of 1360 (lost again 1368)—but for
most of its medieval history, Beynac was French territory. Conducted tours
are in French (English pamphlet). The castle has double walls protecting
the 'landward' side, and a drop of 150m to the river taking care of the rest.
Enter via an impressive if fanciful gateway. To the left the ancient donjon
with living quarters and the first of many fine views. To the right the stables
of 1650 lead on to the upper courtyard. From here the main block is well
seen with its machicolated top and restored wooden guardboxes projecting

from the walls. To one side is the former castle chapel, now the parish church. Note the stone roof slabs (*lauzes*). A number of other castles can be made out from the terrace, most obviously Castelnaud. Enter the keep, which is probably 14C and may have been built during the brief English occupancy. Many of the interiors and some whole parts of the buildings are 19C while others are modern restorations 'in keeping'. The stone of the area ages very rapidly and many of the additions will quickly pass for medieval. The ground floor has tanks for watering horses, the entrance to the original stair, and a *pisé* floor of shaped cobbles. The first floor within the keep is reached via a modern oak stair. Here are sets of rooms on two levels, a large room plus a smaller, private room with *garde-robe*. Note the pointed barrel vaults. The vaulted great hall was remodelled in the 17C for the meetings of the States General of Périgord. Flanking the elaborate fireplace—metopes, ox-heads, fruit, etc—are the flags of Beynac and Biron, who controlled the south, and Bourdeilles and Mareuil, for the north. Opposite, a small chapel has rather crude 14/15C wall paintings including an appropriate Last Supper and the Christ of Pity at the foot of his own cross as seen in the vision of St. Gregory. The interior of the ancient donjon has yet to be restored. A further spiral stair leads to the battlements (no parapets in places, keep children safe) and amazing panoramic views. Down again, and a cistern court of the 17C (the cistern is beneath the paving) has a chunky baluster stair, and the outer gate a drawbridge and suspended wooden guard box.

The path from castle to village passes through the old defensive wall and a tower housing a small museum of proto-history, outlining the early farming and ironworking of the region. The village proper is exceptionally picturesqueand touristy. Boating is very popular, with river trips and boat hire. The valley is glorious and the views from the water are memorable.

The **château of Castelnaud** stands across the Dordogne (from Beynac, take the D703 for 3km then cross river on D57, 1km to the village. The castle access is beyond the bridge, turn left then sharp right as signposted.) The situation is superb, the castle one of the most dramatic and interesting sites in Aquitaine. Children should love it. The river crossing provides an idyllic and popular picnic spot, a wonderful place for a cooling paddle on a hot day. The drive up the twisting road to the pretty upper village provides endless views and there is parking at the Castle. For the best approach, walk back to the village centre, then through the main gate.

Castelnaud was the rival to Beynac for much of Aquitaine's English history. The original 12C 'new' castle was destroyed by Simon de Montfort during the Albigensian campaign of 1214. It was substantially reconstructed after the Treaty of Paris, 1259, when it was ceded to Henry III of England as Duke of Aquitaine. It changed hands repeatedly throughout the Hundred Years War, finally falling to the French King, Charles VII, in 1442. Soon after, the castle was restored to the Caumont family, who carried out repairs and improvements, while further work followed the 16C French Wars of Religion. Abandoned at the Revolution and used subsequently as a quarry, modern restoration of the building started in 1967.

The château's present state of semi-completeness is its principal attraction. Furthermore, it contains a **museum of the Hundred Years War** which is both imaginative and informative, making sensible use of the buildings and grounds. It is very visitor friendly and should be seen. Visits are open access and, while the texts are in French, the displays, audio-visuals and models are self-explanatory and visitors may borrow an ample information-pack in English. The castle consists of a central core, 13C, with a tall, pointy roofed donjon, an inner court and high walls, a ruined artillery tower hanging over the village and a lower court with fine views and a 16C outwork. The visit includes the interior of the great round tower—note the unusual stair snaking around the outer wall—while upper chambers within the 13C core have displays of sieges. In the open courts, reconstructions of medieval weapons evoke the primitive technology of the time, note the recreated *trébuchet*, a wooden 'tea-chest' catapult capable of flinging dead horses and the like into besieged fortresses.

The D703 continues along the north river bank for a further 2km to reach **la Roque Gageac** a picturesque village perilously perched above river and road. The situation was significant as the English were never able to capture it, effectively blocking their passage up the Dordogne. Now, just stopping there is difficult. Narrow streets of golden houses clamber up and down through arches and terraces. There are some fine views, particularly from the simple 12C church. Not all the houses are what they seem. For instance, the Gothic confection at the entrance to village, Château de la Marlartie, is a purely Edwardian invention. The Manoir de Tarde standing near the river beneath the rock-face is everything it seems. Gabled and turreted, it was the home of Canon Jean Tarde, humanist and friend of Galileo.

The D705 leaving la Roque moves away from the river for 3km returning for the bridge and the D46 leading to **Domme** (1.5km; Tourist Office, 24250 Domme).

The fortified town occupies one of the best positions in Aquitaine, originally a fortress but extended as a planned town in 1282 by Philip III (the Bold). It fell to an English siege but was recaptured by the French after 22 years. In the French Wars of Religion, the town fell to the Huguenot Geoffroi de Vivans, who one night, with 30 of his men, climbed the seemingly impregnable, and thus undefended northern rockface and took the place by surprise. After four years, in which he burnt the church, he changed sides, joined the Catholics and sold the town, taking care to set fire to it first. Fortunately, stone towns do not burn well, and much of the medieval centre remains.

While Philip the Bold's town is planned and the grid-street system is fairly obvious, the erratic shape of the hill-top creates an almost triangular development. Hence the walls are not smooth but irregular, though an attempt was made to have a west, south and east gate. The north is a sheer drop. Domme is very small, and though gently sloping, is easy to visit on foot. Parking within the walls is difficult. It is best to park as soon as you have spotted the first town gate. The walls are well preserved, the original gates thin in the manner of *bastide* towns. The east gate, the **Porte des Tours**, is the most impressive, having twin towers with rusticated masonry, diminishing arches towards the entry, double portcullis slides, and plentiful arrowslits. It was rebuilt by Philip the Fair, and the towers were used as prisons for Templars after the suppression of that order in 1307. The walls here were continuously machicolated. All the gates lead quickly to the Place de la Rode (parking), a sloping irregular square with cafés.

The **Grande Rue** (pedestrianised) leads up the slope to the town centre, past numerous attractive and interesting stone houses and shops. On the left is a three-light Gothic window, a corner house to the right with late

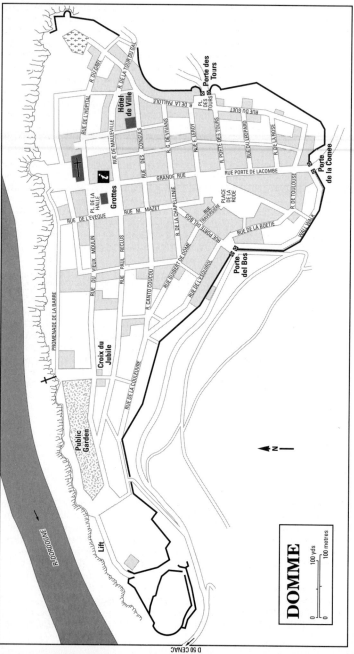

Gothic windows and many shops with medieval vaulted cellars. Specialist shops include foodstuffs from the region. The **Place de la Halle** opens left, with its 17C rustic covered market building and 'Scots Baronial' Governor's House, now the local *syndicat*, all turrets, gables and coloured rooftiles. Across the square, is a small museum of domestic life in an old town house. If you wish to see the famous underground grottoes, it is best to buy tickets immediately as they are timed, then plan your visit accordingly. The little church is dull, though the gabled west front looks curiously Breton. The terrace north of the church commands a broad view of the Dordogne valley. All the side streets of Domme are attractive, with individually pleasant buildings—see the **Rue Marguérite Mazet**, parallel with the Grand Rue. There are public gardens with fine views and a windmill, and a wall walk from Porte del Bos.

The **Grottes de Domme** (open all year round) are some of the most impressive and extensive in south west France, with relatively easy access, though within, it is sometimes wet underfoot and steep. Enter from the Market Hall. There are some large caverns, while in other places trenches have been cut to allow headheight. Plants grow beneath some of the lights. Animal bones including bison have been discovered. The formations are relatively neutral in colour, though special lights have jazzed them up somewhat. Worryingly, many of the monolithic columns were fractured by volcanic eruptions in the Auvergne. One curious section has a dome-like roof, apparently created by an underground whirlpool. The visit ends on a cliff-ledge with a splendid view of the valley, and the exit involves a glass lift up the cliff face into the public gardens, which are about three minutes walk back to the Market.

From Domme it is possible to return to St-Cyprien along the south bank of the Dordogne, using the D50, with its panoramic view, to St. Gybranet (5km), then right on the D57 to Castelnaud (4km), whence the D53 winds its way 10km to Allas les Mines and a river crossing, picking up the main D703 just east of St-Cyprien.

10

Sarlat and Souillac

Sarlat is one of the most famous, and most visited towns in Aquitaine. Despite living off tourists, it is a beautiful place, seen ideally in the early morning or late afternoon. At other times, parking is hard and the crowds enormous. Souillac is not technically in Aquitaine, just a few km over the border. However, a good round trip from Sarlat is easy, and the famous Romanesque sculpture well worth seeing.

From Les Eyzies, Sarlat is 21km along the D47 (29km with detours suggested below). The road is reasonable, the route pretty, the first distraction being the signposted route at 9km to the *cabanos* at **Breuil** (3km signposted). These little round huts are found all over Aquitaine and resemble the *trulli* of southern Italy. Dry-stone, with a door opening and a stone slab conical roof with the occasional dormer window, their appearance is comical. Several of them are joined together, and one has even become the annex of a later farmhouse. They are said to be pre-Roman, but their authenticity is called into question by the mini-*cabanos* supplied for the resident dogs. Given that the material occurs naturally, the shape avoids large corner blocks, and that the tradition persists, they could be any date. Still, the situation is delightful and the current occupants, a noisy mixture of ducks, geese, hens and dogs, add a touch of the ridiculous. When returning to the main road, a right appears just as the D47 comes in sight. Turn right here and in just over 1km give way, turn left and then park at the first right where the turning is marked with a no entry. From here it is possible to walk to one of the most romantic spots in Aquitaine, the **castle of Commarque**. The walk is gently downhill for about 1300m. Always follow the road track.

Commarque was taken by the English in the Hundred Years War. After falling again to the French, it passed to the Lords of Beynac. The original Romanesque donjon was supplemented with another in the 13C plus a fine vaulted hall. It was ruined before the 16C.

Public access to the castle is unclear, though there is a public footpath below. The setting is stunning, with wooded slopes and big vistas, the opposing castle of Laussel being most obvious. The main approach to Commarque is through a small gate with a lost drawbridge. The internal yard, now very ruined, was once filled with domestic buildings, whose remains run along the left-hand wall. Then you come to an inner rock-cut moat, or more correctly a dry fosse, and so through another gate to the inner court which is minute and stuffed with goodies, not least the dramatic views and gaping holes. To your left, stands the great tower with a turret and lots of machicolation. Before you, are the remains of another turret with ruined stairs. Rooms literally fall away down the slope including a ruined chapel.

If you return to the D47, and head east, in 4km signs appear for the **Château of Puymartin** (open 1 July–15 September, closed 12.00–14.00, other dates, pm only. Enquire). Access is via a very steep and narrow lane. It was the successive residence of several family names including the Saint-Clars, the Rofignacs and the Montbrons, though it remained essentially in the same hands, as it passed repeatedly through the female side. It was a Catholic stronghold in the French Wars of Religion.

The approach is dramatic, through a wooded setting. The house looks quite fantastical, with towers and turrets, perhaps rather more than it needs. The entry gate is modern, while to the left, the massive main block is half medieval (right) and half 19C (left). The gate leads into a tight courtyard with a high terrace open to the south. From the upper terrace the main elevation becomes clear—a central block with three storeys, four-square windows and a machicolated walkway. To the left is the big extended square tower, to the right, a fat, round tower, all medieval, with an extension of the upper walkway. The roofs are stone *lauze* in the local manner. There are gun loops in the main façade and over the 19C door, is a 19C St. Louis. The cottage-style buildings to the right look like country relatives at a rather grand do.

The rooms shown include an entrance hall with a big 19C fireplace and Louis XIII and XIV furniture, note the double-gabled cupboard. The stone stairway leads to a fine bedroom with 18C green Aubusson tapestries, a four-poster bed and a painted ceiling. The fireplace wall has one of the curios of Puymartin. It is entirely painted and includes a central scene of Danæ as Mary Magdalene, all dated 1671. In the little room off it, are 17C mythological scenes in grisaille, painted by Phillipe le Maire. This is one of the oddest interiors in Aquitaine.

The *grande salle* is hung with 17C Oudenarde tapestries depicting the Trojan War, and came to the house in a marriage dowry. It has another huge painted fireplace, this time depicting Venus and her three suitors whose moral is, 'Love fades in time'. Upper rooms include a vaulted turret chamber complete with a ghost—la Dame Blanche—traditionally imprisoned here by a jealous husband. It is also possible to visit the machicolated wall walk near the round tower and to see the massive roof structure of the main block. There are no gardens as such. Two period bedrooms are let.

SARLAT (8km) is a showpiece. It was a pioneering attempt to rescue and rehabilitate an ancient, crumbling and de-populating village. Now, 'Sarlats' exist all over Europe, spruced up, gentrified, full of identical tourist shops selling identical tourist trash. Sarlat did it first, and did it rather well. It resulted from a new law protecting and encouraging the restoration of historic villages, piloted by André Malraux, French Minister of Culture under de Gaulle from 1958. Sarlat was given as an example in the law. By the mid-1960s it was all but transformed. More than half the ancient centre has been repaired, though not too prettified.

Hotels are plentiful but tend to be expensive. If parking is required, stay on the edges and walk. Restaurants fill almost every nook and cranny, especially around the cathedral, in the small alleys and along the Rue Fénelon. The Office du Tourisme is at BP 114—Place de la Liberté, 24203 Sarlat. Tel 53592767, fax 53591944.

Sarlat began as a monastic community in the 8/9C. Under Charlemagne it acquired the relics of St. Sacerdos (Bishop of Limoges, died 520) and of St. Mondane, his mother. A town grew, controlled by the abbots, until a reform of 1299 placed the government of the town in the hands of consuls. It became a bishopric in 1317, when the monks of the cathedral were replaced by canons. It was ceded to the English in 1360 though generally sided with the French. After the Hundred Years War it was granted favours by the French crown, and much rebuilding took place. The great bulk of Sarlat's historic buildings date between c 1450–1550. It was a Protestant stronghold in the French Wars of Religion, costing the town much of its ecclesiastical heritage. Since the Revolution, Sarlat has gently crumbled.

Crowded or not, Sarlat is a beautiful medieval stone town, largely pedestrianised, with individual and groups of buildings of interest. Parking is a problem—try the signposted parks around the old centre.

This route will commence at the Place de la Petite Rigaudie on the road from Les Eyzies and is intended to maximise the number of interesting streets and buildings without too much walking. Some of the streets lack name-plates.

Before setting off, note a number of early medieval stone buildings on the north-west angle of the square at the beginning of Avenue Gambetta, well outside the medieval centre. Enter the town on the main Rue de la République and take the first left, Rue des Consuls. The streets are narrow and the buildings surprisingly tall. At the end of the curving street, is the

Hôtel Tapinois de Betou (right); if the door is ajar, go in. The interior court has fine late Gothic windows and the most extraordinary 17C wooden stair and balustered open landings reminiscent of Lyon. Continuing, note the little inset **Fontaine St-Marie** (left) and opposite, a fine row of medieval hôtels, see the **Hôtel Plamon** with 13C traceried windows.

The little **Place des Oies,** with its appropriate sculpted geese, opens to the left. Behind you (left) is the **Hôtel de Vassal**, with corbelled turret and stair tower. Next door stands the immense late medieval **Hôtel de Gisson** with early plate tracery windows of c 1200. As you pass diagonally around the geese, you come to the almost theatrical arrangement of stairs and entries and the curious stump of a church (right) and into the main Place de la Libertà. The stump is the nave of the church of Ste-Marie, begun in 1365; the chancel was demolished. Deconsecrated after the Revolution, it has been a bakery, a coal-store and a post office. It is now offices.

The main square is full of interest including the **Hôtel de Ville**, begun in 1618. The street to the left, Rue Fénelon, has fine 16/17C buildings and looks inviting but resist this and take the little passage immediately right of the Hôtel de Ville and climb the narrow Rue de la Salamandre. On the left the **Hôtel de Grezel** has stone sides but a pretty timber-framed and jettied façade plus the ubiquitous stair turret and fancy door. A turning left into Rue du Présidiat, and then the first right reveals the garden and rear façade of the *Présidial*, the Royal Court of Justice, established here by Henry II in 1552. The back of the building, propped on a large arch, is rather odd.

Retrace your steps back to the top of Rue de la Salamandre, then turn left along the Rue d'Albusse and left again by the 15C Hôtel de Génis, 15C, with a massively machicolated upper floor, and then to the turreted front of the *Présidial*. A lane directly opposite the Génis leads to a garden gate. Go through and enter the gardens east of the Cathedral. To the left on a slight rise, is the **Lanterne des Morts**, a curious, elongated beehive in stone, probably 12C and completely inexplicable. Only the lower chamber has ever been accessible, it has a domical vault and a pointed wall arcade. From here, the view of the Cathedral apse is most striking, bar the seasonal staging erected for the Son et Lumière. When erected it blocks the route around the church. The chapel left of the main church is that of the Pénitents Bleus, while around the main apse is a rock-cut necropolis.

If the staging is up, then leave the garden via the same door and walk down the Rue Montaigne to the main door to the **CATHEDRAL**. The church of St-Sacerdos was Romanesque until 1504, when Bishop Armand de Gontaut-Biron knocked most of it down for a new one. He should not have bothered. The Bishop was elevated in 1519, and the project hung fire, being completed only in the 17C. Fortunately, the Romanesque tower survives, all arcades, some pointed, then a late medieval stage plus a silly 17C topnot. Lower down are remains of late Romanesque sculpture. The west door is 18C. To the right is the façade of the former bishop's palace, with large six-square Gothic windows, elaborate buttresses, topped by a Renaissance loggia and matching windows, all very rebuilt. The Renaissance additions were by Cardinal Niccolò Gaddi, Bishop from 1533. Just inside the door of the Cathedral (right) is a section of Romanesque wall with corbel table.

The Cathedral interior lacks imagination: the fat piers rise up through the walls as bulges, the arcades seem to spring from nowhere, and the vaults burst through the wall—all very predictable. The windows have the dullest

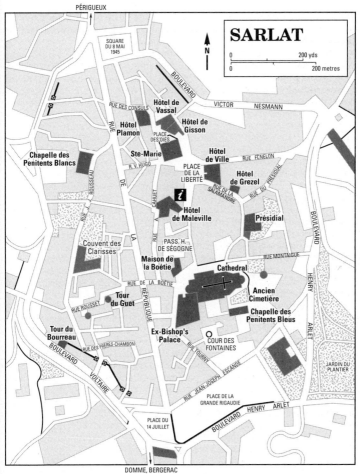

PÉRIGUEUX

SQUARE
DU 8 MAI
1945

SARLAT

0   200 yds
0   200 metres

N

BOULEVARD

RUE DES CONSULS

Hôtel de
Vassal

VICTOR   NESMANN

Hôtel
Plamon

Hôtel de
Gisson

RUE

PLACE
DES OIES

RUE DE

Chapelle des
Penitents Blancs

Ste-Marie

R. V. HUGO

Hôtel
de Ville

RUE FÉNELON

PLACE
DE LA
LIBERTÉ

Hôtel
de Grezel

RUE DE LA
SALAMANDRE

RUE DU PRÉSIDIAL

ROUSSEAU

RUE A CAHUET

Hôtel
de Maleville

Présidial

BOULEVARD

Couvent des
Clarisses

PASS. H.
DE SÉGOGNE

RUE DE LA

RUE MONTAIGUE

Maison de
la Boétie

Cathedral

HENRY

RUE DE LA BOÉTIE

Ancien
Cimetière

RÉPUBLIQUE

Tour
du Guet

RUE ROUSSET

Chapelle des
Penitents Bleus

ARLET

Tour du
Bourreau

RUE DES FRÈRES-CHAMBON

BOULEVARD

Ex-Bishop's
Palace

RUE TOURNY

COUR DES
FONTAINES

JARDIN DU
PLANTIER

VOLTAIRE

RUE JEAN-JOSEPH ESCANDE

PLACE DE LA
GRANDE RIGAUDIE

PLACE DU
14 JUILLET

BOULEVARD   HENRY   ARLET

DOMME, BERGERAC

tracery, though some of the piers have slender pilasters spiralling around
them, just crashing into the capitals. Only the planning of the east apse
shows any interest. It turns in five straight sides, the side chapels banged
straight on, while the ambulatory walkway is created by standing the ranks
of stalls away from the outer wall. The side chapels end up with skewy
tierceron vaults, the axial chapel is tunnel-like and mesh vaulted and the
whole thing has a slightly drunken unexpectedness. In historically Protestant territory, fittings will not be ancient. Some of the glass is 17C—see the
east window of the apse—and there is the odd Baroque altarpiece.

A south door leads into the site of the cloister, revealing the southern flank
of the church. Immediately left, notice fragments of re-used masonry in the
wall. Here on the left is the Chapel of St. Benedict, known as the *Pénitents
Blanc*, a Romanesque chapel unfortunately kept locked. Pass on beneath

the adjoining arch into the Cour des Fontaines, the water supply here is said to have tempted the first monks to settle in Sarlat in the 8C. The rather shabby state of the courtyard comes as a relief.

The exit west of the court leads into the Rue Tourny, where a right takes you back past the Cathedral and opposite to the famous **MAISON DE LA BOÉTIE**, the most photographed thing in Sarlat. It is not only striking but quintessentially Sarlat. Built by a magistrate, Antoine de la Boite, in 1525, it was the birthplace of Etienne de la Boétie, writer and friend of Montaigne. The house says everything about the domestic architecture of the town. It is quirky, pretty, interesting, a mixture of styles and very, very showy. The ground floor has a shop-front flanked by classical columns, while off to the left, a through-arch carries half the house over a side street. All the windows are too big, four-square and with early Renaissance pilasters and archi-traves. Note that all the left-hand window pilasters have dribbling, Italianate detail, while all the right-hand ones, have bolder strap-work shapes. The zippy, crocketed gable is pure Gothic, as is the idea of the top window crashing straight through it. The side dormer is flouncy. The chimney looks like a toast-rack.

Pass beneath the house into the Passage Henri-de-Ségogne which leads into a series of alleys and courts (monument to André Malraux, died 1976, to the left). All around are interesting and arresting details. A building to the left with stairs leads to a balcony and a wooden stair turret. In an alley to the right stands a tall narrow four-storey house with a Renaissance door and many windows—lots of architecture here, squeezed into a small space. Continue through the alleys until you return to the main Place de la Liberté by the side of the **Hôtel de Maleville** with its Doric doorcase, classical busts in roundels (said to be Henry IV and his wife, Marie de Medici or his 'favourite' Gabrielle d'Estrées) and the inevitable stair turret. On the square, the Office du Tourisme, or Syndicat (left), occupies a perfect early Renaissance building. It is very classical and has an original shopfront, Corinthianesque capitals, fluted columns and scrolly designs in the pediment. Opposite, is a late medieval version of the same thing. Passing back to the left of the Office du Tourisme and through a passage beneath the Hôtel de Maleville, turn right on the Rue Albéric Cahuet and arrive at the west front of the **former parish church**. The tower is most odd, all buttresses and turrets. A left passing along the short Rue Victor Hugo brings you to the main street, Rue de la République, and modern reality.

So far, only one side of Sarlat has been examined, the area most restored. Across the République lies another story, mostly unrestored, partly derelict. For those with time, the following route will cover the most interesting streets.

Walk back (right) 75m towards the point where the walk began, but then cross the street and take the **Rue des Armes** opposite the Rue des Consuls. Here are picturesque buildings of character and interest including a fine timbered façade and to the right a twin arched stone building with four-square windows. Then, keeping above the Rue de la République, walk back into town but up the ramp until the Rue Jean-Jacques Rousseau. Here is the **Chapelle des Récollets**, a 17C chapel with a Baroque doorway and containing a museum of sacred art. Continuing along these quiet lanes, notice the alleys either side, mostly untouched. A little further on the left after the Côte de Toulouse, the convent wall of the **Abbaye Ste-Claire** begins (under restoration). Note the fine house on the corner of Rue de la

The Hôtel de Genis, Sarlat

Boétie, with its corbelled corner turret. The range (right) along Rue du Siège has interesting medieval details, see **No. 6** with medieval shop-fronts and **No. 8**, with its blocked door, two large blocked arches on the first floor and its splendid traceried windows at the side. Directly opposite, the Rue

Rousset winds down to the Tour de Guet or watchtower, a round tower, turret and machicolated walkway combination.

Retrace your steps to the Rue du Siège and turn left. Passing under an arch, you reach a triangular place, where a turning right reveals a town gate and the wall. Pass through it. For the best view of the high town wall and the Tour du Bourreau (Executioner's Tower) built 1580, cross the busy road. Then walk downhill and re-cross the road when the next town gate comes in sight. This leads back into the relative calm of Rue des Frères Chambon. From here, the Rue de la République is quickly regained. The little Rue Lakanal opposite leads back to the Cathedral while a right leads into Place de la Grand Rigaudie, another market place. At the rear of the Palais de Justice (left) are the **public gardens**, to a 17C design by le Nôtre. Saturday is either to be avoided or savoured—Sarlat has a vast street market that makes visiting almost impossible, parking totally so.

From Sarlat, a 78km half-day round trip may be made to the eastern extremities of Aquitaine, crossing the border briefly to see Souillac, and returning along an upper reach of the Dordogne. Leave by the D704 the way you entered. Only stay on this road for 9km until a right is signposted, the D60. Turn right and after a few hundred metres a left turning takes you to St. Geniès in 4kms.

St-Geniès is very attractive, especially seen from this approach. It climbs up a slight hill to the church, all stone and mellow. The centre is a rambling square next to the church. Parking is no problem. The roads north of the church have been raised to assist traffic, resulting in the burial of some ancient buildings to some depth. The effect is almost comic—you can touch the church roof. The church exterior has particularly silly heads on the corbels of the apse. Inside, the simple unaisled church has a Romanesque apse with damaged sculpture but little else. A Baroque wood carving on the north side depicts Angels carrying the Cross. Next to the west front rises a whimsical little château, all turrets and towers, of the 15/19C.

On the very top of the village stands the tiny but abrupt **Chapelle du Cheylard**. The Gothic chapel, built in the 14C is commonly called Sante-Marie de Sarlat. It is usually open. Intended as a funerary monument for the family of La Chaminade, it was founded on 6 April 1329, by permission of the Bishop of Sarlat and built soon after. It is of principal interest for its painted interior.

The chapel is vaulted in two bays, and has two tiers of painting. Starting from the north wall, west end (left of entry), in the lower register, is the Martyrdom of St. Andrew, followed by St. Michael weighing souls at the Last Judgement. In the next bay, St. Valerie is about to be beheaded and beyond the window is St. Peter with the keys. Above this, is an unidentified and faded female. The east wall has St. John at the gate of Rome (lower left) flanked by the Baptism of Christ, with above, the Annunciation (left) and the Crucifixion. The window splays have the signs of the Zodiac. The south wall begins with St. Paul (lower left) and St. Maurice with Christ and the Cross and the Flagellation above. In the second bay is a depiction of the Martyrdom of St. Catherine (lower left), and appropriately beneath, the arms of the family Massacré, and next to her, St. George. Three scenes above include, from left to right, Christ mocked, Peter cuts off the servant's ear, and the Betrayal by Judas. The entry wall has St. Christopher (lower left), the Stoning of St. Stephen over the door and St. Francis of Assisi (not common). Above is a much defaced Last Supper. Thus the Christ scenes run oddly from over the west door to the south side of the east window. Presumably the accompanying Annunciation began a Nativity cycle. It is all very unusual, though the theme of Death seems plain enough. The style is mid-14C, the settings elegantly Gothic. The colours, refinement of drawing and general quality mark out this chapel as something special. Add the lost vault paintings, stained glass and sculpture and it must have been truly fabulous.

From St-Geniès, the little D61 leads towards Salignac, picking up the D60 after 5km. **Salignac Eyvigues** (7km) is a small hill-top town with a rambling, ruined château. (Tourist Office, 24590 Salignac.) The town lies left of the main road and centres on a stone market hall, flanked by huge, semi-derelict medieval buildings. The church is a little out of the town and is perhaps not worth the trouble. It has a 19C tower, a 15C nave with a tierceron vault and a painting of the Crucifixion in a little niche behind the altar.

The **château** (open July/August and perhaps September) is still the home of the Salignac family, whose most famous member was the writer, François de Salignac de la Mothe-Fénelon, Archbishop of Cambrai. The castle dates from the 12C and was possessed by both sides in the Hundred Years War. It was siezed and sold at the Revolution, and the Salignacs bought it back. Much of the medieval building remains including the sections of the inner circuit wall, tall towers and a ruined Romanesque chapel. The grounds are pleasantly overgrown, with wild flowers and sweet-peas gone to seed. The raised terrace about the château stands on the top of the old outer walls. The main block has a round and a square tower, much rebuilt after 1450. The interiors are well worth seeing, partly for their decrepit state (repairs are under way)—this is surely how many of the 17C French aristocracy actually lived—and as a house lived in by one family for many centuries. Inside, a number of rooms are shown including the kitchen and larder— note here the depth of the outer walls— a living room with a large fireplace c 1600 decorated with bulbous shells and pictures including a gloomy portrait of Louis de Salignac, died 1598, who became Bishop of Sarlat aged 22 (cousins, uncles the lot, all had bishoprics somewhere), a murky portrait of Louis XIV as a child, another of the duc de Biron, executed 1602. The furniture in the family rooms includes several pieces of the chunky Louis XIII period, notable for their diamond patterned doors. A Renaissance spiral stair leads up to bedrooms with Louis XIII fittings.

The D60 out of Salignac has good views of the château. After 2km turn right on the D62 (D15) for Souillac, which is reached in another 16km. Alternatively, follow the D6 south from Salignac for 2km then right at the signs for Les Jardins du Manoir d'Eyrignac (3.5km). The 17C manor, built by Antoine de la Calprendre, Consul of the Présedial in Sarlat, is principally famous for its period gardens (open every day, am/pm). The house is a modest stone-built affair like some Yorkshire rectory but the gardens are sumptuous, with topiary, groves, pools and vistas. Return to the D6 and after 3km, a left on the D47 leads to the main D60, where a right will reach Souillac in 8.5km.

Souillac is in Lot, just 5km out of Aquitaine, but as the road circuit passes through, it forms a convenient routing. It also possesses one of the great Romanesque churches of France. The town is no Sarlat; it is alternately bustling and silent, depending on the time of day. Some of the streets north of the abbey are interesting but hardly picturesque. The big, aisleless, vaulted and abandoned parish church has a dramatically broken tower.

Behind, in the Place P. Betz, it is possible to park right up against the apse of the abbey (Eglise Ste-Marie). The **church** is usually open all day and is entered from the north-west end.

Souillac is one of the best examples of the domed churches of south west France. Huge, aisleless, striding in great leaps towards a spreading transept, a broad apse clustered about with radial chapels and with repeated rows of windows. The exterior is a little scraped. The interior is splendid if antiseptically cool. Imagine it all painted up and lit through stained glass. The domes are majestic. But it is the **sculpture** that puts Souillac on the map. Behind you, within the west door, an assortment of Romanesque figures and scenes makes a confusing picture (light by door). Of course, such a grouping belongs on the exterior which is where this may have been until the French Wars of Religion. Possibly, all this was reset inside in the 17C. The main scenes above the door tell the story of Theophilus, who, wrongly accused by his abbot, makes a pact with the Devil for the return of his post as Treasurer. Repenting of this, the Virgin appears to him in his sleep and returns the damning document. The high setting of the story makes it rather difficult to see. Easier to admire are the richly ornamented columns, probably designed as the central support of the door, which show monsters with sinners and the Sacrifice of Abraham, and the two flanking figures of Isaiah (right) and Joseph (left). The **Isaiah** is universally recognised as one of the world's great works of art—his dancing step, elegant pose, magnificent head and hair. It was originally painted, and traces of red remain. It is a pity about Joseph. In the church, is a 16C woodpanel, the Mysteries of the Rosary (left) and a later painting, Christ on the Mount of Olives, by Chassériau. The monastic buildings, burnt in the French Wars of Religion, are mostly 17/18C. Next to the church, is a museum of automata.

The return to Sarlat or Les Eyzies/le Bugue may be made along the Dordogne river, taking the D703 along the north bank, or the prettier D43(D50) along the south bank. On the southern route, **Fénelon** (14km) has a fine **château** formerly belonging to the Salignac family and birthplace of the famous Fénelon (Open 1 March–31 October am/pm; not Tuesdays). With great foresight the family sold up in 1780. The house is well situated, standing high above the surrounding trees. You can park below the château; the house is only a short walk away. Enter by the small side door (right), ring the bell and wait. The guided tours take about 45 minutes.

The tour starts in the waiting room, a vaulted hall which was formerly a guard room. In future, the visit will include the tunnel leading from here into the outer bailey. At present you proceed through the main gate into the *lice*, or area between the walls. Fénelon has three courts or baileys, though the walls of the outermost one look dubious. In many places the inner walls sit directly upon the exposed rockface. Many of the towers have been cut down. It all looks a bit severe but the roofscapes relent a bit. After a stroll around the walls, you reach an inner gate shaded by a fine cedar, which is said to date from 1651, the year of Fénelon's birth. The gate bears the family arms, and from here you can see the façades of the main house.

The central block has two storeys and the usual four-square windows, here in pairs. There are 15C machicolated end towers and the dormers all have late-Gothic details. Peeping out from behind the towers are others, added sometime later, which make the whole ensemble look overstuffed. If you are told that the crack in one tower is where it was hit by an aircraft do not laugh, it happens to be true. The north façade, the main entrance, is softened by the 17C addition of a terrace and a horseshoe stair. The inner court is tiny and dominated by the large arches necessary to carry the raised terrace. There is a fat stair turret and a door to the right and a well nearly 80m deep. The rooms within are a mixed bag and will be subject to change when current restoration work is complete. At the moment the tour visits an armoury with the expected suits of armour and weapons and, surprisingly, a fireplace with a bread oven. Another room is currently empty but will house tapestries now displayed elsewhere, and there is a large chamber with a big ceiling and huge walnut fireplace wall, all of which are 17C. You can also see 17/18C furniture and Dutch and Chinese porcelain, then a bedroom with another fireplace in walnut, a portrait of Fénelon, tapestries and 17C furnishings. The bedroom leads to a tiny room which contains a sinister waxwork of the aforesaid writer and a stunningly good inlaid chest. In the yard, an interesting door leads into a small chapel which, though 17C, could pass for Romanesque. Odd fittings include the bone figure on the Crucifix and a late-Gothic chest.

In another 6km the D50 reaches Rome and the D704. Sarlat is 11km to the north, while once over the river, a left finds the D703 to la Roque Gageac (39km to le Bugue, and in 42km to Les Eyzies).

An alternative route to Sarlat still involves crossing the river at Rome and on to **Carsac-Aillac** (2km). The tiny Romanesque church here has an apse with rather damaged carved corbels, a dumpy tower and a curiously rebated west door. From Carsac, a left on the D703 leads towards la Roque Gageac and Montfort (2km) and the dramatic view of the **Cingle de Montfort** (signposted). Parking is very restricted but the view of the Dordogne, with almost sheer drops to the water, is impressive. On the far hill, stands the **Château Montfort**, a fantasy of 19C towers and roofs, but majestic none the less. The village is quickly reached and has some interesting houses and roofscapes. Montfort seems to have belonged to just about everyone except the Montforts. In 1214 it was held by Bernard de Casnac, who fled before the crusading army of Simon de Montfort. Having seized the castle, Montfort destroyed it. By the time of the Hundred Years War, it was in the hands of the Turenne family, who became Protestant in the 16C. Hence, the château became a stronghold for the armies of the Reformed faith. Most of what you now see is 19C though there is some 15/16C work hidden away (not normally open but easy to view from outside).

From Montfort, the D55 turns right from the D703 once you leave the village, and heads for **Vitrac** (1km). The little village clustered around the church is called Vitrac Bourg to distinguish it from the area at the river crossing below. The little church has the remains of a fortified east block, while the west front has damaged Romanesque sculpture. From Vitrac, descend to the D46, where a right turn leads along a quiet road, reaching Sarlat in 10km. Alternatively, from Vitrac, La Roque Gageac is 6km.

11

Les Eyzies/le Bugue to Bergerac, or a round trip via Biron

This route offers a choice—a round trip of 106.5km from the Les Eyzies area, visiting abbeys, *bastide* towns and two stars of the region, Monpazier and Biron, or a one-way route to Bergerac. The latter also offers a choice, either leisurely or direct. They each begin by heading for the river Dordogne at Limeuil.

The Circular Route via Biron

Take the D703 west from le Bugue (pass to the right of the riverside hotel, then go left) and after 2km turn left on the little D31 to **Limeuil** (3.5km; Tourist Office, 24510 Limeuil). Just outside Limeuil is the tiny Romanesque **chapel of St. Martin**, built by Henry II of England as part of his penance for the murder of Becket. The French attribute Henry's conquest of large areas of south west France, including the Périgord and Agen, to the exploits of Becket when still Chancellor. After his murder in 1170, Henry was forced to build many churches. This one was completed in 1194 and dedicated to SS. Martin, Catherine and Thomas of Canterbury.

The simple building has an east apse, see the cow corbel over east window, and a very plain exterior. The interior is semi-derelict but usually open, and contains a display charting the story of Henry and Becket. The aisleless nave may have been intended for domes, now it has a wooden roof (just). There is the usual dome over the crossing and a half-dome over the little apse. There were to be, or have been, transepts. The interior is principally interesting for its paintings. In the apse, there are pictures of the Crucifixion and Deposition (right of east window) and Flight into Egypt (left), perhaps 14/15C. Other fragments include coats of arms, and architectural painting on string-courses etc. On the east side of the north crossing pier is a later painting. On the north wall of the nave, a consecration tablet records the event and participants. The 'credits' include Pope Celestine, Kings Philip of France and Richard of England, the Duke of Aquitaine and the Count of Périgueux. There is a French translation adjoining it and English notes on the church on the opposite wall. The upper village, Haute Limeuil, is easily reached. It commands a fine view. There is a private château. The parish church has a very crude tower while above the south door, a classy, sculpted Virgin and Child of c 1400 wrecked by the most hideous modern head for the child. Descending to the river, take both bridges, one over the Vézère, the other over the Dordogne, and head off on the D51E and D2 for Cadouin (10km).

Cadouin is famous for its abbey church, and especially for its cloisters. The **abbey** was founded in 1114 by Robert d'Arbrissel, and became

Cistercian in 1116. In 1214, there is mention of a Holy Shroud, long believed to be Christ's burial shroud. This became the object of great devotion, attracting royal pilgrims to the church. It was spirited away during the Hundred Years War but returned by Louis XI. The pilgrimage was discontinued only in 1934. Though damaged by the English, the church remains essentially that of the 12C and is the most important Cistercian work in Aquitaine.

The **west front** stands in a small square, with the abbey buildings to the right, a market hall, a Tourist Office and a few shops and houses. This was once the abbey yard. The main façade was to be very grand but the scheme seems to have foundered. The door is now very plain, the capitals having all been lost. The north exterior is visible, plain at first, then slightly richer around the transept and apse. The east end can be seen from the road, but do not climb the easy fence into the gardens, though the view of the east apse with its Romanesque decoration is very good.

The **interior** of the church seems dark as, in the Cistercian manner, there is no clerestory. The nave is very plain, with compound piers, pointed arcades, a pointed barrel vault sitting tight on the arches, and hardly any decoration. There is a short choir with an apse, a transept with apses on the east side and a crossing with a dome. The monks' night entry door within the south transept appears part-way up the wall. In the north aisle, the original floor level is revealed, indicating that the present floor is over 1m higher. The capitals throughout are of the simplest, decorated with just the odd volute. The exception is the south aisle, where fancier items appear only to be dropped. The 19C paintings are unforgivable. Near the cloister door is a Virgin and Child with donor, in stone, c 1500, actually made up from shattered fragments.

The **cloister** is something of a showpiece (closed Tuesdays). The monastic buildings were seriously damaged in the Hundred Years War, causing the cloister to be rebuilt. Older work survives, as in the Romanesque arcade and door in the east walk with zig-zag patternings, and the little Romanesque chapel. The present cloister dates from the reigns of Louis XI, Charles VIII and Louis XII—see the royal door with their arms and those of Brittany (Anne of Brittany, widow of Charles VIII, married his successor Louis XII to keep his French hands on her Breton lands). The Flamboyant tracery is particularly lively, and the interior is enriched with incidental detail, niches, pinnacles and sculpted scenes from the Old Testament with Renaissance detail occasionally creeping in. The north walk has an elaborate Abbot's throne and a fresco of the Annunciation. At the south west angle, a carving of the Crucifixion tops the doorway. The tierceron vaults have carved bosses. There is now a small museum.

Across from the abbey west door, the little monastic gateway is called the Porte St-Louis.

A further 8km along the D25 brings you to **St-Avit Sénieur**, a small hill-top settlement centred on a big **church**.

The former Augustinian house was founded in the 11C in honour of the hermit St. Avitus. The saint was captured by the non-Christian Clovis in 507, whereupon he proceeded to convert the saintly Queen, Clothilde. The present building (under restoration) dates from the very end of the century and is one of the oldest domed churches in France, though its original domes are now lost. The relics were translated into the new church in 1118.

The church was obviously fortified in the Hundred Years War, and its battlementation is visible even at a distance.

The **west front** is asymmetrical, the left tower partly ruined, with a machicolated wall-walk guarding the door. The south side of the east end is more elaborate with exterior arcading, but the scheme was soon dropped. The interior (under repair) is wide, with massive wall piers intended to carry domes. They now support 13C Angevin rib vaults—it is said that the original church suffered badly in the Albigensian Crusade. The lateral walls have arcading which support a mid-height wall-walk as in the churches of Périgueux, and the passages cut straight through the wall piers. The window design groups twin openings with a single opening above. The replacement vaults have traces of painted schemes and carved bosses. The simple chancel is square-ended.

The **exterior south side** of the church shows evidence of the two phases of the building, the original and the 13C repairs, with buttresses slicing through the outlines of earlier windows. A small geological museum operates in what is left of the claustral range, note the detachment of the chapter house. This dormitory range also provides access through a barrel-vaulted arch to the exterior of the east end of the church. The rear of the east claustral range is very burnt. In the outer court, you can see the foundations of the refectory, and other buildings, and beyond that, a two-storey range with a well. The building has a cellar, a loggia and more evidence of fire damage.

From St-Avit, the D25 moves to **Beaumont** in 5km. (Tourist Office, 24440 Beaumont.) The town was an English *bastide*, founded in 1272. The west side of the little town still has traces of walls near the Porte de Luzier, and the centre has a square, though few of the typical arcaded buildings survive. The fortified **church** is a monster, with twin towers east and west, visible for miles around. There are arrow-slits galore and the windows are kept high. The east window is a vast Rayonnant piece. The south door is defended from above, while the huge west door retains little of an elaborate sculpture scheme save some small Evangelist symbols and some foolish-looking animals in a frieze. The interior is big. It is an aisleless church, six bays long and flat-ended. The present vault is a replacement of 1869. Little chapels have been cut north and south in the second bay to act as transepts and a further chapel exists opposite the side door but the interior is still what was intended, a barn. Beneath the north-west tower, a little room (light) contains some interesting sculpture; a carved boss from the original vault showing Christ in Majesty, c 1300, and fragments with St. Front (the dedicatee), and the Virgin. The actual sculpture of the tower-room is also fine with dragons, monks, and crumpled men. In the sanctuary is a small wall painting of a man and a woman. It is worth wandering around the back of the church to see the north side and the nearby building with its elaborate late Gothic window, coats of arms and the large cellar door. The Tourist Office is to the north of the west front. The main square retains a few arcaded buildings, now sticking picturesquely into the square (market second Tuesday of the month).

Those making a circular route and returning to the area of Les Eyzies may go south for two of the region's great sites, Monpazier and Château Biron. Alternatively, these may be seen separately as a half-day excursion. The problem with these two famous places is that they are remote, being only in Aquitaine by a bulge of the border. From Beaumont, take the D666 south to Monpazier, which is reached in 16km.

To many, too many, **Monpazier** is the perfect *bastide* town. (Tourist Office, 24540 Monpazier.) It has a grid-plan, gates and some walls, a big church and above all, an almost intact arcaded *bastide* square. The centre is small, containing barely four blocks, and parking is recommended outside—try the southern side and walk in along the Rue Nôtre Dame.

Monpazier was founded on 7 January 1285 by the English king, Edward I, to protect the road up from Agen. The town was intended as part of a chain of fortified centres. Disputes soon arose with the Lords of Biron, and the town's future began to look uncertain. Worse still, no one side secured the town in the Hundred Years War, resulting in both sides sacking it. It was the centre of a peasant's revolt in 1594 while in 1637, Buffarot, another revolutionary leader, was horribly executed in the town square.

The **central square** lives up to all expectations. Best of all, it is car free. All around are stone houses slung over dark recesses, with arches of varying widths fronting the shaded walkways. Interestingly, the houses are truly individual, each carefully sliced from the next. This means that most have their own independent side walls and this is reflected within the galleried walkways where the transverse arches are doubled. This may indicate the piecemeal development of the original town. The covered market hall contains the old measures for grain etc. The houses in the angle nearest the church are especially attractive, with varying roof lines, four-square windows and tiled roofs. The cut-away to the church is picturesque. Next door, a much restored upper floor four-light window c 1300. The next building is a cheeky intruder while the next neatly abandons the gallery, forming an inset square.

The **church** dates from the 1280s though it has been revaulted, see the elaborate apse vault. The choir has Gothic stalls with misericords. The painting of the Nativity is said to be 'after' Pietro da Cortona—quite a long way after. The west front and rose window are from c 1550. See the Revolutionary inscription proclaiming that despite everything, the people of Monpazier still believe in God. The block north of the square has passages and alleys, including the Maison du Chapitre, c 1300, which was the town's tithe barn. The Rue Notre Dame ends to the north with a town gate, and there is another gate one block away.

Market day is Thursday, while Chestnut Fairs are held on Thursday and Sunday mornings from October to December.

Château Biron is 8km to the south and well signposted. From Monpazier take the D2 and after 5km the D32 leads to Biron. The distant view is impressive. The Château has a very vague connection with Lord Byron's family and is one of the most famous castles in Aquitaine. It rises skyscraper-like above a tiny village (parking is difficult here). The castle dates from many periods, with basic work from the 13C and extensive reconstruction after c 1490. A scheme to recreate the castle as a Renaissance palace never quite came off, though sections of the plan continued to be built into the 18C. This explains the bitty nature of the site. Biron was one of the four great baronies of Périgord, becoming a dukedom in 1598. The site was fought over by both sides in the Hundred Years War.

The castle is irregular in plan, a lower court to the south and a tighter upper court standing on a raised terrace. Enter through a gatehouse with

Renaissance dormers. The outer court is dominated by the mass of the castle to the left and by a surprisingly big church on the right. Visits are guided (usually in French), but the lower court is unsupervised. The 16C loggia forms part of the abandoned Renaissance scheme. The chapel is really a double church, the one beneath and out of sight is entered from below and acts as the village church. The building is late Gothic/early Renaissance with big buttresses and fancy parapets. Inside, the vaulting has stellar patterns, while the Gothic piscina and Renaissance aumbry neatly catch the 16C dating. There are two damaged Renaissance tombs. One commemorates a knight, Pons de Gontaut-Biron, died 1524, with a frieze that includes a scene of the Raising of Lazarus. The other tomb is for Armand, Bishop of Sarlat, who built the church. This is decorated with three seated Virtues. In the far left-hand corner of the court, the burnt remains of the kitchens are clearly seen, with the damaged donjon of the ancient castle rising above.

The main entry to the inner castle is Renaissance and leads to an inner court containing a vast Doric loggia cut into the older buildings in the 18C. The east side of the court is late Gothic, with an elegant stair turret and strange fluted window mouldings. It was the main living area. The interiors have decorated fireplaces and there are gun loops beneath some of the windows. The rooms often house exhibitions. The stair ends with a top vault—note the beautiful handling of the under surfaces of the treads above your head. The ranges opposite appear to be 18C but have earlier work. The main stair leads up to the wood-vaulted great hall, while the basement houses the soldier's refectory, a huge room with a pointed barrel vault. The exterior walls may be viewed by passing through the loggia. Most of the elevations are late Gothic with masses of roofscapes and some quirkily placed *garde-robes*.

If you are returning to le Bugue or Les Eyzies, a brief stop may be made at **Belves**, which is reached by leaving Monpazier from the north side, and heading straight up the D53 for 17km. The route is very pretty but with no villages—the sign to Fongalop may prove irresistible. Belves is a funny little town which does not quite work as an historic centre. (Tourist Office, 24170 Belves.) It stands above the Nauze river, and looks promising from a distance. It has a medieval market hall on columns, with a little museum opposite, while in the narrow streets behind are the Renaissance Hôtel Bontemps, the guts of a Templar's building, a little passage (formerly the entry) to the castle and a Museum of Spiritual Arts. The Syndicat (on the main through road) and the adjoining *mairie* are housed in the former Dominican church. There is a market every Saturday.

The River Dordogne is reached in 4km by continuing north on the D710. Once across, the D703 turns left and reaches Campagne on the Les Eyzies-le Bugue road in 12km.

Beaumont to Bergerac

77km from Les Eyzies.

If you are on a leisurely drive from Les Eyzies to Bergerac, leave Beaumont on the D25 and drive 15km to **Issigeac**, a small, pretty town with overhanging buildings mixing stone and timber. (Tourist Office, 24560 Issigeac.) The walls along the east side remain, with buildings breaking through here and there. The town has barely spread an inch beyond its medieval confines, and though the church is commonly locked, the centre has a quiet air that makes it most attractive. The late Gothic church was burnt in the French Wars of Religion and had to be rebuilt. It has curious barley-twist columns on the west door. To the north of the church, the big 17C palace of the bishops of Sarlat has towers with extra corbelled turrets. It was another residence of Fénelon. There is a tile-nogged market hall (Sunday market), narrow streets and shady trees.

The D14 leaves Issigeac to the north west and after 8km meets the N21 to Bergerac. After 4km a sign points left for **Mombazillac**, one of the most famous châteaux and wines in the region, whose pungency can overcome any tendency to be cloying.

The **château** stands on a high bluff with distant views of Bergerac. Yet the feeling as you approach is that it is down in a hole. Built in 1550 by François d'Aydie, Viscount Riberac, it now belongs to the local wine co-op, who have commercialised the whole place. Visits are guided (in French), the groups far too large for the capacity of the rooms. The main façade, made famous from the label, has an almost Breton ruggedness. The stone seems encrusted and on a fine day, takes on a distinctly green tinge. The façade consists of the usual two storeys plus battlements and dormers, with fat towers each end sporting pointy roofs, all machicolated. The effect is surprisingly austere for the date, bar the random roofline, and only the dormer pom-poms hint of the Renaissance. The raking fire positions from the corner towers show that even in 1550, this fortified house meant business.

The interior resembles an Edwardian girls' public school. The internal arrangement is surprisingly modern. An entrance hall leads to the stair, with two rooms on either side, all repeated upstairs. The rooms are rather dreary, though the displays of historic viniculture might interest some. The cellars are fine. Mombazillac became a Protestant stronghold in the French Wars of Religion and this is reflected in a small Museum of Protestantism, potentially interesting but not in the manner offered. Generally the rooms are tatty, though enlivened by the odd piece of Louis XIII furniture. There are some flashy fireplaces and a small collection of Roman bronzes. You might think of saving the rather high entrance fee and splashing out on a good bottle!

Return to the N21 where Bergerac is reached in 6km.

Les Eyzies to Bergerac direct

57.5km.

Follow the earlier route as far as Limeuil and there take the tiny D31 to **Tremolat** (7km) which has a 12C Romanesque domed church with a large belfry and, in the churchyard, a second Romanesque chapel. If you wish to see the view from the **Belvédère de Racamadou**, above Tremolat, then a signposted route to the north of the village will take you to the hilltop viewing platform in 2.5km. The view of the great meander at Tremolat, with its cliff edges, is impressive. Returning to the village, turn right for Badefois-sur-Dordogne by taking the D31, then the D28 and D29, which is easier than it sounds. Basically, stay south of the river.

Badefois-sur-Dordogne (7km), is a little village overhung by a cliff on which are the scant remains of a castle. It has fine views. Following the south bank of the river, take the D29 and head west, crossing the Dordogne at St-Front for Lalinde, which is reached in 4.5km. **Lalinde** (Tourist Office, 24150 Lalinde) was singled out by the Germans for destruction during their retreat in 1944. However, the medieval brick gate and a section of wall survives on the Bergerac exit, as well as the Porte Romane, plus one or two old houses, including the Governor's House of 1597.

Lalinde was an English *bastide*, founded by Henry III in 1270. The restored Market Cross dates from 1351 (Market Thursdays plus fair, every second Tuesday of the month). Leaving Lalinde on the main D666, head west for 3km and cross the river once more, heading for Couze et St-Front (papermaking).

For **Lanquais**, take the D37E1 to the right as you approach Couze, and turn left after 2.5km at Varennes. The village is reached in another km. Lanquais is a delightful little place, scattered about a valley.

The **château** is very special (check opening times, it is closed on Thursdays but open on weekends in October). It can be approached from either side, with equal parking and access. Approached from the valley floor, pass the great medieval barn (open), you get the best idea of the curiosity in store. If you are standing before the exterior north façade you will see instantly that Lanquais is a chimera, a mixed-breed of a building, half medieval castle, half Renaissance palace. What is odd is the way it changes from one to the other. The left side is massive and fortress-like, with a big fat tower and battlements. But as the façade proceeds towards the valley it is transformed into a rather fancy late-16C house so that the right-hand tower does not match the left-hand.

The medieval castle, home of the Mons family, was transformed from c 1580–90 during and after the French Wars of Religion, shell holes on the façades are souvenirs of a siege. The builders, Marguérite de la Cropte and Gilles de la Tour de Limeuil, never completed the project. Not only does one side survive from the Middle Ages, but only one wing and a corner of the new work was ever achieved. The house became the property of the present family, the de Brandois, in 1737, and they still live in it, having kept their heads down, and on, during the Revolution. The earlier façade has late Gothic windows inserted into it to soften the effect, while the original machicolated walkway is mostly ruined. The Renaissance work is much fancier, with a predeliction for panelling and flouncy dormers. Note the gun loops, showing that the French countryside was still a dangerous place. The intrepid will walk the narrow path around the right-hand pavilion to appreciate the position and lake views.

The house is entered from the south court, where the façades are reversed, with the addition of a big late Gothic stair turret against the fat tower. The roof texture is magnificent. The Renaissance façades are richly panelled, and again have gun loops. You go in by the medieval turret, which has a fine vault at the top. Four doors lead off the stairs, one per step. At the top, the wall walk may be visited. The rooms which are open give the appearance of being only part furnished but this is probably the state they were in throughout the 17C. Fortunately, Lanquais manages to avoid being a modern idea of a stately home—it simply has not been touched for generations. Where there is furniture, it tends to be Louis XIII. There are fireplaces from the Louvre school. The main bedroom retains its cabinet *toilette* and twin beds from the early 17C. Like most rooms, the ceiling is timbered and the fireplace enormous. The picture of St. Paul on the road to Damascus is an odd subject matter given the use of the room. There is also a Louis XVI room with a painting of the castle over the fireplace. The dining room is mostly Louis XIII except the 19C dinner service. The billard room has a table with no holes. It contains a flint collection. Other rooms shown include a drawing room, the kitchens, what is called a fencing room, and a garrison refectory, complete with gun emplacements. The medieval sections of the basement include a sally-port and access to a well 25m deep.

For Bergerac, head back to the D37E1 by forking left and avoiding Varennes, then cross the Dordogne at St-Germain-et-Mons (6.5km). Picking up the main D660 at Mouleydie and heading west for Bergerac (10km) enables you to avoid the worst traffic problem in town, the single river bridge.

BERGERAC (Hotels/Rest. Tourist Office, 97 Rue Neuve-d'Argenson. Train connections, Limoges, Périgueux, Sarlat) has a traffic problem, with a number of main roads all attempting to cross the Dordogne by a single bridge. One day this may be remedied. Parking is also difficult, but try the Place Foirail, a short walk from the old town. Bergerac is a prosperous centre for wine and shopping. The medieval town exported wine from the river frontage, which remains one of the town's attractions. It became a notable Protestant centre and was the capital of Périgord until the Revolution. Its commercial future must be in some doubt, as it is the French centre for tobacco production.

From the Place Foirail, the Rue Junien Rabier leads to the major **Rue Neuve d'Argenson**, where a left turn takes you in one block to the Hôtel de Ville, set within a garden. Opposite, the narrow Rue d'Abret will lead directly into the **old town**. The character is quickly established—stone ground floors, timber-framed and sometimes jettied upper levels, lots of brick nogging. At the end of the lane, there is a stone block with arches and 14C windows. Turning left on the Rue Boubarraud brings you to the **Musée du Tabac**, which will in future be something of a curiosity like Poor Houses or torture chambers. The building is very fine and was the Maison Peyrarède, built in 1603. It has a huge entry, four-square windows and a pretty turret, which are best seen from the adjoining square. Beyond the museum, a left turn along the Rue de Château leads to the riverside and the **Quai Salvette**. Turn back to see the ancient port buildings, some with lifting gear for loft storage.

From the river, take the Rue des Récollets and enter the **Place du Dr.**

D709 MUSSIDAN

BERGERAC

0   100 yds
0   100 metres

BORDEAUX, AGEN   SARLAT-LA-CANEDA, CAHORS

Cayla. This pleasant square contains a statue of Cyrano de Bergerac. Here, in the **Convent of the Récollets**, is the *maison du vin*. Enter through the passages and arrive at the incomplete two-storey cloister, dominated by a magnificent tree. The timber upper levels of the cloister are supported by 18C Doric columns on one side, and 16C Ionic on the other. The building is occasionally open for visits and includes cellars and upper rooms and a great hall. It now houses the regional wine centre. At the other end of the square, here called the Place de la Myroe, the **Musée du Vin** occupies a picturesque timber-framed building. The inside is very spruced up and contains model boats and vinicultural implements.

From the statue of Cyrano, turn left into the Rue de Mazeaux and into the rambling main square, the **Place Pelissière**. It is dominated by the church of **St-Jacques**, a strange looking affair with turrets clinging on to the tower. Given Bergerac's religious history it comes as no surprise that the church is virtually a 19C rebuild. Tiny fragments of older fabric occur along the south side. The Rue St-Jacques leading from the east end of the church, has a fine house at **No. 23**. From the **Rue des Fontaines**, a main shopping area, a right turn leads to **Nos 27–29**, a huge medieval block with arches along the street. Other houses in the street are also worth a look. The street will lead back, via the Rue des Farges, into the Place Cayla, where a left turn will pick up the far end of Rue d'Albret. There are more old houses here, including a large timber-framed block. Continue along the street until you return to the Hôtel de Ville. The other sections of the town, (left up the Rue Neuve d'Argenson) are mostly modern, and contain the bus and rail station.

Market Wednesday and Saturday plus an Easter Fair and St. Martin's Fair, November.

12

Bordeaux to Agen via Bazas

This route may be taken one-way, or as a round trip from Bordeaux to Bazas and back. Bordeaux to Bazas round trip 138km. Bordeaux to Agen via Casteljaloux 157km.

Leave Bordeaux by crossing the Pont de Pierre and turning right on the main D10. Once clear of the city, the road is quite scenic though the traffic is often heavy. Alternatively, take the Autoroute A64 and head for Toulouse. Leave at the second exit and head for the river crossing at Portets (N113/D115). Turn right on the D10 and at 5.5km a right turn leads to **Rions** (direct from Bordeaux, 30km). You will already have seen the pretty north gate of the town, which comes as a welcome sight on rather a hectic road.

Rions is a pretty, quiet *bastide* town, with substantial walls but most of all, an unspoilt character. The main gate, the Porte de Rhyan, bulges out at the visitor, with its glowering low arch and big battlements. It dates from 1330, the walls hereabouts earlier, c 1295. Head for the little church where it is possible to park near the east end. The Romanesque church is usually locked, which is a pity. It has an uncommon exterior, particularly over the chancel roof where the nave east wall rises higher and has two mysterious openings looking into the roof. It is worth having an amble about Rions, especially if the drive from Bordeaux was an ordeal. You will find perfect, shuttered medieval shop-fronts, and an 18C arch, a small *mairie*, a defensive tower with *garde-robe* and a view across the fields.

Return to the D10 to continue to **Cadillac** (5km; Tourist Office, Hôtel de Ville, 33410). As you see the town walls, follow the road around the dog-leg right and left, then park in front of the south wall. This is the original river frontage of the *bastide*, and from here there is a fine view of the walls and of the Renaissance **château** rising dramatically over the town. Cadillac was an English foundation of the 13C. Later, it became the seat of the Dukes of Epernon. Enter the town via the slender south gate. This has machicolations and a wall-walk while the rear has a sentry box over the upper entrance. The flood levels are marked within the arch; that of April 1770 must have drowned everyone. The grid-plan leads quickly to the central square which retains a few arcaded buildings plus a huge market hall, shops, cafés and Hôtel de Ville. There is another dramatic view of the château. Further up the slope and the château is reached. (The tourist office is to the right.) It is a big and rather splendid building of the late 16C approached over a dry moat. The ticket office is in the porter's lodge.

The house was constructed between 1598 and 1620 for Jean Louis de Nogaret de Lavelette died 1642, friend of Henry III and leading figure in the successive reigns of Henry IV and Louis XIII. He was Governor of a number of provinces including Guyenne, Admiral of France, Colonel-General of the Infantry and also Duke of Épernon, all this despite refusing to give up his Protestantism. After the Revolution the château became a women's prison, and some of the cells remain.

The main building (the wings have been demolished) is severely restrained, with a central block and pavilion ends. The wall/roof colour contrast is particularly pleasing. The two-storey elevations have six-square windows while the central door features sculpted reclining females. At present, the interiors are unfurnished, though on occasion, 26 Aubusson tapestries depicting the life of Henry III are displayed. The internal arrangements are those of a palace, a great stair with one major apartment on either side, repeated at both levels. Each apartment begins with a major audience chamber, and is succeeded by a smaller, private room, then smaller and smaller ones. The main rooms have spectacular fireplaces dating from 1616, the work of Fontainebleau artists, possibly including Jean Langlois. They are packed with marbles, trophies, fruit and floral swags and are memorable, despite Revolutionary damage. Some rooms also have painted timber ceilings. The principal hall is on the upper floor, to the right of the stairs. Descending to the bottom of the stairs, the kitchen arrangements may be seen. The north end basement room leads to a marvellous spiral staircase. A back door gives access to the rear elevation and the formal garden. The back of the house is more impressive still, rising directly from the dry moat.

Nearby the château, the **church** is a dull affair, with a 19C façade, and a 17C interior. The south chapel is another matter. Built in 1606 for the tombs of the ducs d'Epernon, it is extremely ornate. The great tomb of the founder, designed in 1597 by Pierre Biard, was smashed up during the Revolution. Fragments exist in the château while the main figure is now in the Louvre.

From Cadillac, take the D10 for 5.5km to Ste-Croix-du-Mont, where you turn left on the D229 for Gabarnac. The first right in less than a kilometre leads to Labal and **Verdelais**.

The village sits in the gently rolling countryside. It is mostly a 19C planned settlement, with a tree-lined main street ending at the church. It is a pilgrimage centre for two reasons—the Virgin of Verdelais has long been an object of devotion, and the churchyard contains the tomb of Toulouse-Lautrec, died 1901. A minor work by the artist hangs in the local hotel.

The **church** is more curious than interesting, and could not be accused of being beautiful. It was founded by Géraud de Graves, who became a hermit following his return from the Crusades in 1109. It later became a house of the Grandmontine order. The present church is post-medieval. The interior is liberally coated with votive plaques, many of great interest. There is a thank-offering from the Duchess of Angoulême for a safe sea-crossing in 1823, several relating to plagues in 1643/44, and one for a man blind since childhood who was cured in 1626. Many of the plaques date from the 17C, presumably when the present church was inaugurated. To the left of the door, there is a monument thanking the Virgin on behalf of sailors rescued from all the storms between 1629, 1661, 1695, 1702, 1703, 1706, 1710, 1736 and all the rest up to 1862. Some of the plaques, though 19C, relate medieval cures, such as the miracle of Blandine Duvet, who was cured of

The Renaissance château at Cadillac

paralysis 'in word and all her limbs'— presumably a bed-ridden case. Across the road lies the cemetery containing Toulouse-Lautrec's tomb. Above, stands a Calvary or outdoor Stations of the Cross. The gardens are pretty though a glimpse at the first monumental sculpture may suffice for all but the insatiably curious.

The little road passing the church joins the D19 and **Château Malromé**, where Toulouse-Lautrec spent many years and where he died, is 3km north from this turning. A medieval château built by the counts of Béarn, it is open afternoons mid-June/mid-September, Sundays and holidays Easter– 1 November. A right turn off the D19 brings you to St-Macaire in 3km. Crossing the railway and the main road looks awkward but follow the signs. Park at the first, north gate.

St-Macaire is an amazing survival in an unpromising position. (Limited Hotel/Rest. Camping. Tourist Office, Hôtel de Ville, 33490. Tel 56 63 03 64) Now happily bypassed, it sits on a small hillside above the river, quiet, almost asleep. Yet it is one of the region's most attractive towns. Where are the tourists? A fortress occupied the little bend in the Garonne during the 11C and a century later the settlement also had a large monastic church. By the reign of the English King, Henry III, St-Macaire was an established town and had probably received its walls.

Enter the town by the 14C Porte de Benuage and on the first corner (right) the Tourist Office occupies a beautiful 16C shop with its original shop-front. Enquire about the opening times of the church.

Continuing straight down the Rue de l'Eglise, you arrive at the west front of the **church** and a little garden containing the remains of the monastic buildings. From the Benedictine house, the south walk of the cloister plus another building survive. The terrace south of the church commands an attractive view towards the river. It also reveals the true scale of the church—big, aisleless, with a tall nave, a shorter apsidal choir and a similar transept. The tower is oddly placed against the north flank. The east apse has some Romanesque decoration and the buttresses are finished with colonettes. Passing round the outside to the north, the octagonal tower is tucked into the angle of the nave and north transept, and nearby, the square-framed tracery window is clearly a 14C intruder. The west front is rather grand, or was before the loss of much of the sculpture. The elaborate 13C door has lots of angels in the arch, all relatively unrestored. Beneath, in the tympanum, are the figures of Christ, the Virgin and John and below, the Apostles. The door jambs are unusual, a two-tier design with trefoil arcading, the upper level having standing saints while the lower tier reveals colonettes descending from nowhere. The whole thing is topped with a rose window and is very typical of northern France.

The **interior** is vaulted throughout, the rib-vaults of the nave and crossing sitting uncomfortably upon their supports. The trefoil at the east end is most obviously Romanesque. The apse has a double-arcade. The crossing piers have blank arcades, as in the domed churches, and suggesting that this was also to be domed. Certainly, all the apses have half domes and the first bay of the nave has huge wall piers as if for domes. The rest of the nave is all of a piece with the present rib vaults. Possibly the scheme was changed when St-Macaire became the property of Ste-Croix, Bordeaux. Alternatively, the building may have taken so long to erect, that domes simply went out of fashion.

The **decoration** is important. Many of the Romanesque capitals are painted, see Daniel in the lions' den being comforted by angels (south transept). In the nave, the capitals change from Romanesque figurework to Gothic volutes. The vaults are extensively painted, though unfortunately restored in 1828. The apse contains a great Trinity, with God the Father holding the keys of Heaven, and the disc of the Earth and the sword in his mouth symbolic of His power over unbelievers—this is Albigensian territory. The angels beneath reveal the poor standard of restoration, the right-hand Angel, c 1320, has been retouched, the left-hand are 1828, repainted. The other subjects seem endless but include Apocalyptic scenes, standing saints, the Golden Legend (on the crossing), the lives of St. John, St. Catherine (south transept), St. James (north transept), and coats of arms. The west door within the internal porch retains an ancient wooden door with extensive ironwork, 13C?

The town is well worth exploring, especially the much photographed, though little visited square. To reach this, pass to the east end of the church and take the Rue Carnot, taking note of the little castle in the alley off to the left with a passage to the riverside meadows. Walking north along the Rue Carnot, you pass on the left a fine 13C house with traceried windows and post holes, the latter intended for external wooden structures.

The square, **Place du Mercadiou**, opens on your right. And what a square. Actually, it is a long, rather rambling oblong, spasmodically closed at the far end. All the buildings are worth examining in detail yet they blend into a perfect whole. Nearly all have the typical *bastide* arcading though

Typical bastide arcading at St-Macaire

St-Macaire was not a true *bastide*—it is here simply a question of fashion. The internal ceilings are of wood, the only tragedy being that the locals can find no other use for the covered spaces than car parking. On the southern side is a three- storey building with blocked tracery, and yet more with second floor traceried openings; indeed, St-Macaire gives the impression of having substantially more 13C houses than most other *bastides*. The north side is truly picturesque and better lit. Of particular note is the old post office, a Renaissance post house of almost building-block simplicity. It contains a local post office and a postal museum. There is a pretty courtyard within, and a fine spiral stair. The continuation of Rue Carnat will bring you back to the Tourist Office—note the big, late medieval building on the left with a machicolated wall walk hanging over the street.

Alternatively, St-Macaire is very pleasant for an amble. The far end of the square leads another 14C gate, the **Porte du Thuron**, with the remains of an extensive outwork. Another gate, the **Porte Rendresse**, survives at the opposite extremity of the town. The back streets recall the state of all the Sarlats of Europe before the 1960s.

What you do next depends on the time and whether this is a round trip or a specific journey to Agen. Just south of the Autoroute, the A62, lies a group of monuments and sites, some of which open at set times. If it is lunch-time then head for Bazas and eat. Either stay until the cathedral re-opens at 15.00 and then head for the group of papal monuments—Roquetaillade (open afternoons Easter–1 November, then Sundays and holidays, pm plus July/August 10.00–19.00), Uzeste (usually open but may shut lunchtime), and Villandraut (at present left open, but this will change). Alternatively, skip the cathedral interior at Bazas or go back later, as all these sites are very close together but do not form a neat circular route.

The route from St-Macaire to Bazas takes you back towards Bordeaux in order to cross the river. Leave St-Macaire on the N113 and use the Langon bypass heading for the autoroute (4km). Ignore the toll entry, swing left and join the D932 at 2km. Turn right here and head for Bazas, just off the road, and another 12km. (At 5km the D125 heads (right) for Roquetaillade, 3km.).

Bazas is a quiet, unspoilt town, where it is possible to have a simple lunch, a pleasant stroll and to congratulate yourself for avoiding the crowds. (Tourist Office, 1 Place de la Cathédrale, 33430. Tel 56 25 25 84, fax 56 25 18 30.) It was a Roman town, and a bishop's seat from the 6C until 1790. Now it is a small agricultural centre where little happens. There is parking as you arrive before the Hôtel de Ville. The small pedestrianised street just ahead leads into the biggest surprise of the town—a vast central square, sloping up towards a cardboard cut-out cathedral, and straggling off in unpredictable ways. Market day (Saturday) would be the time to come. Better still, would be the Thursday before Ash Wednesday (Jeudi Gras) when the local cattle process through the streets. Bazas beef is considered the very best in the Bordelais, though it is rather hard to find locally.

The square contains some fine buildings—the **Alchemist's House** is now the Tourist Office, and there are several arcaded blocks. On the left as you approach the cathedral, is a late Gothic house with stepped gables and windows which look rather Chinese. This is the **Maison Andraut**, also known as the Astronomical House after the Sun and Moon over the first floor windows.

The **former cathedral** is very impressive from outside, but less so within. This is not the fault of any architect but of the Protestants who singled it out for extensive destruction. The main façade is very satisfying; it has three broad doors, the raised central section with Flamboyant rose and Renaissance pediment, lacey flyers and an odd, almost detached tower with a nobbly spire. The Renaissance work derives from the post-Religious War restorations, 1583–1635. The doors retain lots of damaged sculpture while the jambs have the same two-tier arcades revealing inner colonettes as St-Macaire. It all looks 13C. All of the major free-standing sculpture has been lost, the central trumeau is Renaissance, the figure modern. The door depicts the life, or rather death of St. John the Baptist along the lintel, while in the tympanum above, are Christ and the Last Judgement, the Blessed and the Damned and surrounding angels, mid-13C. The right-hand door shows the Death of the Virgin on the lintel with the Coronation of the Virgin over. The voussoir blocks forming the arches have the Tree of Jesse and the Labours of the Months. The haloes from lost free-standing figures survive built into the fabric here and there. The left door has the story of St. Peter, with Christ walking on the water, St. Peter released from prison, Christ gives Peter the keys and his upside down crucifixion. The earlier Nativity scene with Shepherds is an odd piece from somewhere else. The gardens south of the west front offer views of the little valley with its mill race, and of the south flank of the church (excavations in progress). There is no transept.

The **interior** is bound to be a disappointment. Smashed, burned and partly demolished by Protestant zeal, it is a wonder that anything is left at all. The west end is nearly all 17C, the middle, 15C, while the east end, including parts of the nave, is 13C. The change in the upper clerestory windows from east to west says it all. The crossing piers have 13C leaf capitals. The apse was redone in the 15C with a new vault and boxy side chapels. The main elevations are uncomfortable. To begin with, the arcade arches are too high; there is an abandoned middle storey (recalling Rouen Cathedral), and the vaults sit uncomfortably, especially in the choir aisles. As there are no capitals at main springing level, these vaults must be 14C, not 13C. Further west is evidence that a rebuilding or remodelling of the nave was under way c 1500, look at the pier bases. Now the piers rise as fat drums, most unpleasant, as is the glass throughout—come back Calvin, and bring your hammer. At the west end, south side, late Gothic stellar vaults have crept in.

Bazas retains impressive sections of its fortifications, especially north of the main square, see the Porte Guisquet, 13C and 19C.

If you have not yet visited the papal monuments, now is your chance. Roquetaillade is reached by retracing your route back to the main D932, ignoring it by proceeding straight ahead on the D3, and taking a right after 3km on the D223 through le Nizan. You will arrive by circling the estate gardens, and there is parking at the gate (Bazas to Roquetaillade, 10km).

The castle at Roquetaillade

Roquetaillade is one of the showpieces of the Gironde. The present **castle** was built from 1310 by Cardinal Gaillard de la Mothe, nephew of the French Pope, Clement V. The building survived remarkably well into the 19C when the Mauvoisin family, whose descendants still occupy it, called in Viollet le Duc, the most famous architect of the day, to modernise the interiors, which he did. Roquetaillade is a dream palace for lovers of 19C interior design, a monument to the architect's taste and pioneering vision. That it is also a splendid site, with magnificent parkland and setting comes as a bonus.

The house is approached from the north down an avenue of trees. It is at first a little forbidding, lying low in its rock-cut hole, with end towers and a huge central donjon. The effect is softened by tall 17C windows, Gothicked up by Viollet. Passing to the right you see the main façade, crowded with bastion towers and hardly any intervening wall. If it reminds you of Bodiam Castle (East Sussex), this may very well be the model. The gardens (open and free all day) were laid out in the English style by Viollet; while to the right, on the edge of a scarp, perches the old castle, founded—so legend has it—by Charlemagne. The garden about it was once a village, the nearest gate (1302) being that to the village centre. All this went later in the 14C. The old castle is dominated by a huge square tower, plus sections of high ruined walls linking to another, shorter tower. Much of it is 12C. Also, catch a glimpse of the stables, which are a combination of market hall and railway station also by Viollet.

The **gardens** circle round the main house towards the 19C family chapel, which is a shrine to the Gothic Revival. The architecture is Picturesque Romanesque, with a little bell-cote, an odd chimney and tiny windows. The inside is quite exotic. The altar of Pyrenean granite is set about with enamels, stained glass and metal work. The 'mosque' lamps are but one reference to Islam, another being the harem screens at the west end. Amid the myriad of quotations, including the Muslim style of the Capella Palatina, Palermo, the font is unbelievably modest. The chapel prepares you for what is to come inside Roquetaillade.

Tours of the house are guided, sometimes in English. You will have grasped already that the new castle is square, with corner towers, and a great tower rising from its centre. The exterior walls are medieval for virtually all their height, including some of the battlements. The big windows are inserts, as are the corbelled sentry-boxes above, a little fancy from Viollet. The north façade has an additional entry, converted by Viollet into a loggia. The drawbridge slots low down suggest an original side door. The main entrance façade is most impressive, especially its arrow slits and *garde-robe* exits. Within is a tiny court—the great tower occupies what would normally be open space. Notice the semicircular windows set high up; they look 1900, but are in fact 1860s. It is useful to grasp the original layout of the house. In the 14C, rooms lined the interior of the walls on three sides, not the entrance side. The great tower is slightly off-centre to allow for the court in which you stand. Many of the original first-floor chambers must always have been lit by windows on the exterior walls as the great tower blocks their internal façades. What the Cardinal arranged was an entry with stair at the base of the tower, leading to a large room on the first-floor back, with another higher in the tower.

The plan was largely preserved by Viollet. The main door has carved headstops, the 19C patron and his wife plus Viollet on the right and the

Madonna on the left, who has a typical Viollet copy of a 13C Parisian face. The stair-hall is worth seeing alone, though it is definitely not for the faint-hearted. Rising nearly half the internal height of the tower, it is an essay in Victoriana *à la française*. It dates from 1867, and cleverly combines a grand stair up, with a descending stairs through the middle. Note the 'Medieval' washing tanks—there was no drainage—and the painted decoration, probably after 1874 but still years ahead of the Arts and Crafts movement. The bat motif was Viollet's trade mark. The stair-hall is topped by a great stellar vault, said to be 14C and certainly recalling an English medieval chapter house.

A number of rooms are shown including the dining room, a garden conceit with sky-blue walls, trellis work paintings and trailing plants. The style and details are all Gothic but the notion is strangely Roman for Viollet. Still, it is great fun though the painted linen-fold ceiling is a bit much. Amongst the furnishings is a splendid English 1930s silver tea service, modernism's answer to the likes of Viollet. The Pink Room is named for obvious reasons, and is filled with lacquer-wood furniture. It has an interesting bathroom attached. The Great Hall on the first floor was designed in 1868, probably within the medieval hall. It was to have had great arches supporting a wooden roof, as you can see from the artist's impression, which has been preserved. The interior is dominated by an imported fireplace that apparently rises through the roof. It is in the style of Fontainebleau and resembles those in Cadillac, except that this is pristine. There are coloured marbles, standing and reclining ladies, broken pediments and lots of fruit—surely the top with angels is by Viollet. Like many of the 19C rooms, the hall was left unfinished. The Franco-Prussian War of 1871 and the collapse of the wine trade following grape disease led to financial ruin for many families in the Gironde. The present owners have lovingly restored what was achieved and clearly appreciate their inheritance. A bedroom of the 19C and a superb period kitchen complete the tour.

What you visit next depends on the direction in which you are heading. If you are returning to Bordeaux, then see Uzeste, if your destination is Agen, then see Villandraut.

Take the D125 on from Roquetaillade to Roaillan (1.5km) then a left on the D222 brings you to a crossroads with the D3. Ahead is Uzeste (3km) while turning right brings you to Villandraut (5km; Tourist Office, Place du Général de Gaulle, 33730).

Villandraut is another huge early 14C **castle**, here built by Pope Clement V in his birthplace. Clement, whose real name was Betrand de Got, was made Archbishop of Bordeaux in 1299. He became Pope in 1305 and began work immediately upon Villandraut. Whereas Roquetaillade is a complete château, giving a clear idea of a great house, Villandraut is a wreck, hardly touched for centuries, and very impressive. It stands hard on the village, fronting close on the road, and approached over a rock-cut moat. It is rectangular with big round corner towers and a gatehouse, a sort of crouching Roquetaillade. Begun in 1305 and completed within a year, it formed the model for many others in the region. The main façade is dominated by the gate—two closely sited round towers with evidence of a smaller gate trapped between. The smooth sloped battering of the lower walls is remarkable and note the *garde-robe* exits down into the moat. The wall to the west, left of the gate, had a curious two-tier arrangement with a lower wall-walk slung on an arch, and the approach doors to it are still visible. This sophisticated layout permitted a double machicolated walk-way. A walk around the perimeter as far as possible allows the visitor to grasp the scale and magnificence of the work. The family relationship with Edward I's Welsh castles is obvious. The north west angle tower is in a near-perfect state. The north (rear) façade, with lots of latrines, was extensively altered in the 17C with the addition of large windows. There is evidence too of a rear salley-port or surprise exit. The south east tower was reduced to its present height by order of the *parlement* of Bordeaux in 1592.

The **interior** is presently a mess. Two great ranges of rooms flanked the court, while a 17C(?) range filled the flank facing the gateway. The entry range has many features of interest and may be extensively explored. Beware of sudden drops, walks without railings and straightforward holes. The west range on the left seems to have a double hall arrangement on the first floor with back to back fireplaces. A spiral stair now leads into the south-west angle tower containing an octagonal rib vault, with Christ in Majesty on the boss. The fireplace and latrine passage show that the room was lived in. Stairs lead up to a similar room above with an intact *garderobe*. From here, a wall-walk crosses to the main gatehouse, where a further stair goes both up and down. The plaster within the turret has painted masonry lines in need of protection. As with all the others, the tower wall-walks are derelict and grass grown, but the views from them are good. The twin entry towers flanking the gate are extremely close together—look down and see the narrow gap. This section of the castle could be made visitor friendly by replacing the lost wooden floor and by installing a few railings. The stair down (you might need a torch) leads to a chamber above the entrance which housed the portcullis mechanism, the only remaining sign of this is the slit in the floor. Crossing to the far side, the chamber in the second tower has a rib vault. Back at ground level, the tower left of the entry has a lower room with an octagonal vault and a bread oven, and there are cellars below. The east range is difficult to read. A stair led somewhere and connected with the later gallery (16C or 17C) along the south entry range, and there are fireplaces on both levels. The north range has intact corner towers and archaic rammed rubble barrel vaults. The salley-port faced the main gate directly, as at Bodiam (East Sussex). The north-east corner tower has another octagonal vault and an intact loo. Villandraut is interesting as a relatively untouched medieval château of a VIP, especially so as the builder was a pope. But its ruined state does limit the information to be gleaned. However, it seems that even for a pope, defensive requirements still came ahead of comfort.

From Villandraut, take the D3 back towards Bazas, but 1km from the village turn on to the D110 for Uzeste (5km).

Uzeste would not be visited but for its **church**, and that, not but for the tomb of Clement V. The tomb was wrecked in the French Wars of Religion, but the Pope began a rebuilding of the church to befit the burial of a pontiff and that makes it interesting. The church is tiny but has pretensions. It was raised to *Collégiale* status in 1312. The nave is partly earlier, Clement died in 1314 before they got round to it. The apse was to be very grand but remains incomplete. It has lots of tracery and flyers. Over the south door is a carving of the Coronation of the Virgin with kneeling angels in the voussoir arches.

The interior seems by some trick to be larger than the outside. It has a choir, no transept and a stumpy nave. The apse is very ambitious, with five straight sides canted around the semicircle and tiny radiating chapels—a cathedral in miniature. It may be ambitious, but it is not beautiful. The Virgin and Child in the east chapel may be 13C. The nave has alternating drum and compound piers and six-part vaults. There is hardly any clerestory. The aisles also squeeze in six-part vaults, all to look grander than size permits. Behind the pulpit, is what looks like a little figure of the Pope. The outer walls here belong to the earlier church that was gradually being replaced by the 14C work. The west end of the nave seems 18C.

The Pope's tomb (1359), behind the High altar, is sadly damaged and incomplete. The black marble chest carries a smashed white marble figure of Clement which recalls the Stratford figure in Canterbury, c 1340. Clement wears elaborate vestments and shoes and there is a naturalistic depression in the pillow caused by the weight of his head. The whole thing may once have been contained within an openwork canopy. Other tombs within the radial chapels include those of the Grailly family, 14C.

If you are returning to Bordeaux it is possible to visit one or two châteaux en route. From Villandraut, the D110 to Origne (12km) becomes the D220 to Cabanac-et-Villagrains (14km). Here, turn right on the D219 until at 3km the D220 leads of left to **la Brède** (various opening times, at present pm only). This romantic, moated and fortified **château** was the home of the philosopher Montesquieu, 1689–1755. The house dates from the 12C though much of the present structure is 15C. It is approached over a little bridge and through an arch by a barbican tower, then over another bridge leading to a tall gatehouse with machicolated sentry box over the door. The exterior walls rise sheer from the water and have large four-square windows. On the far side where the moat is widest, stands a tall machicolated tower with dark pointy roof. The medieval inner court was opened up during the Renaissance when one side was demolished. The original must have been very dark. The façades are quite plain though attractively overgrown, and the irregular plan and odd stair turret is all very picturesque. Among the rooms shown are the philosopher's chamber with period furniture, and his vaulted library. The park and gardens with their rustic towers and dovecotes were also laid out by Montesquieu.

From la Brède it is possible to pick up the Autoroute A62 in 4km Bordeaux centre is 19km.

Alternatively, from Villandraut, the D8 going north passes Sauternes, just off the road to the left at 9km, while 2km further north is the famous **Château d'Yquem**. The present house was built in the early 16C and remodelled a century later. It has a little gatehouse with a sentry-box above it, some round towers and a variety of roof shapes and colours. The views and wine are marvellous, but that is all you get. The house has been lived in by the Lur-Saluces since 1785, and they like their privacy. From d'Yquem, the Autoroute A62 can be reached in 8km by following the D8 straight to the tolls (Bordeaux 44km). From here it is also possible to drive the other way and head straight for Agen (95km, autoroute all but 6km).

If you are heading from Bazas to Agen and prefer a country route, then the D655 from Bazas is reasonably quick and very rural. **Casteljaloux** (29km

Hotels/Rest.) has a fine timbered centre with attractively tumbled back lanes. (Tourist Office, Place du Roi, 47700.) The first square has hotels and restaurants, while at the far end of the town there is a pretty grouping of houses around the church, including the Tourist Office. In the little park, the Maison Jean d'Albret, is a modest pavilion formerly the property of Henry IV's mother, of whom more later.

From there, the D11 will pick up the motorway in 18km or the main N113 to Agen across the river another 6km further, with 22.5km remaining to Agen centre. Another option would be to take the N113 all the way, either by returning to St-Macaire, leaving some 90km to Agen. This is only recommended for those wishing to see la Réole, 18km from St-Macaire, with its church and town hall.

La Réole, the Roman *Regula*, looks impressive from a distance rising on its hill top, especially the monastic buildings to the west which recall nothing less than the Escorial in Madrid. But it is a traffic nightmare. A bypass will provide some relief in the near future. The town is quite pleasant, the suspension bridge remarkable. (Tourist Office, Place de la Libération, 33190.) Head for the church and park in the Esplanade du Général de Gaulle which has fine views.

The monastic church was founded in Charlemagne's day, while the English built a castle just west. The present **church** looks no earlier than 1180. The apse has lancet windows. The entry, via a late Gothic door, is in the north transept. The interior is wide, unaisled, and low. It is all vaulted in three lots of six-part rib vaults, an alternative to domes, though it was rebuilt after 1687. Whether the original vaults were so disastrously low is open to question. The supporting wall piers alternate. The apse interior is a later remodelling. The south transept seems 14C but was restored in 1608 after the French Wars of Religion—la Réole was distinctly Protestant. Not surprisingly, all the fittings are later: choir stalls, 17C, the grotesque pulpit, c 1680, organ loft, 18C. Many of the fittings were stripped out and taken to Bordeaux at the Revolution. The painting of the Marriage of the Virgin is by Jean de Batse.

The attractive monastic buildings date from c 1700 and lie on the south side of the nave. From the cloister court, rose windows can be seen set low into the nave wall. The buildings, now civic, retain ironwork of 1756 and a fine stair hall. There is also a pretty 17C garden court.

Further west are scant remains of Richard I's castle, demolished in 1629. A route to the ancient town hall leads off from the small Place Albert Rigoulet, fronting the north transept of the church. From the north east corner, the Rue Numa Ducros joins the Rue Jacques Duprada and within 50m the tall stone building comes into view.

La Réole is notable for its Romanesque town hall, built perhaps in 1200. Very few civic buildings survive in Europe from such a date. It lies on a distinctly nasty bend in the road (key kept in The Maison du Vin opposite entry). It is a two-storey structure, opened by a ground floor arcade on its east face. The upper floor is supported by twin arcades with good capitals—the effect resembles a mosque. The upper façade has windows of many periods including some original twin-light openings. The interior, reached by external stair, is a large room, measuring perhaps 9 x 20m which has obviously been floored up at various times. Various window openings and fireplaces have been opened up and may be inspected. The houses in this part of the town are quite interesting. Return to the church via the Rue Peyssequin from the corner of the timber-framed and jettied *maison du vin*. This street joins the main shopping area along Rue Armand Caduc, where a left leads to the town centre, Place de la Libération (tourist office), while a right will return you to the church.

13

Agen

Agen (Hotels/Rests.) is connected to Paris by rail (TGV 4 hours) Toulouse and Bordeaux. Lines also connect the town with le Bugue/Les Eyzies and Bergerac. The airport (la Garenne) has flights to Paris daily. It also lies on the A62 connecting Bordeaux, Toulouse and the Mediterranean coast.

Tourist Office, 107 Boulevard Carnot, 47000. Tel 53 47 36 09, fax 53 47 29 98.

AGEN, the *préfecture* of Lot-et-Garonne, is a pleasant town, well situated on the banks of the Garonne, with sufficient old town to be of interest, a good art gallery and museum. It makes an ideal centre for visits to the surrounding sites and countryside.

Agen was Roman *Aginnum*, though nothing remains from this period. It was captured by Clovis in 502 and came to Henry II of England via Eleanor of Aquitaine. In 1196, the Agenais passed to Raymond VI, count of Toulouse, as part of the marriage dowry of Joan, sister of Richard I. Though notionally under the control of the French Crown, Agen was occupied by the English in 1360 and held until 1444. In more modern times it has become an agricultural centre, world famous for prunes.

The town stands on a low bluff almost entirely east of the river. There is a long and attractive **waterfront**, partly tree-shaded, with pretty gardens and a bandstand and ample parking. Notice the narrow bridge, **La Passerelle**, built on the site of a 12C crossing. It was opened in 1840 but unfortunately, the chains broke, casting 20 people into the river. It was re-opened the following year. At the top end of the parking is the Esplanade du Gravier, a popular place for *pétanque*, a skilful, and in Agen, aggressive form of *boules*. The Péristyle du Gravier, the 19C shopping arcade facing the park, seems a failed attempt to merge the town with the waterfront.

Walk up the Rue Lomet by the clinic, and take the second left on the Rue Richard Cœur de Lion, soon to reveal (left) the east end of the great, 13C red-brick Dominican **church** (Jacobins). It is double aisled beneath one great roof, the mid-buttress showing the internal division outside. The windows look a bit bashed, indeed the church is used now only for occasional exhibitions. There is a Virgin and Child at the east end. If it is open, go in. The interior is a barn which provides huge spaces for public preaching with minimum interference from the architecture. Four spacious bays rest on tall drum piers. In the south east angle is a porch with a mesh vault, dating it from after the mid-14C. There is also a projecting chapel on the south side. The 14C painting includes simple patterns, ribbon motifs, and foliage. The east arcade respond is painted on the wall with fake marble patterning. There is some 19C glass.

Further down the Rue Richard Cœur de Lion, the **Hôtel Montesquieu-Suffolk** at No. 55 is very Parisian 18C, with a fine stair. In the turning right just opposite on the Rue Beauville, the star **domestic buildings** of Agen are immediately upon you. A tiny quarter of topsy-turvey, twisted and jettied timber framing, beautifully and sensitively restored and used. The main interest comes in the buildings forming an island site, with big jetties, brick nogging and tall top storeys. Some of the timber window details look original. It is surprising how deep these blocks were. The first corner is turned like a ship's prow. Passing all round the block, enter the Place Dr. Pierre Esquirol where, to the left, the view is dominated by the theatre and adjoining museum and art gallery.

The Théâre Ducourneau, 1906 by Tronchet, was the first in France to use reinforced concrete. The **Musée d'Agen** (including very civilised Thursday evening openings) is based in a line of town houses dating from the 16C and 17C. The main entrance is in the Hôtel d'Estrades, c 1600, a stripey thing of turrets, angles and lots of roofscapes. Maréchal d'Estrades 1607–86, was an ambassador for both Louis XIII and XIV, and a signatory of the crucial Treaty of Nijmegan. By contrast, the next house, the Hôtel de Vaur, is very Italianate, and played host to Nostradamus amongst others. There follows the Hôtels de Monluc and de Verges (1575), all good examples of rich town houses of the period of the Wars of Religion—the Monluc was the home of one of the Catholic army commanders. The rear of the ensemble is equally interesting and can be seen from the Rue des Juifs, to the left and behind the main building. Note especially the Renaissance details of many of the windows, the attractive setting of the stair turrets and the sober Louis XVI gateway

The collection is well displayed and labelled. It begins with medieval items from the region including metalwork, Romanesque capitals from the lost cloister of Agen Cathedral (notably like Moissac) and a reconstructed Romanesque fireplace. The Roman collection contains some important marble works including the 1C **Vénus du Mas** and the figure of Silène. There are also Roman glass, mosaics, sarcophagi and Merovingian metalwork. The courtyards are occasionally open. A further medieval section includes a 15C bust possibly by Mino da Fiesole. The important prehistoric display is down in the cellars, interesting in itself and apparently containing prison cells.

The fine Renaissance spiral stair leads up to period rooms with pictures and furnishings of the 17C including French and Venetian schools and some French miniatures. The Holy Family, School of Raphael might be better labelled Infant School. See also the alcove room containing **Goya's** Self-Portrait, 1783, painted when he was 37, in the tradition of Velasquez. There is also a prototype black picture, full of floating cows and elephants, and his Mongolfier Balloon Flight, set against a Constable sky which may not be a genuine Goya. See too, the study for an equestrian portrait of Ferdinand VII. Other notable pictures include **Tiepolo's** Page Dying (not a moment too soon), the portrait of the child Louis Alexandre de Bourbon by François de Troy died 1730, and a scene-stealing **Corot** lake view. The top

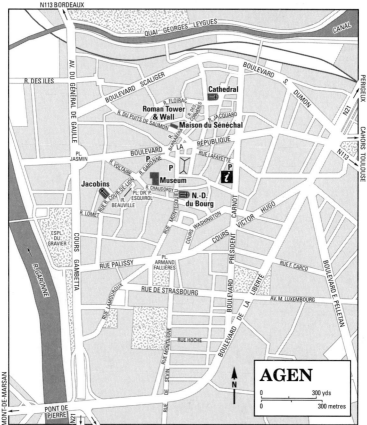

Map labels:

N113 BORDEAUX

QUAI GEORGES LEYGUES

CANAL

BOULEVARD S. DUMON

PÉRIGEUX
N21

AV. DU GÉNÉRAL DE GAULLE

R. DES ILES

BOULEVARD SCALIGER

Cathedral

R. FLOIRAC

Roman Tower & Wall

R. DU PUITS DE SAUMON

R. DES CORNIÈRES

R. JACQUARD

CAHORS TOULOUSE
N113

Maison du Sénéchal

RÉPUBLIQUE

PL. JASMIN

BOULEVARD

R. VOLTAIRE

R. GARONNE

LA

RUE LAFAYETTE

P

P

i

Jacobins

RUE COUR DE LYON

R. BEAUVILLE

R. ESQUIROL

PL. DR.

R. CHAUDORDY

Museum

N.-D. du Bourg

R. LOMET

RUE MONTESQUIEU

COURS WASHINGTON

RUE VICTOR HUGO

BOULEVARD E. PELLETAN

ESPL. DU GRAVIER

COURS GAMBETTA

RUE PALISSY

PL. ARMAND FALLIÈRES

COURS CARNOT

COURS PRÉSIDENT

BOULEVARD DE LA LIBERTÉ

RUE F. CARCO

R. GARONNE

RUE DE STRASBOURG

RUE LAMOUROUX

AV. M. LUXEMBOURG

MONT-DE-MARSAN

RUE HOCHE

RUE MONTAIGNE

RUE DE SEVIN

AGEN

N

0   300 yds
0   300 metres

PONT DE PIERRE

N21

A62 E72 TOULOUSE, BORDEAUX

floor includes a view of the Seine by Frank Bogges of Oldham, born 1855, and a **Sisley**. The Renaissance stair leads on up to a viewing platform providing a vista of the city. Easy to miss is a small room on the upper floor containing a private bequest, Room 27. Here are a pair of pictures by Clouet of Charles IX and Elizabeth of Austria, tiny but finely detailed, and a self-portrait of **Van Dyck**. A portrait by **Hans Meuelich**, died 1573, could be a late Holbein. There is also a splendid **Tang Dynasty** figure of a man on horseback (7C), a bronze Buddha of similar age, and rare 15/16C **Italian artists' sketchbooks**.

Passing round the back of the theatre and left into the Rue Molière, a turn right on the Rue Garonne, takes you into an undistinguished pedestrianised shopping area, including a multi-storey car park. This leads quickly into the Place des Laitiers, with remnants of an arcaded square now sliced by the modern Boulevarde de la République. Some of the interior arches are definitely medieval, even where the frontages have been rebuilt. Cross the square and the boulevard and head for the **Rue des Cornières**, the most consistently arcaded street in Agen. Despite modern refacings, the arcaded walkways beneath the buildings are evocative, recalling such Italian cities as Pisa. There is a flower market here Saturdays and holidays. Some of the buildings are arcaded on modern RSJ's while others rest on ancient timbers. The unnumbered block opposite No. 24 is completely medieval though barely recognisable as such. It does have Gothic arches and the remains of moulded windows on the floors above.

A turning right leads straight into Place Barbès and then a left leads into Place du Maréchal Foch and the **Cathedral of St-Caprais**. This is a strange animal, stumpy and abrupt, as if great sections are missing. The square offers a view of the entire south side. The east end is Romanesque and impressive and there is a tall apse with tiny radiating chapels. The double row of windows predict that the interior has no internal arcade, so that the lowest windows light the apse interior, and the upper ones light a roof-space above a half-dome vault. The chapels are dressed with pilasters and blind arcading. An early cemetery was revealed beneath the apse, but covered 1993.

The south flank continues with a tall transept façade and a rather mean tower squeezed between it and the oddly truncated nave, against which stands a funny little house. The main entrance is on the south transept.

The **interior** is distinctly gloomy. The apse has a ribbed semi-dome, the crossing piers have Romanesque capitals (restored) and carry pointed arches—perhaps to support a dome. The transept is very shallow and was presumably meant to have pointed barrel vaults. None of this happened, or if it did, it collapsed. Now the interior has Gothic vaults. Evidence that the scheme hung fire can be seen on the north west crossing pier which starts as Romanesque, and ends as Gothic. The nave has only two bays, with rib vaults supported on strong wall piers. The whole interior cries out that it was to be a domed church. Also screaming is the ghastly 19C painting which smothers the whole interior. The fittings are 19C. The north transept door to the chapter house (enquire) has a collection of Romanesque bits and pieces.

From the west front of the cathedral, cross the street and enter the Rue Neuve des Augustins, then pass left into the Rue François Arago and see the **Tour du Chapelet**, 11C on Roman foundations revealed in a garden to the left. Turn back and walk down the short Rue François Arago and, crossing the top of the Rue des Cornières, a right leads into the **Rue Florac**. The Italian feel of this area is shattered by No. 1, the Hôtel Amblard, 1773, which is very French and very severe. It was built by the banking brothers Pelissier. A left into the Rue du Puits de Saumon presents you with an early medieval house with a stair turret and the remains of an entry now zapped out for garages. On the first floor, there are remains of round-arched windows, the arches shaped from single blocks, all c 1180. Then on the left comes a spectacular stone façade, the **Maison du Sénéchal**, with ground-floor pointed arches and curious long slits. The open loggia above has four lights with twin arches, each trefoiled and carried on columns and capitals, with holes punched through the tympanums dating from around 1220.

Proceeding towards the increasingly crowded and jettied buildings, cross the Rue des Cornières once more and enter the Rue Banabára. Turn right into to Rue Jaquard, with timber-framing, then crossing the Boulevard de la République, follow the signs for the Hôtel de Ville and enter the old **market square**. The replacement of the market buildings by the present

Agen: Rue Beauville with its fine medieval timber-framed buildings

structure defies belief though the market within is still lively and local. Quickly passing the market buildings on your left, enter the Rue Montes-quieu with several medieval houses. Many are timber framed but not of the kind ever intended to be seen because they would have originally been plastered over. In the little square on the left, off the Rue du Droits de l'Homme, is the tiny brick church of **Notre Dame du Bourg**. This 13C church has been raised dramatically, as you can see from its north side along the street. The window sills have been blocked at the bottom while the walls have been raised some 3m. The walls were banded, brick and stone; now all the upper parts are brick. It has a little bellcote. A 13C door leads into the vaulted interior. The church was badly damaged by the Huguenots to good effect—now it is stripped clean and bare. The main vault has four bays plus an apse of later date. The windows are simple lancets and the capitals 13C. The vaults may have brick webs. There is a three-bay aisle along the south side—the last bay east is later than the rest. The latter has been cut through an earlier scheme, see the previous clerestory window. The chapel has a curious entrance arch and inside, a net vault. The middle chapel has a tierceron vault, English style, and the last one has a simple rib vault.

The Tourist Office may be reached down the Rue du Droits de l'Homme, and into its continuation, Rue de Raymond, where a left on the main Boulevard Carnot will find the office in c 100m. This modern section of the town is unlovely, but contains shops and banks.

From Notre Dame du Bourg, the **Rue Montesquieu** continues south where No. 12 is a fine and remarkably complete 18C Parisian hôtel—entrance pavilion, horseshoe court, three-storey austere elevation and stables and carriage sheds all blocked up. You soon arrive at the large and shady Place Armand Fallières, with the big Palais de Justice, opposite, designed in 1869 in the style of Napoleon III by Juste Lich. Next door (right) is the **Préfecture**, formerly the bishop's palace of 1773 by Leroy. Arranged around three sides of a court, the façades combine the Doric and Ionic orders and triangular pediment. It is not very homely. There is also an 18C Public Library on the side you came in. Note the exotic and characteristic street furnishings—kiosk, lamps and poster carousel. The street beyond the latter, **Rue Palissy**, heads west towards the river, along a pleasantly gentrified route.

The turning right into the Rue Louis Vinvent, leads to the **Hôtel Hulot de la Tour**, 1755, (left, off a small yard) decorated with pilasters and pediment. Continue to the Rue Mirabeau, where a left turn leads straight to the river and the parking area. At the corner you will notice the terraced gardens and rear façades of the Hulot, and the Tour de la Poudre, part of the 11C fortifications transformed in the 18C into a music chamber (enquire at the tourist office for admission). You return to the Esplanade du Gravier.

14

The Romanesque Route

Agen provides an opportunity to visit the important Romanesque site at **Moissac**, just over Aquitaine's regional border. This corner of Aquitaine has Romanesque sites of its own, several of which can be taken in with this circular route of 111km. Moissac can also be reached direct from Agen by train.

Leave Agen on the N113 for Moissac and at Lafox (8.5km) turn left on the D16 for **Puymirol** (8km). (Tourist Office, Mairie 47270. Tel 53 95 32 10.) The view approaching the hilltop village is positively Tuscan, though the circular *campanile* proves to be a water tower. The village is very quiet. Lying on the main road from Agen to Clermont Ferrand, it has been inhabited since Roman times. A Merovingian rock-cut cemetery was discovered here. It was refounded as a *bastide* in 1246 by Raymond VII, count of Toulouse, when it was given the classic walls plus four gates arrangement. The characteristic arcaded square, here an oblong, is also characteristically full of parked cars, even caravans. The humble church has a rather abrupt tower and an amazingly deep 13C south portal. The landscape view from the north side is splendid. The back streets to the south of the church have a certain rustic charm.

Continue on the D16 for another 8.5km where a sharp left takes the same road another 1.5km to **St-Maurin**, an exceptionally attractive village just inside the Aquitaine frontier. (Tourist Office, Mairie 47270.) The village seems deserted. Find the central square, neither square nor very central, and park. All about you are scenes of 19C rural life. The village buildings have a mountain chalet air about them, with flower-decked galleries and shutters. See also the timber market hall.

You have probably parked on or near the nave of the Cluniac **abbey of St-Maurin**, the reason for the existence of the place. The nave is of course no longer there, though plans are afoot to excavate it. The tall stone tower north of the square, now the *mairie*, was the entrance to the abbot's house. The right-hand corner joined on to the west end of the abbey. To your right is a tiny chapel with a tower which is actually the south transept of the abbey. All will become clear if you go on an organised tour (ask in the *mairie*), not strictly necessary but informative, and perhaps a little eccentric. What you will also see are some interiors which are otherwise kept locked.

The layout of the abbey was unusual in that the cloister lay north of the nave, with the chapter house north of the cloister. Sections survive in the little garden right of the *mairie*. The cloister was evidently two-storeyed, the upper section made of timber. The nave was possibly domed and had an arcaded exterior. A low tower completed the west end, possibly with a projecting west apse. What survives is the ruined chancel, the south transept now kept as a chapel, the north transept, very ruined, and parts of the claustral buildings. The tall tower of the abbot's house, flanked by a stair turret, is entered by an ogee-headed door. The upper machicolated wall-walk has all but collapsed. Within are splendid late Gothic fireplaces, especially on the first floor, some now marooned in corridors. The barrel-vaulted basement (shown on tour) contains a museum of rural life. The vaults are mixed brick and stone, possibly 13C. The tour takes you into the south transept which is amazingly tall being shorn of its crossing. The single bay is topped by a later tower, while the apse also received Gothic windows. Inside, there is ample evidence that the transept was domed, with pointed supporting arches. The apse carries a semi-dome, the voussoirs still painted. The Romanesque capitals are funny rather than fine. Over the door, a consecration inscription commemorating the event in January 1097, conducted by Simon, Bishop of Agen and Pierre, Bishop of Lectour, the church was comphrehensively dedicated to the Holy Trinity, St. Croix, St. Marie, St. Maurin and all the saints of God. There is a model of the church in a late Gothic stage.

Leaving the transept, proceed east around the end of the block and arrive before a small low-walled garden. Inside the chancel is nicely overgrown and domesticated. The apse has collapsed. The two-bay chancel has a pointed barrel vault, supported by sculpted wall piers. The capitals here are of better standard and include the Decapitation of St. Maurin, note how he picks up his head and walks off—they did that in those days—and the inevitable beasties. There is a pointless-sounding plan to remove the house lodged in the crossing, and to expose whatever is inside.

Leaving the garden, head north past the ruins of the north transept and its apsidal chapel. No pristine lawns, manicured stonework and helpful signs, these ruins are ruined, and much the better for it. Keeping the abbey wall on your left, proceed into the country and glimpse the meadow spring (left) that watered the abbey. Circle left around the wall and enter the abbey orchard through a gate. This reveals the back of the abbot's house and is also a lovely spot. The ruined section to the left of the house was the abbot's chapel, 13C. The tour, lasting about 90 minutes also takes in the village church, which usually locked. It is a quiet little building, heavily restored in the 17C.

If you can tear yourself away from St-Maurin, head towards Moissac by heading back on the D16 for 1.5km until the sharp turn, then take a left on the D27, and turn left again after only a few hundred metres on the D28 to **Castelsagrat**, which you reach in a further 5km. This is a pretty and quiet *bastide* village, with an arcaded square which is almost intact, one house replaced by a timber frame. The unaisled church has a big tower, and within, chapel recesses the length of the nave. The interior is dominated by a huge altarpiece, big, bad and Baroque, all saints, cherubs and peeling paint. The views from the ends of the side streets are inspiring.

Leaving Castelsagrat on the D28, turn right after 2.5km on the D7 and stay on it to Moissac (15.5km) crossing the main D953 en route.

MOISSAC is one of the principal Romanesque sites of Europe (covered in full in the Blue Guide Midi-Pyrénées). (Tourist Office, 6 Place Durand de Bredon.) It lies in Tarn-et-Garonne just a stone's throw from Aquitaine but provides a convenient stop for sight-seeing, lunch, and crossing the river for a return trip to Agen on the south side. What follows is merely a resumé of the church. Moissac, a Cluniac abbey, possesses a huge church and a famous cloister. The **church**, open all day, is a great pink pile of several periods.

The early 12C church was domed, that much is clear. At some stage the domes either fell or were demolished, and the church was then remodelled with Gothic rib-vaults, the bays not necessarily corresponding with those of the previous design. This accounts for the wayward appearance of the exposed south side, all windows, brick raising and blocked bits. However, the church takes a back seat when it comes to the entrance, one of the set-pieces of medieval Europe. The **west end** is a tower-porch, that is a large entrance bay, here with two doors, west and south, above which rises a fat tower, clearly made defensive.

The interior is vaulted with primitive ribs. The **south door**, apparently moved here from the west end in the 13C(?), is dominated by Christ in Majesty, seated amid his Heavenly Court. The scene of c 1115 may be drawn from the Revelations of St. John but the flavour is distinctly that of an Islamic *diwan*. Note the characteristic poses of the evangelistic symbols surrounding Christ, and the various contortions of the Elders eager for a glimpse of the Almighty. The heady stylistic mix is continued with the Persian-like circular frieze motif in the lintel below. The carved tympanum is supported by a central column or trumeau, containing one of the greatest figures in Romanesque art, **Jeremiah**. The ease and grace with which he sweeps down the jamb is staggering, as is the delicate stylisation of the face and hair. It is a pity that no-one glances at **St. Paul**, his pair. To the left and right are other scenes within the jambs. Those to the left tell the story of the beggar Lazarus and Dives the rich man—notice how the rich man feasts while dogs lick the sores of the recumbent Lazarus, who is comforted by an angel. Above, the dead Lazarus is taken up into the bosom of Abraham while devils fight for the soul of Dives. Opposite, the Annunciation is an appalling piece of modern restoration. There is also the Adoration of the Magi and the Flight into Egypt, Presentation at the Temple—note how St. Joseph is warned to flee. Above the door are figures of the abbot, Roger, and a trumpeting angel.

Inside the porch are a series of fine **capitals**, all worthy of examination. They include (starting on the left side, west door, at the north-west corner) Sampson and the lion, monsters (north west corner), foliage including deer (north-east corner) and wolves and other animals (south east corner).

The Gothic reconstruction of the church **interior** makes it look like Albi, though not as spacious. The deep vault piers allow for chapels beneath, while the walkway and some Romanesque windows survive from the earlier scheme. The choir is completely Gothic and very straight-up. It has a polygonal apse and low side chapels. It is dominated by a hybrid Renaissance screen of c 1600, which creates a processional ambulatory walkway where none exists architecturally. The stone screen is very fretted, with balasters, figures and a central garden-pavilion like structure. It stands partly on the exposed foundations of a Carolingian apse. There is a foundation stone of 1063 to the left through the gate.

There are a good number of fittings. Starting at the east end south side, an Entombment of Christ, carved in wood, c 1480. Everyone seems to have big heads. Note Mary Magdalene and her ointment pot. Then an early-Christian sarcophagus, plain and set into the wall. The third chapel retains traces of late-medieval paintings which are rather crude. On the wall pier between chapels 4/5 is a wooden crucifix, the cross-arm of knarled twigs. The tenon sticking out from the base suggests it came from a group, perhaps a 12/13C rood screen. In the fifth chapel is another wooden sculpture, the Flight into Egypt, 15C in painted wood, though St. Joseph is a 17C replacement. In the sixth chapel is a very Germanic Pietà plus donors, all out of proportion, but very powerful. It is dated 1476. In the seventh chapel is a hideous St. Roch.

In the second chapel on the north side is a 17C image, the Martyrdom of St. Ferreolus, a Roman soldier killed for refusing to worship idols—some unintended irony here. In the third chapel are two late-Roman capitals and an early-Christian sarcophagus, perhaps 7C. The stalls look as if they were made in c 1600.

The **cloisters** of Moissac contain one of the largest collections of Roman-esque sculpture anywhere (closed lunchtime). They are also most attrac-tive. The cloisters lie on the north side of the church, and have low, pointed arcades and a simple tiled roof. There are no vaults. The effect is rather Italian, though their present appearance is evidently not original. The capitals certainly are, all 76 of them. Their date is debatable, but c 1110 covers most opinions expressed. There are too many to describe in any detail but some shout out for attention. The scheme has single and twin columns in alternation, though the capitals tend to ignore this syncopation. The abacus decoration is superb throughout. The angles are turned on piers, decorated on the insides with large and splendid marble plaques or re-cut sarcophagi carved in low relief. A similar scheme decorated the mid-point piers along each alley.

Beginning in the south-west angle and proceeding along the south alley, the fifth capital illustrates the **Temptation of Christ**, with Christ shown on a stone tower. Next to the east, are the **Horsemen of the Apolcalypse**. Some of the inscriptions here are actually 18C graffiti. The south east angle has tall plaques with named figures of **Peter** and **Paul**, very much in the manner of St. Sernin, Toulouse, especially the fold types, the classicising heads and the flattened aspect of the figures. The capitals detail the life of **St. Peter** and the **story of Samson**, see the upsidedown **Crucifixion of St. Peter** at the start of the east walk. Further north, are the **Adam and Eve cycle** and a capital in the distinctive Mozarabic style of northern Spain. The sixth capital moving north has the **Martyrdom of St. Lawrence** (or St. Vincent), complete with a man with bellows, the seventh has a design on the abacus taken from an early-Christian sarcaphagus. The ninth repeats the **story of Lazarus and Dives**. The second capital beyond the mid-point pier features the **Marriage Feast of Cana**, two further north, the **Adoration of the Magi** with an inscription. The north-east angle turns with plaques of **St. James** and **St. John**. At this point, see the small vaulted chamber opposite, housing further architectural and sculptural fragments including Samson and the lion.

The north walk continues the wealth of interest and design. Third from the north west angle are **St. Martin of Tours** and then a classic Islamic pattern. The west walk has **Daniel in the lions' den** before the mid-pier, which alone retains an external marble plaque, **St. Simon**, with the dedication of the cloister on the back. Fourth from the south west angle are **Cain and Abel**. There is no obvious iconographic sequence dictating the choice of subject mattern or position.

Back in the south west angle, a steep stair opposite leads to the upper level of the west tower-porch. The well-lit interior has a 12-rib domed vault centred upon a compression ring, quite sophisticated for the date. All the capitals are Corinthianesque. The stairs leading down into the church, may have been part of a processional route including the upper stage of the tower. More stairs lead up to the wall-walk around the exterior, with good views especially of the cloister. There are other delights in Moissac, including the early-20C market hall.

From Moissac head west along the river towards Agen on the N113 and after 5km take the bridge over the Garonne on the D15. The river here is very wide, particularly to your left. Here the Tarn enters the Garonne, making a considerable lake. Passing St-Nicolas de la Grave (3.5km) head on over the Autoroute A62 to the crossroads at Laparguère (3.5km) and turn right on the D12. This quiet road bumps along parallel with the autoroute, finally passing beneath it just before the hill-village of **Auvillar**, which is reached in 11km.

Auvillar looks attractive from a distance, and is utterly charming close to. Head for the **church**. The building, of brick and stone, has a dramatic, partially collapsed west tower that is very picturesque. The west and north walls stand, the rest hugely buttressed, while a brick turret perches precariously on the top. The church itself is brick, enormous, not fine but striking. The chancel interior has a tierceron vault in the English manner, and a big, blousy Baroque altarpiece in someone else's. The sprawling aisled nave is rib-vaulted but has no clerestory, and the big compound piers have been altered. Only the south east pier is Romanesque, all the others are late medieval. The size of the later piers suggests that an earlier, Romanesque unaisled nave was smashed into for arches. The north aisle has a Romanesque apsidal chapel with a period entry and semi-dome. This tends to confirm that the early church c 1150 was unaisled, and had a transept with east chapels, a standard enough plan in these parts. The terrace north of the church offers glimpses of the riverside below.

Walking from the south west angle of the church, enter the village proper. It is almost a sin to reveal the secret of Auvillar but the expected *bastide* **square** is triangular. If your heart does not stop at the sight, you have not got one. Brick and timber, crowded and erratic, the arcaded buildings squeeze a circular market hall within their arms. How can it be used as a car park! Without them, this would be the most lovable *bastide* square (sic) in France. The **market hall** is an oddity. Round, with a central drum, it is surrounded by a Doric colonnade, recalling the format of ancient Gaulish temples. The central section features curious shutes and bins cut in stone, which may have been measuring devices. All about are marvellous vernacular buildings, some with country Renaissance doors and details. Pass to the north of the market and admire the great view, river, hills, trees, nuclear power stations. What you see is actually a large island in the Garonne, the town in the distance, Valence, is on the far bank. Note the suspension bridge and tiny château.

Leave Auvillar and head for St-Loup, still on the D12, crossing the D953 in 3km. Ignoring St-Loup village stay on the D12 heading for Donzac (5.5km) where, having just passed a brick church, a give-way at another brick church involves turning left and then right before heading for St-Sixte which is still on the D12 though no longer the main route.

At St-Sixte (3km), a left at the church heads for **Caudecoste** (2.5km) and back in Aquitaine. This little *bastide* has another pretty square, almost all of timber framing and quite a contrast with Auvillar. On the far side of the village you can pick up the D129 for Layrac (8km). Note the view shortly after passing beneath the autoroute. Another fine view greets you as you approach **Layrac**, almost Italian in setting and in the position of the great domed church. Turn left for the town centre when you arrive and follow the signs, past the Gers riverside with its tumbling weir. (Tourist Office, Villa 'La Paririe', Rue des Jardins 47390. Tel 53 67 02 96.)

The centre of Layrac is another triangular *bastide* square but there the similarity ends. The town is pleasant enough, but it is the **church** that offers the interest. From the square, head down the Rue Joseph Danglade towards a tall gate-tower, one of the abbey entrances. It is square below but octagonal above and is picturesquely random in its use of material. You approach the abbey church from the south east, and the terrace offers good vistas.

Layrac developed around its Cluniac abbey, a dependent of Moissac. The most obvious 12C feature on the exterior is the enormous east apse, which is arcaded throughout and has no radiating chapels. This promises an interesting interior. There is a transept with apsidal chapels, the south with damaged Romanesque capitals, while the nave has Speyer-like tall blind arcades running the whole length. There are no aisles but still a massive west front. Clearly, some sort of west block has been demolished. Enter via the big door. The interior is instantly attractive, especially in the afternoon, despite the extensive 19C painting scheme. The crossing carries a dome, the weight having pushed the support piers outwards. It has interesting curved triangular pendentives which are typical of Aquitaine, with a segmented dome in eight panels which has a compression ring in the centre. But what is its date? The crossing piers have big Romanesque carved capitals depicting beasties, but the north west pier is later, yet another construction that held fire for some time. The chancel space is very impresssive, being unbroken and luminous. A single barrel-vaulted bay goes straight into the semi-domed apse. The low wall arcade has good Corinthianesque capitals. It could not be simpler. The transept suffers from a strange hiatus, which squashes the apsidal chapel almost into the corners. Their west walls have huge blind arcades with erratically set windows. This architect has obviously seen many major Romanesque buildings, but his memory is not too good. The nave marches off confidently, covered with a pointed barrel vault, the transverse arches carried on half-shafts with odd, capitals which are probably later. There is a magnificently silly altarpiece in Pearl and Dean neo-Classical. Outside, the remains of the claustral buildings lie to the north, a characteristic arrangement in this part of Aquitaine. They are mostly 17/18C with cool, shaded gardens. The exterior of the dome is very obvious, its odd bell-shape explained by the actual form within.

Leaving Layrac, take the main N21 for Agen, cross the autoroute, admire the views and after 4km turn on a sudden left, the D268, for **Moirax** (2km; Tourist Office, Mairie 47310 Laplume. Tel 53 95 14 54). You may well feel that you have suffered a surfeit of beautiful places and dramatically interesting Romanesque abbeys, but this last will revive you. Moirax is tiny and almost circular. In fact, the tight circuit of streets reflects the original near-circular wall of the **abbey**. Head for the church where there is parking. The outline as you approach is most odd—a bizarre dome-shape to the east, and a drawbridge-like silhouette to the west.

Moirax was Cluniac, founded in 1049, though the present building is early 12C. The west front of the abbey church seems enormous, with a tripartite division, the central section projecting. The large central door has been extensively damaged, the sculpture left unrestored. The flanking half-shafts have good monster capitals. There are more capitals on the blind arches though the window details have all been got at. There is a little bellcote above with a daft roof. The exterior should be examined first. The south side has little to offer. The cloisters and their associated buildings have gone, though the spaces remain. Passing north from the west front, the north flank and east end can be inspected from the adjacent field. Mind the sheep. The apses are heavily decorated, with capitals, half-shafts, carved corbel blocks and inserted carved plaques. The chancel bay is further decorated with a scallop design. The dome stands not over the crossing but over the chancel bay and is accompanied by twin east stair turrets. The cone-like dome has a red-tiled pepper-pot top, not original. Next door is the stump of what looks like a central tower.

The **interior** is a dream, restored but not wrecked. It feels very spacious

Inside the church at Moirax

though is not in fact so large. It definitely wanted to be Cluny III on a tiny budget. The **east end** is apsidal with arcading and windows. There are capitals everywhere, mostly foliate. The straight bay preceeding the apse has a double wall arcade with capitals, mostly beasts. Above, the wall gets thicker and is punched by three windows on each side. These also have columns and capitals and chevron-decorated arches. The wall then sprouts squinches, little triangular arches supporting an octagonal opening. The spaces below have circular windows north and south, but only openings east and west. All this supports a dome rising in two parts. The present structure was possibly rebuilt in the 17C, though the model for the whole bay design was clearly Cluny III from the early 12C. It is very ambitious and deliciously wonky. Next, the crossing bay proper has yet more monster capitals, these partly painted, and the space is now covered by a later rib vault. It may have originally been another dome.

The **transepts** have a most unusual feature for Aquitaine: doors between the apsidal chapels on the east wall and the chancel bay. This is very Germanic but could also have happened at Layrac—remember the erratic transept chapels? The apsidal chapels have wall arcades, and yet more capitals. The wall before the north chapel must have failed; it has been rebuilt. Again, the present vaults are ribbed and constructed later. The transept west walls have interesting schemes suggesting that the nave was to look rather different from now. The nave aisles enter the transept with a giant order, an arch encompassing both aisle entry and a twin-arched opening above. The latter now looks into the dark roofspace over the aisle but what was it supposed to do originally? The initial scheme for the nave may have been two-storeyed, with an arcade and tribune or upper aisle beneath a barrel vault. This is the scheme of St-Sernin, Toulouse, Santiago de Compostela and many of the Pilgrimage churches. Why not here? Look into the nave—the hacked-down first pier was clearly a change of mind.

The **nave** is almost Cistercian after all this talk of Cluny, apart from the inevitable sculpture. The piers are compound but not consistent, with capitals on the arcade sides, while the vault shafts zip up higher to spring the pointed barrel vault. There is no clerestory and the whole thing falls outwards quite nonchalantly. The most easterly bay suggests a removed screen between monks and laity, or perhaps another change of mind. The aisles are groin-vaulted, and have wall responds with carved capitals. There are no fittings of note, and the stalls, now in the nave, look 18C.

Returning to the main N21 (2km) Agen centre is reached in 7km.

15

Agen to Bayonne

This route travels 266km diagonally across much of the width of Aquitaine and includes a variety of landscapes and sites. The first part could be made into a day excursion, returning to Agen. Equally, the last part could be implemented the same way from Bayonne.

Leave Agen on the D656 and just after the autoroute, pick up the D7 for **Nérac** (29km). You can park near the river. (Tourist Office, Mairie 47600.

Tel 53 65 03 89.) The Baïse becomes quite wide at Nérac, and flows through a deep cutting, not quite a ravine (boating). Cross the high bridge and head for the château before you. The fragment of **Château Nérac** is picturesque rather than informative. It now contains an archaeological museum and an exposition of Henry IV. The house was the home of Marguérite of Angoulême, sister of Francis I, and later, of her daughter, Jeanne d'Abret and her husband, Antoine de Bourbon. This was a crucial marriage in the history of France—a son, the future Henry IV, became the heir to the French throne, his Protestantism causing the French Wars of Religion. You can escape neither Henry nor Jeanne d'Albret in this part of France, indeed, the area you are traversing is called the Pays d'Albret. The house was used by the young Henry, the surviving wing dates from his mother's lifetime.

What you see is one internal façade of a lost courtyard. Up to your right and now exposed and hanging, are the fireplaces and access doors to a lost corner block, served by the little stair turret. The façade is dominated by the first floor loggia, the arcade carried on a curiously coved out section of the lower wall. The columns then project down through the coving, terminating in sculptured bosses—quite attractive. The capitals all look late Gothic, the basket-handle arches, early Renaissance. If all the missing wings had such tall roofs, the overall effect must have been still quasi-medieval. Inside are a number of rooms, vaulted on the ground floor, including a small chapel, a council room (which was possibly the scene of the Nérac Conference called by Catherine de Medici in 1579), and a guard room with an odd fireplace. The riverside park opposite was the château's hunting ground. The distant bridge is 16C. Nérac has little else to offer but is a pleasant stop for coffee. The **church** immediately behind the house is an 18C monster, its twin-towered façade recalling St-Sulpice in Paris. The interior is grotesque and the stained glass gross.

Opposite the west front, the little alley has a fine 16C house around a courtyard with galleries at three levels, sadly abandoned. A block away in the central square, the grandiose **Hôtel de Ville** contains a fine Roman mosaic floor, one of the most intricate and delicate in the region.

From Nérac it is possible to make a quick detour to see two other sites of interest. They lie either side of the nearby town of Lavardac (take the D930 north from Nérac for 6km, then continue right within Lavardac for the Autoroute but then follow the signs for the D642 for Vianne, 3km). After a pretty riverside stretch, the approach to **Vianne** is awful. But if you persevere, you will suddenly see a town gate and sections of medieval wall. (Tourist Office, Mairie 47230. Tel 53 97 54 14.)

Vianne is a *bastide* town with all the gates standing. It was founded in 1284 by agreement between Edward I of England and the local lord, Jourdain de l'Isle. Drive through, head straight for the gate opposite and park. The gates are very simple and rather abrupt with very prominent roofs. Near here, the little church (locked, try hunting for the key, it is a good way of seeing the village if not actually, the church). The **church** has a big west door, a big central tower, a big blocked south door, strange when the whole thing is so tiny. The tower is defensive, the firing lines passing easily over the nearby wall. The interior is fancier than you might expect. The nave, all barrel-vaults, has vigorously carved Romanesque capitals and a narrow chancel arch. There is a small square with a part-medieval Hôtel de Ville.

Make a circuit of the walls and gates by car; notice especially the 14C west wall, the evidence for lost jettied wooden structures on the gates, the attractive view of walls, towers and church from outside the north-west angle of the wall, and the suspension bridge over the Baïse.

Return to Lavardac (3km) and take the D655 to **Barbaste**, really only a suburb. (Tourist Office, Mairie 47230 Lavardac. Tel 53 65 84 85.) As you approach, a wide vista opens to the left, revealing the riverside and its buildings. Keep bearing left within the village and head down a cul-de-sac towards the river. On foot, cross the long bridge and descend to the water's edge. The **bridge** can now be seen to have ten arches and to be Romanesque, a rare survival. Before you is a small mill, with the water glugging up from the submerged tunnels. Next, a miniature Romanesque **castle**, looking like a child's toy. It is perfect but gutted internally, and the combination of buildings and unkempt setting is memorable.

The castle keep has corner turrets and *garde-robe* chutes but few other openings. At the rear of the block is a pretty overgrown garden, with sunken boats, water lilies and flowering shrubs, all running wild, and an eccentric 19C miller's house. Plans are afoot to do something with the ensemble, though one hopes not too much.

From Barbaste, take the back route D109 to Gueyze (20km) where the road becomes the D656 to Gabarret (14km). From Réaup, 13km from Barbaste, take the D149 to **Mézin** (8km), which has an attractive Romanesque church, a restored but fine central tower, medieval houses, a town gate and museum. Mézin has later established itself as a centre for forest walks (hotels). Forest routes throughout have green signposts. (Tourist Office, Mairie 47170. Tel 53 65 77 46.)

From Gabarret, take the D35 to Créon-d'Armagnac (9.5km) and on to **Labastide d'Armagnac** (8km, joining the D11 some 4km after Créon). This famous little town is very charming but lacks any real intrinsic interest. It was founded by Bernard IV d'Armagnac in 1291 with the permission of Edward I. The town retains the gist of its grid plan but no gates or walls. The principal interest and attraction lies in its central **square**, a classic arcaded *bastide* market. Unlike most others, the church plays an important role in the make-up of the square, the west end occupying almost an entire side. The rest is full of stone-arched buildings mixed with timber and brick, quite lovely but for the parked cars. Pretty side streets lead off in most directions, some maintaining an arcaded theme. At one point the opposite sides of the street get so close as to collide. There seem to be few tourists in Labastide, and it is difficult even to find a place to have coffee.

The **church** has a monster west tower, strongly buttressed, with a defensive top, arrow slits and a whimsical roof. Within is a big west Gothic doorway from the 14C. The interior is really just a big vaulted box, covered in four bays, with a square end. The vaults are tierceron, with ridge ribs in both directions, never quite managing to connect bay to bay. However, nothing distracts the eye from the painted illusionistic horror within the choir, inflicted upon the church by a certain Ceroni in 1831. The altar is 17C. There is also a polychrome wood *Pietà* of c 1500 near the door. Just outside Labastide, on the D626 towards Cazaubon, is the tiny 11C Notre Dame de Cyclistes (3km). It means what it says. The apsed chapel stands on a 4C Roman villa.

If you are travelling all the way to Bayonne, then the next move is the D11 heading south west from Labastide, joining the D934 outside Villeneuve-de-Marsan (14km), which is another 22km to Aire.

Aire-sur-l'Adour is a bustling town, popular with tourists and bus parties and good for food. (Tourist Office, Place du Gal de Gaulle, BP155 40801. Tel 58 71 64 70.) Much of the centre is pedestrianised and there is an ample supply of food shops and eating establishments. It is a regional centre for geese and ducks, and every conceivable thing you can do with them. Its riverside position is also an attraction. The historical interest in Aire lies in two churches only one of which stands in the centre.

The main church stands next to the Hôtel de Ville and a little park (car parking). This was the cathedral of the diocese from c 500 to 1933 (now moved to Dax). It is a large Romanesque pile, formerly Benedictine. If you approach from the Hôtel de Ville, you are confronted by a substantial south transept, all brick. To the right is a big 18C chancel. The interior is dark and complicated. What you need to know is that the Romanesque church of 1060–92, was aisleless, had a transept with apsidal chapels, and presumably an apsed choir. The latter went in the 18C. The nave had holes smashed into its lateral walls to make arches when the aisles were added later. The crossing retains a barrel vault over the north transept arm, but has a rib vault over the south arm. The transept chapels have some good capitals including two knights in helmets, but they all look late, perhaps c 1180. There is also a square chapter house with four rib-vaulted bays supported by a central column. Near the main door, around to the right, is the face of an early Christian sarcophagus depicting the Good Shepherd and great heads at the angles.

The other church of the town is hard to find but worth it. **Ste-Quitterie** (pronounced Keytree) was and is still a place of pilgrimage. It lies south west of the town centre (take the car) and is reached by leaving Aire on the D12 towards Pau for about 1km and just as the road gets wiggly, a small sign points to the left and uphill to the church. Once there, you cannot avoid the gargantuan structure. It is a huge and molested thing, stone and brick, much repaired and yet still wounded. There is parking outside. The exterior is dominated by the brick west tower with many levels and trapped by great flanking rooflines. The west door is huge, but gives the feeling that the whole scheme was somehow never quite finished. Go round to the north and see the flank of the church, stone below, from the church of 1092, brick above, clearly a raising of the entire structure from 1309.

The **west entry** has a deep porch with a plastered brick vault, all 14C. The two tiers of arcading flanking the entry are severely burnt. The central column or trumeau (claimed to be Roman) has lost its figure; so have all the lateral niches. The arches above had angels, apostles and elders, but they have been smashed. The tympanum carries a Last Judgement with Christ, the Virgin and John and the usual Blessed and Damned. Traces of blue colour remain here and there. Beneath is the Fall of Man.

The **interior** (key from nearby house) might seem disappointing but what is on offer takes some finding. The nave was burnt out by the Huguenots in 1569, and replaced later by the present uninteresting classical design. However, there is a holy water stoop to the right supported by a boss from the earlier nave vault. It carries the arms of Foix. The opposite stoop rests on a Roman capital and a section of post-Roman sculpture. The crossing reveals the first indication of the richness of the medieval building. There is a great deal of Romanesque arcading here with many capitals. The arrangement of this area has been changed since the initial 1090s building. Then, only the projecting choir was raised high over a crypt; now the raising engulfs the lower sections of the crossing, the transept and their apsidal chapels. This explains why the wall arcades are at floor level within the choir, but virtually out of sight elsewhere.

The **choir arcading** is amongst the most lavish and decorated in French Romanesque, though many of the capitals are damaged. Designs include the usual beasts, an angel with sword stopping Balaam on his ass(?), and a devil hanging a woman etc, all of good quality. The altar is by Fedele Mazetti, and is signed and dated 1771. The north transept contains a modern stairway through the apsidal chapel, permitting a good view of yet more Romanesque capitals. The stairs lead down to a damp crypt and the centre of the cult. The floor is made up from smashed fragments of Roman material, and part of the paving is said to be the platform of a Roman temple of Mars. There is a well in the centre (it could be an early total-immersion font). The east crypt is full of bits and has Romanesque masonry lines painted on the surfaces. The rest of the crypt is a confusing mass of Roman, Merovingian and later fragments, giving no clear idea of a layout but undisputably part of an early church, apparently built on the platform of the temple. The reason for this layout is the **sarcophagus of Ste. Quitterie** which stands at the west end.

Ste. Quitterie's history is rather vague, though by tradition, she was martyred by her own Visigothic family. The Visigoths swept southern France on their way to the conquest of Spain and eventual conversion to Christianity. Of unknown origin, they were amongst the many north-Euro-pean tribes who brought down the western Roman Empire in the 5C. They were driven from this area in 507 by Clovis. Legend has it that Quitterie, died 476, was of royal blood, and a secret Christian. Refusing an arranged pagan marriage, she fled to Aire but was chased, found and beheaded. Predictably, she jumped up, collected her head and continued her flight. Her sarcophagus is a princely piece though her bones were thrown out by the unromantic Huguenots in 1569.

The marble tomb is of high quality, and may be 4C. It is crowded with incident. In the centre is the Good Shepherd plus others (the veiled female figure is said to be Synagogue). To the right are God, Adam and the Tree of Knowledge. In the next scene, God creates Man, while round the side, Jonah is thrown up on the shore. To the left of the Good Shepherd, is a Daniel in the lions' den plus the Raising of Lazarus, and on the end, Jonah cast into the sea. On the lid, from the left end are depictions of the sacrifice of Abraham and Isaac, Christ telling the cripple to pick up his bed and walk, and of Jonah and the whale. The corners have large heads with wild hair, like the sarcophagus in the cathedral.

Returning to the main N134, drive away from Aire and in just over 1km a right on the D2 heads for Hagetmau. The road is quiet and wooded, occasionally hilly. At 9km the D62/D11 turns right for **Eugénie-les-Bains** (5km; Tourist Office, Rue René Vielle, 40320. Tel 58 51 13 16), quite the most discreet spa in the region and one preserving a strong sense of 19C gentility.

At **Samadet** (24km, a faïence museum with a good collection), the road takes an unexpected turn right and in 10km you arrive at **Hagetmau**. (Tourist Office BP 44, 40705.) You are probably wondering why, but lovers of Romanesque will not want to miss the extraordinary little crypt, which is in fact, most extraordinary for there is no church. The crypt is known as

Detail of one of the capitals in the Crypte St-Girons, Hagetmau

the **Crypte St-Girons**, after the 4C apostle of the area. It lies on the far side of the little town, off the D933 bypass (signposted). It seems to be left open all day. Park by the funny little building which seems to be all roof. The entry leads into a small space and a side door. (Light switch.) The stairs descend into a splendid Romanesque crypt. The plan is that of a four-square mosque, the nine vault compartments resting on four columns and wall piers. The coffin of the saint lay precisely in the middle. On closer inspection, the east wall is canted through two sides, creating the feeling of an apse (the present vault is later). Beneath the east window is a small niche, perhaps for relics. The arrangement of the crypt with two entries suggests a cult centre with a one-way traffic system. The great height comes as something of a surprise though the sculpted capitals are not too high for inspection.

All the free-standing capitals have figure sculpture. The marble columns are all different and presumably re-used. The captials are varied and worth examining—men fighting monsters and giant birds which are pinching grapes. The cutting is very deep, suggesting a date of c 1140. There seems no trace of paint. Some scenes presumably convey a message, for example the angels with two seated men, the angel throwing stones at a monster and the knights fighting a duel. The only obvious iconography is the angel releasing Peter from captivity and scenes from the story of Lazarus and Dives. The setting away from the road is leafy and pretty, and would make a good picnic spot.

The main D933 alongside the crypt runs north to **St-Sever** in 12km. Ascend into the town centre and park in the square. (Tourist Office, Place du Tour du Sol, 40500. Tel 58 76 34 64.) St-Sever is a hilltop town established around an abbey. It is known as the Cap de Gascogne from its elevated position. The centre is pleasant if not beautiful, and there are plenty of shops and cafés. The tourist office is diagonally opposite the church door.

The **abbey** was founded in 988 by Guillame Sanche, Duke of Aquitaine, and was a stop on one of the pilgrim routes to Santiago de Compostela. St. Sever was yet another beheaded Christian missionary, who met his end in 407. The abbey became Cluniac in the 11C and was rebuilt after a fire in c 1060. The High altar was consecrated in 1072 though the nave was finished only in the 12C. It was damaged in the Hundred Years War and again by the Huguenots in 1569; much of the monastery and church was rebuilt in the 17C.

Apart from the remodelled east apse, the plan is classic Cluniac of the mid-11C based upon the second church of Cluny, not the last and most famous one which was built after 1088. Hence, St-Sever has a splendid group of seven east-facing apses, though only the four on the north flank are visible. The apses are staggered in the characteristic arrow-head or chevron plan. The nave is short and rather dumpy. The oddly placed bell tower was rebuilt in the 19C. The west front is a bit scrubbed and also looks renewed. The information table records that in 1884, the time in Paris was 11 minutes 38 seconds different from St-Sever, and that in the age of the train!

The **interior** is gloomy but of great interest (you will need a torch). The barrel vault over the tall nave is a 17/18C replacement. The tall crossing is flanked by barrel-vaulted transept arms stepping down in height. Perhaps Cluny II did this. The two-bay choir has tall arcades into the aisles, the arches with foliate capitals. Above are lunette windows and barrel vaults. The apse interior is pure Pearl and Dean. The side aisles have an odd feature in that the apses are shifted into a corner (as at Moirax) yet no door or any other feature seems to blame. The wall arcades with painted Romanesque capitals become pierced in order to link through to the longer apsidal chapels of the transepts, a most attractive and unusual feature. The capitals in the south transept resemble Hagetmau. The **transepts** also retain a feature rare outside Normandy and the Pilgrimage churches—first-floor gallery walkways to connect the upper levels over the choir aisles and transept chapels with galleries over the nave aisles. The south transept gallery is closed off by a pierced screen recalling Hildesheim—St-Sever put itself amongst classy competition. The arcades here are pointed, as are the barrel vaults. Also, as at Moirax the nave aisle entries have upper arches leading to the galleries. The opposite north transept arm follows suit— notice the men squashed beneath the column supporting the gallery bridge.

The nave is the result of several builds. The bay nearest the crossing is the earliest, with round arches and the upper gallery. Possibly there was a circular clerestory above that. The other bays have fat piers along the south side, evidence of a rather clumsy rebuild. To the left of the main west door, is a capital of Salome at the feast, and another with men having piggy-backs. Beneath the organ loft, on the north side, at the end respond, the capital shows Daniel in the lions' den. Many of the capitals along the north side of the nave are worth a look. In fact, St-Sever has about 150 Roman-esque capitals, many of good quality. The 19C paint is unfortunate but closer to their original appearance than we might expect. Try playing 'spot the Gallo-Roman capitals', starting with the apses of the north transept. The sacristy (door off south choir chapel) has good woodwork and trapped in the passage, the exterior of one of the Romanesque apses.

The fittings are a mixed bag. Beginning at the west end, north side, are a 16C screen and 17C wooden altarpiece. The choir fittings are 18C though the stalls behind the altar are c 1600. Slightly earlier stalls flank the altar. There is a good 16C panelled door on the north side. Beneath the apse floor, fragments of late 11C mosaic decoration have been found.

The town offers other diversions including a few medieval defensive towers. The most rewarding walk is from the back of the church, the Place de Verdun, and the **Rue de Général Lamarque** leading from it. This street contains the best ancient houses in the town, mostly on the right, while the neo-Classical house No. 11 on the left, was the home of the said general. You will arrive at the other main interest of St-Sever, the convent of the Jacobins. This was the Dominican church and convent, and now houses a small but interesting local museum. More significant, the shell of the Dominican **church** survives remarkably intact. These are rare. The convent was a royal foundation of Edward I of England, c 1280. It suffered variously, much at the hands of the Huguenots, and the monastic buildings were extensively rebuilt c 1660. It now belongs to the town. The plan is erratic but then friar's convents often are. The early-14C brick church is a long oblong box with no surviving aisles and no divisions. A glimpse around the north-west corner will reveal that in its original form, the nave or western part was double aisled in the usual friar's manner, but this northern section has been demolished. The **cloister** is not quite square. It was entered by the door next to the west front, reworked in the Louis XIII style. The present cloister dates from c 1660. The chapter house and refectory occupied the opposite, east range, the dormitory possibly over the west range. Go in any door to the church that you find open and you will be struck by its spaciousness even though one side has been lost. The interior is dominated by a fine wooden roof, said to be 14C. The windows have simple tracery, the walls retain traces of painted patterns. Next to the choir, the long east range has been gutted internally. The north section formed a chapter house, the rest, the refectory. Note the remains of the reading pulpit built into the east wall, and sections of medieval painting. The **museum** on the first floor over the main entry contains Roman and later architectural fragments from the region, plus more painted remains. There is also a huge illuminated display illustrating the famous **Apocalypse of St. Sever** (sadly, the original is in Paris) a remarkable Romanesque work produced in the Cluniac abbey, contemporary with the commencement of the present church.

To the north of the town the **Promenade de Morlanne** offers extensive views.

From St-Sever, follow the signs for Dax, the most attractive and probably the quickest route being the minor D32. This passes through Mugron (17km), an attractive village with a fine view from behind the church, and Montfort-en-Chalosse (9km), another village with good views. Here is a museum of peasant life and a great market square, big enough for one of the region's most famous goose fairs. Dax is reached after another 18km.

Dax is a busy shopping town. (Tourist Office, Place Thiers, BP 177, 40104. Tel 58 90 20 00.) Parking is hard, so be prepared to walk.

It was a Roman town, *Aquæ Tarbellicae*, famous for its healing hot water which still flows. Dax stands on the south bank of the Adour, where there is an attractive riverfront, though there is far too much traffic.

The town has extensive Roman and medieval **walls**, now mostly exposed. Notice the Roman brick stripes on the bastion towers. Within the pedestrianised area is the **cathedral church**, a rather forbidding structure of the 17C close to a tree-lined square. The building is curiously antiquated and rather repellent, with chapels on the east side radiating from the apse and flying buttresses. The interior has a giant order, big clerestory and groin vaults. The real surprise comes in the north transept where a complete Gothic doorway from the previous church was re-erected in 1894 inside the present one. The 14C portal was badly damaged by the Huguenots. The main subject matter is the Last Judgement, with Christ, the Virgin and John, the Blessed and the Damned, a set of unconvincing Apostles and seated elders, angels and saints in the arches. The modern figure on the central column (trumeau) is horrendous. Otherwise there is little of note. The painting of Christ and the Poor Man in the ambulatory north side was given by the Emperor (Napoleon III) in 1864. You can see why he did not want it. The south transept has a very swagger altarpiece in the style of Bernini, with lots of red marble and a broken pediment.

The other—and to many the only site in Dax—is the **Fontaine Chaude**, the hot waterworks. This lies in a rather scrappy square, Place Borda, near the riverside park. The outdoor tank is fronted by three Doric arches, which are falling to bits. The water is kept at 64 degrees C and may be felt, or tasted (at your own risk) from a set of taps. It is pleasantly hot and must have made for pleasant bathing. It is said to flow at 2,400,000 litres a day.

Wandering about the town, you realise that Dax is full of thermal spa hotels and public benches occupied by the genteel. Most of the hotels are run by ladies with perms for ladies with perms. The rather rowdy people in the streets are mere day-trippers.

For the insatiable, Dax has a small Romanesque church of some distinction, but notable mostly for being difficult to find.

St-Paul-lès-Dax lies across the river and must be reached by car. Cross the Adour on the main D947 to Bordeaux. Drive up the hill and over the railway. At the junction with the N124, turn left for Bayonne—the **church** is marked on your left. It has a very suburban setting but the building dates from the 11C and is tiny. It comprises a bulbous tower, small nave, chancel and apse, all highly decorated, though much of the nave work is 19C. The east apse exterior is lavishly adorned with sculpture and inset plaques. The wall arcades have marble columns and rather damaged capitals, including what we would call waterleaf. The plaques resemble the marble sculptures of Toulouse from the 1090s, though here they are very restored. The scenes include the usual monsters and serpents. The Three Marys appear wearing crowns at Christ's empty tomb, a grumpy angel heaving up the lid. (The Marys look pretty grumpy too.) Another scene may be the Last Supper. There are depictions of the arrest of Christ, the Crucifixion and scenes from the Apocalypse. Inside, the chancel has foliate capitals and a barrel vault. The apse has a series of seats in niches, eleven in all.

From St-Paul, the main road heads for Bayonne, which is reached in 49km (main road or Autoroute A 63).

Bayonne: the waterfront along the River Nive

BAYONNE (Hotels/Rests.) is an historic city, spread across the confluence of the Adour and the Nive. Lying close to the sea, it makes a handy centre for both the beaches, the mountains and the surrounding historic sites. A visit to Bayonne is strongly recommended. Of all the larger towns of Aquitaine, it has the most consistently attractive centre. It also has the most important Gothic church in the region, the best fortifications and the finest art collection. It is not touristy. The attractive old town is densely packed and still sits behind its Roman and Renaissance fortifications. The modern industrial areas have left the centre unsullied, and the transport facilities are good. Once within Bayonne, everything of interest can be seen on foot. Much of the shopping centre is pedestrianised. (Tourist Office, Hôtel de VIlle, Place de Liberté 644100. Tel 59 59 31 31, fax 59 25 70 79.)

Bayonne was a Roman city, as its inner walls confirm. It passed to England with the rest of Aquitaine and became one of the most favoured towns of the English monarchy. What trouble there was came mostly from the Basques, who still make up a considerable section of the population. The Hundred Years War threatened the city's prosperity and its vital English market. It was the last major town to surrender to the French, and only then following what was interpreted as Divine intervention in 1451. There followed a period of decline and repression, the Bayonnais paying heavily for their old loyalties. Later, a nice irony made Bayonne the last city to fall to the Allies in their drive against Napoleon, the French commander Soult resisting Wellington until 1814.

The character of Bayonne can be summed up by its **waterfront** along the Nive. It has tall, mostly timber-framed buildings on stone ground-floors, arcaded sections as if in a *bastide*, narrow, ravine-like streets and no obvious plan. This route will start at the Tourist Office by the theatre on Place Général de Gaulle (by the Adour, opposite the railway station on the far bank). This part of the city looks quite ordinary but cross the road and enter the bustling Rue Pont-Neuf and you enter a world of charming streets and shops. Ahead rise the distinctive twin spires of the cathedral and that is the place to make for.

All the street scenes are attractive though not specially noteworthy. You will enter a rambling square, Place Louis Pasteur, encircling the north flank of the church.

BAYONNE CATHEDRAL was rebuilt in the style of north French Gothic from the 13C. Halted for decades by war and financial shortages, the main structure was completed only in the 16C. The restorations of the 19C included the completion of the west front and the building of the north west tower. The east end is most impressive, standing as it does straight on the street. The usual array of radiating chapels is tempered by the warm colour of the local stone. The style is Reims c 1220. The nave shows signs of its later date, the austere clerestory window tracery giving way to more exotic Flamboyant patterns. The north transept and its 14C porch retain a bronze knocker, commonly called a sanctuary ring. The lower chapels at street level are later additions. The west front is now very fine having spent centuries as an unfinished fragment. The towers and spires look rather English. Beneath the earlier south west tower crouches a curious stump of an abandoned late Gothic scheme for an extensive porch. The north tower and both spires were added by Boeswillwald in exemplary style during the restorations of the 1880s. The present porch recalls Albi, though the 15C west door is quite plain.

The **interior** is unnerving. Such tall, Gothic spaces belong somewhere near Paris not by the foothills of the Pyrenees (much of the interior was under scaffolding from 1992/93). Like most Gothic cathedrals, the plan is

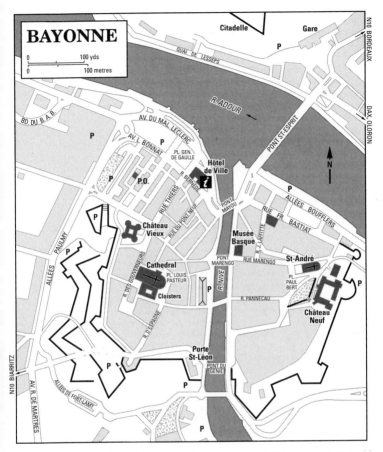

BAYONNE

| 0 | | 100 yds |
| 0 | | 100 metres |

intended to be read quickly—an east apse surrounded by an ambulatory aisle, circled in turn, by apsidal radiating chapels, then a brief transept and crossing, and a long nave with aisles. As with many Gothic churches, additional chapels have been built between the external buttresses of the nave.

The **elevational design** remains pretty constant throughout. The choir has tall arcades, with compound piers, the arches with minimal mouldings. The middle storey is a cage of stone tracery, with twin openings, glazed behind, the whole linked vertically with the windows above, very like the Parisian style of the 1230s known as Rayonnant. The clerestory is extremely simple. The Frenchness of this 'English' cathedral gives way in the vault scheme, where a ridge rib sneaks along the axial line, in a very English manner. The tall aisles bleed straight into the shallow radial chapels, the potential lighting effect ruined by extremely dark and tasteless 19C glass. The transept does not project beyond the main lines of the building. The first bay east of the nave belongs to the earlier campaign and maintains the first elevational design. Thereafter things are on the move. The arcade arches are now very sharply pointed, a bit like Westminster Abbey, and the arch apices sprout strange unidentified bulges, now used to fix light fittings. The cage-like middle storey continues but now very four-square, the spandrels above the arch-heads being pierced. The clerestory shows the most obvious change in both style and date. The second bay east, wider than the rest, introduces a more flowing tracery form, like English Decorated, and from then on the flood gates close, and a more sober pattern is introduced—medieval antiquarianism? The date of the nave is clearly 14/15C as is announced by the heraldry on the simple high vaults. The coats of arms include the Royal Arms of England with 'France Modern' a form introduced c 1405. Other English royal arms suggest that all the vaults were erected before c 1450.

The original form of the nave has been altered by the addition of chapels flanking the aisles. Before that, the side windows lit the wide aisles directly, flooding the nave with daylight. Now, the more remote windows have a hard time of it and the interior is darker than ever intended. As luck would have it, much of the original **medieval glass** survives, especially in the nave clerestory. It dates from late in the Middle Ages and the subjects include the Annunciation and Nativity, at the north side near the crossing, with the Creation cycle opposite. This is an odd reversal of normal iconographic schemes which would place Christ's life on the south, sun-facing side. The rest of the extremely colourful windows seem to follow no special theme, though the style changes progressively from late Gothic to early Renaissance.

Other glass, easier to see, occurs in some of the nave chapels. In the second chapel from the crossing on the north side, there is a replaced window dated 1531, showing the Canaanite begging for his daughter who has been possessed by the Devil. It includes the named donor figures of François de Laduch and his wife, Laurencine de Lagarde, plus their motto, Nunc et Semper—Now and Forever. Above is the Salamander of Francis I. There are few other fittings. At the west end, north side, is a Crucifixion painted beneath an ogee canopy, 15C. The pulpit was made in 1760 of Canary Island mahogany. The organ case was made in 1705.

One of the most interesting features of Bayonne Cathedral is the **south transept portal** which is hidden away in the sacristy where it is not normally on view. But try asking. The south transept portal survived relatively intact due to being locked away. It is a double door with jambs, whose sculpture includes the Virgin and Child, angels, the Apostles with their symbols, and the Last Judgement with the Blessed and the Damned. Somehow the lintels have contrived to be missing. The slightly wincing style suggests sub-Reims, c 1260–1300.

To the south of the cathedral (entrance at the east end, not weekends) stands a magnificent 13/14C **cloister**, the best in Aquitaine. The sober design hints of Salisbury, and the space offers magnificent views of the south flank of the church. Unbelievably the missing north walk was in fact demolished in the 19C to make way for the southern extension of the nave. There are some Gothic tombs gathered in corners, and a classical piece near the north west door to the church, Princess Leopoldine of Lorraine, died 1759. Near the south east angle, the street door bears an inscription recording the name of Auger de Lahet, treasurer of the church in 1515.

From the west end of the cathedral, the Rue des Gouverneurs leads north to the **Château Vieux**, a rather lumpy and unlovely building, which was once the headquarters of the Black Prince. Whatever its date (perhaps 14C), it is rendered incomphrehensible by its modern state. Other than the Black Prince, the château was home at various times to du Guesclin (a French hero, held here as a prisoner of the English), Pedro the Cruel (King of Castille), Louis XI (after the fall of Bayonne in 1451), Francis I, Charles IX and Louis XIV. By going round the back you can see one of the chief glories of the town, the **fortifications**. The city received new walls in the reign of Louis XIV as protection against the Spanish. They are the finest surviving work of the great architect-engineer Vauban, and date from 1674–79. Walking south along the upper terrace will give you some idea of their size and impregnability, the huge diamond-plan gun bastions and deep moats. They get better still around the south east angle of the town.

The southern walls run towards the Nive. The upper street level, along the Rue Tour-de-Sault, preserves sections of much earlier walls, which are basically Roman. Note the tall bastion towers, now built into a variety of structures. They seem to be Roman below, medieval above. You will reach the river by the Porte St-Léon, where you may walk along the west bank, admiring the tall façades and seafood restaurants.

On the opposite bank, a market has been established, while on the middle bridge, early morning unofficial **markets** are held on Saturdays. Here, local farmers set up stall on upturned boxes and sell whatever they have. It is very lively, noisy and a bit smelly, and has all but disappeared by 9 o'clock. The main market building on the west end of this bridge has fallen tragic victim to redevelopment, a black mark for a city that has got so many things right. From here, narrow streets of tall timbered houses snake up towards the cathedral and principal shopping area. Across the bridge lies a different Bayonne, a quarter developed after 1451 for the French, but now predominantly Basque. Do not try your French on the inhabitants, English is much appreciated even if the conversation then has to turn to French. After all, who but the Basques can speak, or even read their extraordinary language. The east bank is arcaded towards the river, with a number of small cafés and shops. Opposite the next bridge, the Pont Marengo, stands the **Musée Basque**, housed in a series of late medieval buildings. The collection examines many aspects of Basque life, including their traditions, costumes, and lifestyles, but unfortunately, structural problems have forced it to close indefinitely.

Take the Rue Marengo and then a left on the Rue Jacques Laffitte and head towards the **MUSÉE BONNAT**, a large rather grey building on the right. The Bonnat Museum contains one of the best painting collections in southern France (open daily in season and at weekends, afternoons mid-September to mid-June, closed Tuesdays). Léon Bonnat, born in Bayonne in 1833, was a portrait painter of limited ability. All his women look the same. But he amassed a considerable collection which has been extended by the city. It is well housed and displayed in chronological sequence. Start at the top of the stairs (lift). The collection starts with **medieval art**, painting and sculpture from the 14/15C. There follow **Florentine** and **Venetian works**, plus **Swabian sculptures**. Notable pieces include an Aragonese painting of St. Martin, from the 15C, a Florentine marriage chest and French medieval ivories. Everything is labelled, even if only with 'School of...'. There follow **French miniatures** of high quality, including two by Corneille de Lyons, 16C, and no less than 15 oil sketches by **Rubens**, well arranged in their own enclosure. Some reveal their underdrawing. His works include a tapestry study for Henry IV, and a powerful Belepheron killing the chimera. The Flemish/Dutch theme continues with **Van Dyck**, including his study for a portrait of Henrietta Maria, wife of Charles I, and his Scowling man. The oddball of this group is the bizarre comic scene from the second **School of Fontainebleau**. There is a very black **El Greco**, followed by a very red El Greco, complimented by a very black **Murillo** and **Ribera**. The the Murillo San Salvador and the Inquisition seem doubtful attributions. The Tiepolo looks, typically, like a ceiling painting. A side room contains the most stunning array of English (sic) portraits and some **Goyas.** The English school includes **Raeburn, William Etty, Reynolds** (a study of Colonel Tarleton), and a **Constable** study of Hampstead Heath. The Goyas include the Last Communion of St. José, black of course, and a portrait of Francisco de Borja, reading a letter, his horse and servant apparently sinking into the mud. Perhaps the best is his self-portrait in glasses. Other works include telling oil studies by **Hoppner** and **Lawrence**, a study for a portrait of Napoleon by Thomas Phillips (quite excellent) and Lawrence's full-length portrait of the artist Fuseli, a splashy work with the artist sitting on a grand chair, and a chaotic 'Fuseli' chasm opening behind.

The French galleries continue the high level of works displayed. There is a whole wall of **Ingres** (his Study of female hands is surely in the style of Rogier van der Weyden). There is also the famous painting of a nude boy clasping his knees by **Flandrin**, dancers by **Degas** and a portrait of Degas by Bonnat. **Géricault** is represented by no less than eleven works, while others include **Delacroix** and a stunning, if mucky **Corot**. The room devoted to Bonnat's own studies of other artists' work is interesting in that all this attention to great masters failed to make Bonnat even a half-decent painter. Works by Puvis de Chavannes include a group of nude men working at a forge—it still retains the artist's working grid. As far as the Impressionists go, Bonnat bought all the wrong paintings. On the ground floor is an atrocious work of 19C soft-porn, called Idylle, plus a number of Bonnat's 'xeroxed' women. The basement contains a small collection of Egyptian, Roman and other objects including small marbles and glassware.

From the corner of the Musée Bonnat, the Rue Fr. Bastiat runs back over the Pont Mayou to the theatre and Tourist Office.

16

Ainhoa, la Rhune and Biarritz

This 84km route offers scenery in vast quantity and small villages of great quality. It also includes a mountain excursion by cable railway and, if you wish, a paddle. It is not rich in great monuments, though it has its moments, and would ideally fill a morning or an afternoon. Check for weather conditions, and do not go if the cloud is hanging low on the mountains. The addition of St-Jean-Pied-de-Port would add 76km and make up a whole day trip.

Take the D932 from Bayonne to Cambo-les-Bains (19km). Alternatively, the panoramic D22 Route Impériale des Cimes towards Hasparren, but right on the D10 is longer, at 30km, but more attractive. On a half day trip you could head for Espelette after Cambo. The more ambitious drivers with good maps may wish to approach St-Jean-de-Port via the more tangled route, passing through Hasparren, and heading along the D14 to St-Esteban (11km), where a visit can be made to the **Grottes d'Isturits et d'Oxocelhaya**. The twin caves feature evidence of man's activity at least as far back as the Magdalenian era, plus natural formations and accretions. From St-Esteban, St-Jean-Pied-de-Port may be reached via the D251, where a right after 4km heads for Helette. In a further 4km, a left on the D22 heads for St-Jean in 21km. It is an interesting but awkward route.

Cambo-les-Bains is a spa town set above the Nive in typically wooded Pyrenean foothill country. (Tourist Office, Parc Public BP15, 64250. Tel 59 29 70 25.) The lower town, Basse Cambo, is a jumble of little white, gabled and wood painted houses similar to many in the region.

From Cambo, the busy D918 heads south-east through increasingly splendid countryside. At 16km, you reach **Bidarray**, across a 14C bridge. The little Romanesque church once formed part of a priory founded 1132 by Compostela. At 18.5km, **St-Jean-Pied-de-Port** (Hotels/Rest.) is a picturesque town, rather too popular with day-trippers and bus parties. (Tourist Office, 14 Place Charles de Gaulle, 64220. Tel 59 37 03 57.) Since the mid-12C it has featured as a resting place for travellers, then of course, pilgrims en route for Compostela. It had a bad reputation for petty crime and hostile natives. It controlled the north end of the pass of Roncesvalles, redolent of myth and Carolingian legend. St-Jean was capital of lower Navarre, though left somewhat in limbo when Aragon seized all of the kingdom south of the Pyrenees in 1512. The town lives on its past and its obvious though perhaps shallow historical interest.

The upper town, north of the river Nive, has medieval fortifications and narrow streets full of typically painted Basque houses, especially along the principal Rue de la Citadelle, which leads to the impressive fort on high. At its lower end, the Gothic church of Notre-Dame, the Vieux Pont with its restored gatehouse, the ancient Hospital (containing a *pelota* museum) and riverside houses form a characteristic and much photographed ensemble. The church has interesting columns. The lower town has walls dating from 1659. The bustling commercial heart centres on the Pont Neuf.

To vary the return to Cambo, leave St-Jean on the D15 towards **St-Etienne-de-Baigorry** (11km), with a Romanesque bridge spanning the Aldudes, typical Basque houses and an ornate, galleried 18C church. (Tourist Office, Place de l'Eglise 64430. Tel 59 37 47 28.) From here, the D948 regains the D918 for Cambo in 8km, with a further 23km before the junction west of the town. Here, turn left and head for **Espelette** (5.5km; Tourist Office, Mairie 64250. Tel 59 93 91 44). Despite the main road, Espelette is charming, a scattered village with streams and gabled houses, many dated over the stone doorways. **Pyrenean houses** are very distinctive and unlike others in Aquitaine. Essentially separate, they stand gable-end on, with deep, overhanging roofs for snow protection, loft entrances under the eaves and painted criss-cross woodwork.

Turn right off the road and park. Head for the little village **church**. From a distance the church looks pretty humble, perhaps 12C with a big fat tower. Closer to, it is evidently 17C but still humble. The porch is dated 1627, the door is of the same period. The interior makes Espelette one of the most memorable buildings in Aquitaine. Nothing can prepare the visitor for what is in store, and it is tempting to remain silent. The interior is crammed, though decked is perhaps the better word, with an astonishing assemblage of **woodwork**. From the moment you enter, the timber fittings spread in every direction, especially upwards. The whole interior is dominated by tier upon tier of galleries, propped, underpinned or just hanging. The building has been designed for nothing else. It is like an Elizabethan theatre and not too far removed in date. The balusters are beautifully turned and everywhere there is something to please the eye. Ironically, for galleries built for a better view of the altar, you must go to the altar for the best view of the galleries. Climb all over them, they only get better. Note the fixed benches and kneelers. From the top gallery you can almost touch the ceiling, which is painted. The other fittings include the 18C panelling surrounding the Baroque altarpiece, all twistings and gilt. To the north of the altar, is a possibly 16C Spanish tapestry in an 18C frame, a gloomy thing of little quality, while on the north wall, St. Jerome, by Ribera, just a gloomy thing.

The commercial centre of Espelette is above on the road junction, where there are pretty shops and hotels. You may catch a glimpse of the *fronton*, the large, usually pink wall for the playing of *pelota*, an energetic ball game and speciality of the Basque country.

In just over 1km the D20 leaves the D918 and heads through hilly scenery for Ainhoa (5.5km, Hotels, Rest.). **Ainhoa** is a showpiece though you will be unlucky if you find any other tourists there. Enter the village, pass the *fronton*, and you see just one main street climbing the gentle slope. All around you are hills and woods. The individual buildings are nearly all worth inspecting; many people leave their main doors open so you cannot be blamed for peeping inside. The basic house combines a farm or workshop with living quarters over and stores in the roof above. Hence, the barn-like doors to the street, often with a stable just inside. The blocks are uncommonly deep, allowing for the storage of farm machinery, fodder and presumably in the winter, livestock. The upstairs accommodation comes complete with flower-decked windows, pretty painted shutters and woodwork details. Check for dates over the doors, one on the right has the date and owner—1641, 26 August, Pierre de Etcheberri. His ground floor is big enough to garage five cars. Quite a few are dated 1641. Notice also the use of the swastika as a decorative motif. It is a traditional Basque symbol and has no other connotation. At the top end of the village, a noticeboard offers details of country walks of one to five hours duration. The village church cannot match Espelette but it is still very attractive. Again, it is 17C and galleried within. The huge Baroque altarpiece resembles some Roman theatre scene.

Leaving Ainhoa, take the D20 another 3km to Dancharia and the Spanish frontier, which is no longer guarded by a customs post. From here, the beautiful Spanish Valle del Baztan leads eventually to Pamplona (80km).

If you turn right to stay in France, the road, now the D4, heads for **Sare** (10km) along a splendid and scenic route. Sare is pretty but touristy. (Tourist Office, 64310 Sare. Tel 59 54 20 14.) It has a big church, a big *fronton*, arcaded buildings, hotels and restaurants. The far end of the village just drops into open countryside. This is the usual staging post for trips up the railway to the **summit of la Rhune**. The train leaves from a small station

Ainhoa

some 3km along the D4 at Col de St-Ignac. The trains usually run every half-hour. Tickets are limited and you may have to wait, but there are cafés. The train runs on rails but is pulled by cable. The journey is highly recommended for the wonderful views en route, the passing flora and fauna, including wild horses if you are lucky, and the panorama from the summit, which is shared with Spain. From the top you can see the coast, St-Jean-de-Luz and, if it is clear enough, Biarritz. You will also notice how lush it is on the French side compared with the barrenness of Spain. It may be a simple matter of rainfall patterns but is still quite remarkable. The journey up and down, plus a reasonable 'look' will take 90 minutes.

From the station, the road takes another 3.5km to reach **Ascain**, another lovely village where the fields squeeze in between the houses. (Tourist Office, Mairie 64310. Tel 59 64 00 84.) It has a big church, dark within and again with galleries. The carving is especially beautiful; notice the pulpit. Oddly, the Baroque altar is raised high over a sacristy room which results in lots of steps. There are simple peasant carved saints and a model ship. From Ascain it is possible to drive to the coast at St-Jean-de-Luz (6km) or continue on an inland route. The coast road, the D918 passes beneath the A63 and joins the main N10 along the coast.

St-Jean-de-Luz was an important whaling centre in English times, though later it turned to piracy. (Tourist Office, Place Maréchal-Foch BP 151, 64500. Tel 59 26 03 16, fax 59 26 21 47.) It is now a busy tuna-fishing centre and modern resort with good beaches. Some older houses survive near the port including the Maison de l'Infante, named after the Infanta Maria-Thérèse, wife of Louis XIV, who resided here in 1660 before her marriage to a reluctant Louis in the local church. Here, too, is the fine Maison Louis XIV (the Maison Lohobiague, 1643) where they spent their wedding night. The interior with fine period rooms may be visited.

The 15C church of St. John the Baptist was extensively remodelled in the 17C and has a rather grand version of a Basque galleried interior with a fine wrought-iron stair. The blocked door right of the entry was sealed after the marriage of Louis XIV to prevent it being sullied by lesser folk. The interior has decks of galleries and a panelled roof often likened to a ship's hull. The raised choir has a fine wrought-iron grill protecting a gilded altarpiece of 1670, which was not the altar at which Louis was married. It is predictably smothered with angels, Virgins and local saints. All these buildings are in the Barre quarter, surrounding the port, now the pedestrianised shopping centre.

The N10 reaches Biarritz in 10km. Alternatively, from Ascain take the D918 the other way to St-Pée-sur-Nivelle (7km) noticing **Ibarron** at 5.5km, with its *fronton* and a wide square. Many of the houses on the far side have interesting peasant designs carved over the doors. **St-Pée** (Hotels/Rest.) is horrid, having been ruined by traffic and tourists. (Tourist Office, 64310 St-Pée-sur-Nivelle. Tel 59 54 11 69.) From here the D255 reaches the centre of Biarritz in 17km on a quieter, back country road.

BIARRITZ is a name enshrined in legend. It conjures images of Victorian aristocracy, of Twenties flappers and characters from Evelyn Waugh. If only it were like that. Biarritz has squandered its fine location and period atmosphere for a quick buck. Clearly, a decision was made some time back to go very down-market. The result is junk-food, trash shops, concrete everywhere and huge, huge crowds. The beaches are packed tighter than the local tinned tuna and the streets are a permanent traffic jam. From that point of view, the decision was a success but unless you like humanity *en masse*, stay away. Tourist Office, 'Javalquinto' Square d'Ixelles, 64200. Tel 59 24 20 24, fax 59 24 14 19.

The resort rose to prominence under the Empress Eugènie, wife of Napoleon III, having for some time been the favoured resort of her Spanish fellow countrymen. In 1855 the couple built the Villa Eugènie, now the Hôtel du Palais. The collapse of France before the Prussians in 1870, and the exile of Napoleon and Eugènie did not halt the rise of Biarritz, indeed even Queen Victoria fell for its undoubted charms during her visit in 1889. This brought the English and their wealth. It continued to be visited by various royals, especially Edward VII, until World War One. The Twenties saw a different group descend upon the place, the newly famous, the film stars, actors, writers and the Prince of Wales, later Duke of Windsor. It was then that Biarritz achieved a slightly risqué reputation.

The modern post-war years have not been kind to Biarritz—Monte Carlo has better weather, Spain better beaches. The casinos still attract those with nothing better to do with their money and the streets are often brought to a stand-still by the sheer numbers of open-topped sports cars driven by the self-publicists and wide-boys. But the glamour has gone and by comparison with the Côte d'Azur, the place is tawdry.

Some former glory survives albeit faded. The Hôtel du Palais is still there, and the dotty Anglican church built by the visiting British in that universal style of the Empire, Melbourne Gothic, but for most visitors, the setting of Biarritz is the main attraction. The town sprawls along a series of rocks and coves, each headland providing fine views of the coast and ocean. The best are around the Rocher de la Vierge on the Plateau de l'Atalaye (there is parking here, though parking anywhere in Biarritz is difficult). Here is also the **Musée de la Mer**, covering many aspects of the marine life of the Bay of Biscay. The terrace has excellent views. The beaches of Biarritz are rather narrow and crowded, and many of them charge for entry.

Bayonne (8km) may be reached on the D260 or the N10, both busy at the end of the day.

17

Bayonne to Pau

This route follows the River Adour as far as its confluence with the Gaves Réunis, which it then follows with odd detours for 134km. The countryside is hilly but by no means difficult. The railway (and TGV) follows the river more closely. For a half-day excursion—90km returning to Bayonne—follow the route as far as Sorde-l'Abbaye, and return via Bidache and Bellocq.

Leave Bayonne on the D312 along the river, turning on to the D261 as soon as the city peters out. This little road hugs the south bank of the Adour, providing endless living Corots. From Urt (15km), the D261 clings to the river, passing the confluence and heading beneath the railway at the approach to Sames (16km) where a tiny side road (left) heads for **Hastingues**. If the name seems familiar it is. This *bastide* was built by Sir John Hastings, Lord Lieutenant of Gascony in 1289. You will arrive in front of the south gate, which is tall, with a machicolated top and arrow slits. The upper hinges for the gate survive as does the portcullis slide. There are sections of the town wall on either side. Park here, as the village is tiny and the views from before the gate are truly rural. There is basically one street but unlike most of the *bastides* of Aquitaine, here the houses are distinctly Basque. Some are ancient, one has huge corbels sticking out for no obvious reason. Another is late medieval with small figures carved on a large ogee arch and dated 1503, and opposite, there is a big house of c 1500. The central square is quickly reached, no classic arcaded rectangle but a loose, rural jumble. The church is disappointingly 19C but south of the church is a fine rambling block from c 1500 with great blocked arches, large four-square moulded windows and a side stair turret. Many of the houses here have vaulted cellars. The houses of Hastingues are built so close together that the resulting gaps must always have caused drainage problems. On the far side of the square there are glimpses of the river way below.

Descending from Hastingues, the tiny D343 (right) leads to the remote abbey of Arthous in 3km. **Arthous** was intended to be out of the way, and it is. The buildings rise up from the valley floor, backed by the steep wooded hillside. It seems remarkably complete from a distance and is certainly very interesting. The **abbey** was Premonstratensian, the order taking its name from their mother house at Prémontré. Like the Cistercians, they settled in wild and uninhabited areas (such as Bayham in Sussex), and their monasteries are often mistaken for those of the more famous order. Arthous was a 12C foundation, the guts of the church surviving from that date. The rest of the buildings, still ranged around the cloister space, date from many periods. They now house a fine museum of more than local interest. The abbey was favoured by the Kings of England in the 13/14C and it assisted Edward I in the foundation of Hastingues. It was burnt in 1523 during a brief war between Francis I and Charles I of Spain (the Emperor Charles V), and ruined yet again in 1571 in the French Wars of Religion, after which much of the abbey was roofless. A general restoration occurred in 1634. In 1766 only five canons remained, reduced to three and a prior by 1789. Arthous was sold in 1791, when it became a farm. It passed to the Landes (the State) in 1966.

Before entering the enclosure (open daily except Tuesday, sometimes closed 12.00–14.00), note the fine simple lines of the east end of the church, and some of the sculpture including the Seven deadly Sins (the Premonstratensians did not follow the Cistercians in their rejection of such art).

Standing in the court, the church occupies the entire south flank, its north transept arm turning the south-east angle. The east range is mostly lost, but would have housed the chapter house and dormitory. The church was divided in two internally, much of the nave given over to the laity. The building is now very derelict though substantial restoration may soon remedy the situation.

The **interior** is unaisled, with a simple crossing, transepts with east chapels, a single chancel bay and an apse. The nave was much demolished, being replaced at the west end by a farmhouse, though the basic shape and spaces have survived. The north door into the church is Romanesque. Note the book cupboards in the adjoining north transept wall. The nave walls have been reduced in height, see the abrupt cutting of the windows. Standing beneath the crossing arches, the history of the church becomes clear. The original church was unvaulted, the present vault fragments date from the 14/15C. The webs were brick. Many Romanesque capitals survive, though some are smashed. The chancel bay is decorated with wickerwork designs and volutes. Formerly, this bay was barrel-vaulted and the apse carried a semi-dome. More capitals flank the windows. The exposed roofs seem old, dating possibly from 1634. The south transept arm has Romanesque capitals of Spanish/Islamic inspiration, while the north arm has fragments of a Romanesque tympanum depicting the Magi. One of the crossing piers has a capital featuring a centaur. Note the mason's working marks near the door. The nave had circular windows (see the south exterior). Also outside the site, the west door survives with columns and acanthus capitals, one decorated with a Dragon.

The other buildings shown are generally post 1634 and contain an interesting **archaeological museum**. The loggia houses fine Roman mosaics from the area, particularly from the 4C villa at Mouneyres à Sarbazan. They are notable for their range of colours, variety of patterns including a jazzy grid-design, and beautiful vine scrolls. Some of the patterns are illusionistic and include intersecting arches within the borders. There is also a model of the Roman villa at Sorde (see below). The exhibits include a medieval or 17C boat cut complete from a single tree, funerary pots from the pre-Christian era, a 2C Roman drain from Gaujacq, and a range of prehistoric finds including carved bone combs. One local find from the Magdalenian IV period, c 12,000 BC includes a small horse carved on a bone, and many other bones finely engraved. There are also human skulls ranging in date from c 9350 BC–1200 BC.

Picking up the D343, the road continues until the intersection with the D19 (2.5km). Head north for Peyrehorade (4.5km) where the road crosses the Gaves Réunis and a right on the main N117 finds a side road, the D29 for Sorde-l'Abbaye, which is reached in 4km from the river crossing.

Sorde-l'Abbaye is another site combining medieval buildings with substantial Roman remains, this time mostly in situ.

Passing the remains of the town gate, enter the main square flanking the north side of the church (Tourist Office). The little town grew around the abbey, and is attractively placed on a slight rise above the Gave d'Oloron. This is excellent salmon fishing country and the medieval abbey took full advantage of that. The church shares a fate similar to many in the region. A large Romanesque abbey church, remodelled in part in the later Middle Ages, it was wrecked by Huguenots and unsympathetically restored. This is not to say that it is without interest. The east end is impressive, with its row of Romanesque apses standing somewhat unromantically in a car park. There is a tower over the north-west angle of the north transept, an odd place. Evidence of burning is everywhere, the local stone taking on a rusty red hue.

The main entrance is via the north transept, of stripped brick and stone, and through a damaged Romanesque door with a smashed-up tympanum. This contained a Christ in Majesty, note the odd pendent hanging over the door.

The **interior** is gloomy but there are lights. The plan is the usual, apsed choir, transept with east apses and crossing, but here the nave is and always was aisled. The chancel and transepts were raised later in the Middle Ages, and they received their present rib vaults probably in the 16C. Genuine Romanesque sculpture takes some finding here but the Christ being led to the Cross and the Man with lions, both in the north transept, look authentic, as do the Virgin and Child and the Magi in the south arm. One of the great mysteries of the church however, is the **chancel floor**. A great mosaic scheme fills the apse, with intricate geometric patterns and jolly figures, including rabbits. It is said to be Roman but the floor gives the impression of being made up from several mosaics spliced together. It would not be unthinkable for the whole thing to be 12C. On the other hand, the nearby monastic buildings contain a splendid array of Roman mosaics from the villa underlying much of the site. There are two sets of stalls from the 16C.

The nave seems mostly 19C though the aisle responds from the 12C. are left stranded along the outer walls, no longer relating to the existing vault scheme. The west front again seems 19C. Adjoining the west end are the gutted remains of the abbey buildings, mostly 17/18C. From here you can walk to the riverside.

The main buildings that can be visited are entered from the car park east of the church. The right-hand gate leads to pretty gardens within the ruins of the later monastic buildings. The main attraction is a galleried walkway flanking the tumbling river.

The left gate leads to a rather more substantial site (ring for entry, guided tour, donation). The buildings are a **late-medieval prior's house** of some distinction, entered by a Gothic door at the base of a stair turret. The gardens contain the outlines of the excavated Roman villa. Inside, some fireplaces survive plus the 'cellar' entry, leading to the galleried riverside passage further west. Much of the house has been gutted to reveal the villa beneath. The major excavation shows a 4C private bath, with swimming pool, warm room and hot room, see the hypocaust sections. The mosaics are of high quality and multi-coloured, with geometrical shapes, vine scrolls, all in need of cleaning. The swimming pool floor has a complex pattern of hexagons and spirals. On another floor, notice the salmon in precisely the right pink tone. Some mosaics were damaged by burials which were cut straight into them. Other detached mosaics line the walls. Altogether it is an impressive collection, with about 15 floors on display.

If you are returning to Bayonne via Bidache, head back the short distance to **Peyrehorade**, which offers food and sustenance, also a stump of the 16C. Château Montréal is near the river, built by the Viscounts of Orthez, and there is the tall and unreachable tower keep of the Château d'Apremont on the hill. Then take the D19 back over the river, pass the turning to Arthous and on to Bidache (6km). The reason for the visit is patently obvious for miles, the great ruined **Château de Gramont** perched high over the little river Bidouze.

The castle was first mentioned in 1040, and was the home of the Dukes of Gramont from the 13C until the Revolution. It was gutted by fire in 1796 and then abandoned. The ruins are reasonably complete and very striking. The present building was probably complete before the visit of Mazarin in 1643. It was later the home of the Compte Philibert de Gramont, died 1707, and his wife, Elizabeth Hamilton, former mistress of Charles II of England. The ruins now house a collection of birds of prey, which may not be to everyone's taste.

The castle occupies a rock promontory—a great gash cut on the 'landward' side completes the defence. (Open afternoons, April–October.) What survives is part of the south range including the ruined gateway, and the very substantial north block, plus underground sections and passages. The entrance façade has a gateway rising from a battered base, with a rusticated arch, pediment, masks, reclining ladies, then two quarter-plan towers turning to square for a lost upper section. A major wing survives to the right, dating from the late 16C/early 17C. This has rustication, dormers, four-square windows with Renaissance pediments above. The interior façade reveals that much of the structure is brick which was plastered over. The opposite range was clearly the main living quarters and has very big windows. It has two storeys plus attic dormers, the latter standing sharply against the sky. There must have been quite a tall roof. To the right is a taller pavilion corner block, obviously once a great stair, dating probably from c 1600. To the left are the remains of a lost west range. The basic walling is composed of rubble, again rendered to resemble cut stone ashlarwork.

Passing through the huge entrance, notice the fireplaces at various levels, left hanging after the collapse of the floors. There is considerable decoration. Within the stair pavilion are remains of the vault that underpinned the lost stair, and shell niches. There is also the remnants of the servants' back stair. Each floor had a large chamber, a fireplace and a room beyond, as at

Cadillac. Pass through the stair hall and arrive on the terrace. To the left, a wing of c 1600 leads to a great fat tower from an earlier castle, perhaps 15C. It has a machicolated top though the windows beneath and the rather clumsy Renaissance doorway are later insertions. Notice that the Renaissance façades have gun loops and firing slits. The panoramic view is fine, and explains why the owners built where they did. Returning through the main wing, turn right and find the entrance at the far end to the undercroft, vaulted galleries beneath a first west wing, which is possibly medieval.

The D936 from Bidache heads west for 10km where a turning left (D10) reaches **la Bastide Clairence** (2km), a reasonably pretty village set on a slope. (Tourist Office, Place des Arceaux, 64240. Tel 59 29 65 05.) Nearby, the abbey of **Bellocq** has a fine modern, wedge-shaped church of 1966 by Duverdier. The design is distinctly post-Vatican II, simple, austere and with subtle concealed daylight. There is a circular sanctuary in the crypt. The D123 passing Bellocq joins the D312 at 2km, where a left will lead to Bayonne in 17km.

If you are pressing on to Pau, take the D29 from Sorde and head south for Carresse (7km) after which, the D17 turns left for **Salies-de-Béarn** (7km), a most attractive spot (Hotels/Rest. Tourist Office, 1 Boulevarde St-Guily, 64270. Tel 59 38 00 33). The town is famous for its salt, hence its name. On a certain Sunday in September, they hold a Salt Fair, which is an excuse for a lot of eating, some drinking, and to dust off traditional dress. There are also many food stalls selling a variety of local produce. The town is charming if not exactly bulging with fine architecture. The centre is a virtual circle of streets, crossing and recrossing the little river Saleys. This provides the principal photographic attraction, lots of timbered galleries swathed in flowers, all placed higgledy-piggledy over the water. It may not be Art but it is certainly pretty and requires no further comment.

Salies is still a spa town and offers treatments. It also has a daily market.

A detour south, time permitting, would lead via the D933 to **Sauveterre-de-Béarn** (6km, Hotels/Rest. Part-time Tourist Office in the Mairie, 64390. Tel 59 38 50 17), another pretty town in a startling position. This time it hangs on a cliff-edge with sheer drops down to the tumbling Gave d'Oloron. Sauveterre offers some of the most picturesque views in Aquitaine but they are hard to find. It also has an interesting church where it is possible to park. The church is large and Romanesque. It stands on a terrace with wide vistas overlooking a bend in the river. Clearly, you are standing on a cliff but the opposite bank is low-lying and wooded. Almost immediately right is the ruined Tour Montréal, a fortified structure of the 12C rising dramatically from the rock scarp. Standing in the water way below are the remains of a **fortified bridge**, the stranded tower washed by the river.

The **church** has a three-apse plan, the Gothic windows intruded into the apse, and a fine Romanesque central tower. The west front has the remains of a large Romanesque door though the jambs are modern. The hanging pendent recalls Sorde. The tympanum features Christ in Majesty with some athletic apostles and squashed angels, perhaps 13C. Inside, there are plenty of Romanesque capitals but also evidence that the interior was raised and rib vaulted later in the Middle Ages. The crossing is lower, reflecting the 12C. overall height. There are transepts with east chapels, their apses still carrying half-domes. The capitals are crude but look unrestored. The short nave seems a little later, perhaps from the end of the 12C. The arcades are pointed and the capitals look c 1180s. Individual capitals of note include on the north-east crossing pier, Gluttony (best to come here after lunch), and on the easternmost respond of the north aisle of the nave, the Nativity.

The **Tour Montréal** has no access and is gutted internally. It is a sheer piece, with arrow slits facing the town, and larger openings over the safer riverside. Further along the pleasant main street are remains of a gate and town walls. To appreciate fully the siting of Sauveterre, it is necessary to get to the fortified bridge. You can walk—it is quite a way—or drive round the one-way system following the signs for the D936 Oloron-Ste-Marie, and as you leave the town on a sharp right bend, stop and pull over. Having parked somehow, follow the path back towards the town and you will arrive at the bridge. On foot, follow the same route, taking a left at the remains of the town gate.

The bridge crossed the river in several spans, one of which survives. How and where it made landfall on the far side is not clear. The picturesque tower has no obvious defensive features—perhaps they were in a lost tower further out in the river.

A **plaque** recalls the story of Sancie, the widow of Gaston V of Béarn. Rumour had it that Sancie had given birth to an illegitimate child born some time after her husband's death. Unable to produce this supposed child, she was then accused of having killed it. Her brother, the King of Navarre, ordered her denial to be tested by drowning, and she was duly bound hand and foot and thrown into the racing stream from this very bridge. As in all good legends, Sancie drifted safely on the water, and was gently lodged on the far shore. Her innocence proved, she was restored to titles and positions. Of course, they could just have believed her in the first place. Not to pour too much cold water on the story, it was said to have happened in 1170—the bridge was built a good 50 years or more later.

Steps lead down to a walk, including another vaulted gallery with fine views of the river and town. Paths in the other direction lead across footbridges to a wooded park, an ideal picnic spot (Camping nearby). For the best view of all, take off your shoes and socks and walk into the fast flowing water. From this angle, the cliff-face, the Tour Montréal and the church with its striking tower form a quite unforgettable picture.

A further detour may be made to the **Château of Laàs**, 8km south east of Sauveterre on the tiny D27. The château resembles rather a large English vicarage and is somewhat surrounded by campers. The house was, until 1953, the home of Louis Serbat, president of the French National Society of Antiquaries, and this is reflected in the opulent furnishings currently displayed. The tour is guided (in French, erratic opening, enquire). The building is 17C though the fittings are of many periods, mostly from other houses of the last family. There are good tapestries and a bed, slept in by Napoleon after Waterloo. Further south east, take the main D936 by crossing the river at Narp, is **Navarrenx** (12km), with some of the earliest Renaissance fortifications and gates in France. (Tourist Office, Porte Saint-Antoine, 64190. Tel 59 66 14 93/59 66 10 22.) Just south of Sauveterre, St-Gladie, on the D23, has one of the largest towers against one of the smallest churches you will ever see. Quite daft. The church has early plate tracery from c 1200.

Sauveterre-de-Béarn

From Sauveterre-de-Béarn, take the D23 to Beüsse (7km) and on to l'Hôpital d'Orion (3km), and after a further 5km, turn left at Pléchot for **Orthez** (Hotels/Rest.), world famous for its production of *jambon de Bayonne* (Market Tuesdays). The Tourist Office is at Rue du Vieux Bourg, 64300, tel 56 69 02 75.

Orthez was the main residence of the Counts of Béarn until the title passed to to the Counts of Foix in the 14C. As you enter the town, park by the first church and head back for the attractive pedestrianised street leading to the river, known as the Quartier Départ. Here is the most famous feature of Orthez, the complete **fortified bridge**. The bridge is probably 14C and is the symbol of the town. For a good view you need to seek out one of the several riverside vantage points. It is asymmetrically arranged, with one large arch in front of the gate-tower, and three behind it. The tower is curiously elliptical in plan and had no portcullis. Note the restored swing shutters between the battlements. The greatest surprise is the positioning of the TGV line directly on the town end of this historic structure. Not only should you take great care when crossing the line, but the vibrations cannot be doing this famous bridge too much good. The town is attractive and has a strange and interesting church.

From the railway track, take the Rue Craverie then go left on the Rue Bourg Vieux where the atmosphere is of 18C prosperity. To the left on the corner of Rue Rosarie, is a 16C house with an L-plan, stair turret, four-square moulded windows and in the garden behind, pretty timber-framed buildings. This is the Tourist Office but was once yet another house of Jeanne d'Albret. A turning left through the shopping area and the Rue de Jacobins, brings you to the huge and irregular market square that surrounds the church. Up to the right, is the tower of the hill-top château, built by Gaston VII, count of Béarn late in the 13C.

The **church** is rather abrupt, and at one stage the north side formed part of the town's fortification. The boxy east end is softened by a polygonal apse, but the whole thing is dwarfed by the huge, single-aisled nave. Walking towards the main south door, the church displays two distinct phases, the 13C apse, chancel and single-bay transept, then the later giant nave with what looks like additional low transepts. The porch and the west end of the nave are modern (1865), built when the earlier fortifed west tower was demolished. The previous church had been dedicated to St. Thomas of Canterbury, though in the rebuilding, they adopted the less English St. Peter.

Inside it looks like a barn with a sawn-off church stuck on one end. What happened is fairly obvious. The 13C scheme was for a normal church, if quite grand. The chancel has a proper elevation, the main space higher than the aisles, and with upper clerestory windows. That scheme was scrapped, the nave aisles raised to the full height of the chancel, the internal arcades abandoned, then the resulting single space vaulted in one leap (as at Gerona, Spain). The choir has a good series of vault bosses, including a knight on horseback, the Agnus Dei, and St. Peter. The south west pier is also decorated with various animals fighting. The later nave vaults have stone ribs but brick webs. The bosses include the famous depiction of the town's bridge—from which hang the keys of St. Peter—and a Passion cycle. The church was damaged by the Huguenots in 1569 but repaired. The lighting of the separate north chapel of the nave betrays that it was once a fortified tower.

The Rue St. Pierre north of the church is a main shopping area and has further views of the river. Passing south the length of the market, a left at the end brings you back to the fortified bridge.

If time permits, it is possible to visit the Château Morlanne, one of the most attractive houses in the region to the north east of Orthez. Take the main D933 north-east from Orthez for 10km until you reach the junction with the D945. Turn right and head south-east for another 10km until at a crossroads, the D946 is marked Morlanne (right). You will reach the village in 4km.

Morlanne is a quiet village of some charm. It has a spacious square with church, market buildings and a Tourist Office. The church actually looks like a castle but the real château is a short walk away. The **church of St. Lawrence** is whimsically decked out with towers, turrets and pointy roofs (if locked, ask in the Tourist Office opposite). It has a simple plan, with no crossing. It was begun in the 14C by Gaston Fébus, Count of Foix and Orthez. The apse dates from his time (see the pretty capitals), though the little vault is 18C. The nave is mostly 16C though along the north side, a range of chapels was built at various times, beginning at the east end. The first chapel has a circular window full of *mouchettes* busy chasing each other, while the capitals are decorated with fish, and crude heads. The middle chapel has the Evangelists on the vault supports. At the west end there is a curious gallery within one of the many southern additions. On the nave vault, St. Lawrence holds up the griddle on which he was barbequed.

Behind the tourist office are the remains of the **Abbaye Laïque**, a slightly derelict but picturesque 16C building with a stair turret. The lane beside the market hall leads over the stream to the **Château de Morlanne**, a charming building and full of interest (open March–October afternoons till 18.30). The castle stands on a tiny, probably artificial mound surrounded by a wet moat. The modern gardens are delightful and have marvellous views. The brick castle was built by Arnaul Guilem de Béarn, illegitimate half-brother of Gaston Fébus. It forms an irregular circle, the walls high and battlemented, the little gate-tower set like the entrance to a fairy tale. Within, some of the buildings have been removed simply to let in the light. The original central court must have been very gloomy. Morlanne represents an important survival of a small, fortified house of the early Hundred Years War. Brick in this part of France was already *de rigueur*. Notice the herringbone pattern of some of the brick-laying and the evidence of *garde-robe* shafts.

The internal arrangements of the house have been thoroughly modernised and the owner, the formidable Mme Ritter, has furnished it with great taste (guided visits take about 45 minutes). Enter through a door dated 1646, and carrying the appropriate motto *expectants*. The collection and rooms shown are all explained. Notable in the entrance lobby are the Romanesque Christ in Majesty, 12C possibly from Toulouse, the medieval lead pinnacle, a Pyrenean Gothic chest and letters and documents including some of Louis XI, Henry IV as King of Navarre and of Marguérite d'Angoulême, sister of Francis I. The dining room has two large Flemish cupboards, 17C and paintings by Van der Velde, father and son. Other notable pieces include a gilded Spanish bureau (hunting room), and an elaborate Henry IV cupboard decorated with scenes and figures.

In the elegant saloon are **Canaletto's** Grand Canal and St. Mark's Square, and Roman views from the 18C. There is also a Japanese lacquered bureau, and a portrait by **Fragonard**. The main bedroom is furnished from the period of Louis XVI, and has a picture by Lenoir. Along the print corridor, note especially that of the Château of Pau as it was before the 19C alterations, and that of the Château of Nérac complete. The library retains medieval features from the 14C castle including the ogee doorway, and there is a bureau with decoration celebrating the short-lived French Constitutional Monarchy, dated 1791 and inscribed 'The King, the Nation, the Law'. See also the huge, fat Dutch cabinet of c 1690. Another bedroom shows more evidence of the medieval castle, while the china cabinet has a plate commemorating the execution of 'Louis Capet' (Louis XVI), shown at the guillotine, a fate shared by the last Baron Morlanne. More bedrooms are shown, one c 1750, another in the Empire style including a portrait of Napoleon's sister-in-law. The last room, with more medieval architectural details, contains a collection of the work of the 20C painter, R. Morère, died 1942.

The prettiest route to Pau is to take the D946 back to the crossroads (4km) cross the main road and continue to Arthez-de-Béarn (6km). On entering the village, a left on the D233 leads down to **Caubin** in just over one km. Here is a tiny church next to a picnic site. The **church** was built by Gaston IV de Béarn late in the 12C for the Knights of St. John. It has a very weird bellcote. It was vaulted but is now roofed in wood. The main interest in the simple interior is the splendid tomb of the Baron d'Andoins who was killed in combat in 1324. The tomb is full of pierced stone-work, cleverly back-lit by small windows. The big crocketted gable is supported by pilaster buttresses that rise to pinnacles. The gable has infill tracery. The chest below is also panelled. The figure is mutilated but notice the lion. What is so interesting about this tomb is that it looks distinctly English, and from a known workshop called the Kent School, whose work can be seen extensively in Westminster Abbey and in Canterbury.

Almost opposite the church, the D233 leaves to the left, and takes a very pretty rural route to Cescau (11km) and on to the main D945 (5km). By turning right you will approach Pau in 12km.

18

Pau

PAU (Hotels/Rest.) is another town with a problem—noise. Traffic booms around the old town day and night, spoiling what could be a most attractive place. It is superbly situated on a high ridge dropping down to the Gave de Pau, giving a spectacular panorama of the Pyrenees, at least on the days when it is not shrouded in mist. If you stay in Pau, and it is a natural and useful centre, find a hotel with sound-proofing or stay just off centre, try the north approaches. The location of Pau is one of its attractions. It has direct rail links (trains to Tarbes/Paris, Bordeaux, Irun, Bayonne, Toulouse, Dijon, Hendaye, Marseilles, Lourdes, Geneva, Nice and more locally, Dax, and Oloron-Ste-Marie), and the Autoroute A64 has routes flying off in all directions and allows easy access to Spain and the mountains. The Tourist Office is at Place Royale, 64000, etl 59 27 27 08.

Pau stands quite high, the bluff edge made into a feature of the town and exploited by the château, the principal monument. Those who arrive by train have the added excitement of using the free funicular up the cliff, a quaint 19C train with a period station directly opposite the railway terminus. At the top, there are fine views, and a shady square. The Tourist Office is on the far side. From here it is a short walk, left, to the old town, with its few narrow and sometimes flyover streets leading to the château (good area for restaurants). The rest of the town needs little comment except that there are lots of shops.

The **Château of Pau** is the reason for the town. In the 11C the Count of Foix built a castle on the end of the ridge, and established a hunting ground on its south-west slope. The park survives in part, semi-wild in the French manner, and offering fine views of the château. The most famous of the counts, Gaston Fébus, enlarged the castle in the 14C adding the great red-brick keep that is so evident today, and his court at Pau was one of the most brilliant of its century. Pau was modernised and enlarged again after 1527, when it received decorations in the new Renaissance style.

This was the period of Marguérite of Angoulême, sister of Francis I, an author, intellectual and great patron of the arts. In 1527, she married Henri d'Albret, lord of Béarn who had the title of King of Navarre. The brilliance and daring of their court came to a sudden end when their heir, Jeanne d'Albret, became a Huguenot. From her marriage to Antoine de Bourbon, she had a son, Henry of Navarre, who inherited the throne of France from his royal father. Of course, the French Wars of Religion were fought in order to keep this Protestant southerner off the throne, but with his pragmatic decision that 'Paris was worth a Mass', he became Henry IV and a Catholic. the rest, as they say, is history. The fortunes of the Château of Pau rest on his fame, not so much in his own time, but from those who subsequently hitched themselves onto this man's popularity. Why Henry IV should be the most popular and well-remembered monarch who ever sat on the bumpy French throne is hard to imagine. He was not a particularly good nor a wise king, and his private life would not stand investigation by the gutter press. Indeed, other than stopping the war, his reign was not favoured with much success. Despite this, popular mythology has created for him a legend of a dashing, heroic sage, with a sex-life quite at odds with the facts. Pau has become a shrine to his memory and if you do not know who he is, or really was, much of the story of the château will be lost on you. Henry IV affected the château more than 200 years after his death.

The post-Revolutionary king, Louis-Phillippe, anxious to ally himself with the revered memory of his royal ancestor, decided to renovate Pau as a royal residence, and to bask in the reflected glory of Henry IV. This did not wash with the public but it radically changed the appearance of the château. The work continued under Napoleon III in another attempt to fictionalise his own reign and the house as we now see it owes a great deal to these two rulers. They rearranged and redecorated the interiors, faked up some of the elevations while demolishing original sections of the castle. It is important to remember that everything we now see, with a few exceptions, is a 19C fantasy on a supposed medieval and 16C theme. It is the image projected by the French 19C monarchy of their supposed past, not the reality of that past. The nearest parallel would be the early-19C sections of Windsor (partly destroyed 1993). Windsor may, in fact, have acted as a model.

The **château** stands on a peninsula of rock, sliced from the city by a dry moat. It is very impressive, truly an idealised French palace. It is roughly triangular in plan, the broad base pointing at the town. As you approach, the red-brick tower of Gaston Fébus stands on the left, and bridging the space before the court, a Renaissance-style loggia. Despite proclaiming itself a work of the early 16C it is a 19C fantasy, and a very good one at that. Previously, a tall range of buildings closed the court from view but the 19C opened it up to the great benefit of the palace. (The château is open every day, with guided tours. Large queues build up, so try to arrive first thing in the morning. The tours are conducted in French, but English notes are available).

The bridge leads to the inner court. On two and a bit sides, the triangle is not quite pointed, and the façades proclaim a 16C date but these should be treated with caution. The restored doorway on the left is basically original, as are the main sections of the short end block. Throughout, the letters 'H' and 'M' stand for Henri and Marguérite. All the dormers are 19C and are excellent fakes. The stair turret in the angle also looks authentic though the busts are 19C. The major range to the right recalls a 19C workhouse, quite the grimmest part of the castle. A large number of rooms are shown and the tour can last 90 minutes. The groups are far too big. What follows is merely a synopsis, and work in progress in some areas may change the route and furnishings.

The early rooms contain two models of the château as it was before 1830. It looks bleak. One room was a **kitchen**, and has a crazy vault pattern, possibly medieval, and animals on the corbelled vault supports including a boar. The **dining room** has tapestries—Gobelin copies of Flemish originals. The **main stair** is an elaborate piece from c 1530, still mixing late Gothic ideas with those of the Renaissance. Again, it bears the initials 'H' and 'M'. **Tapestries** make up a large part of the first-floor room decoration, including designs by Le Brun. Outside the Queen's bedroom are a **Fragonard** and an **Ingres**. Also stranded in a corridor is a real late medieval fireplace. The collection of clocks includes some amusing pieces. The tiny portrait of Antoine de Bourbon, husband of Jeanne d'Albret and father of Henry IV, is by **Clouet**, dated 1557. A temporary gallery contains an appalling strip-cartoon life of Henry IV, including the king clutching the foot of Christ's cross—thoroughly nasty. The ivory backgammon table of 1600 is altogether in a different league. Outside the bedroom of Jeanne d'Albret, Flemish tapestries showing the Life of St. John, 1510. The interior of this room reaches levels of monarchical idolatory that some may find offensive. Some of the fittings are interesting though hardly the turtle shell, the supposed cradle of The Child.

From the court, the stair turret leads to a local museum with some fine rustic furniture, artisanal work and classy Louis XIII pieces together with some models of typical Béarnais period houses.

The gardens and park should be visited. Near the base of the red-brick tower, paths lead to the medieval **Tour de Monnai**, with its free lift down to the mill races below.

The rest of the town offers few historical attractions. The Place Gramont, 18C would be fine without the traffic, and the Place de Verdun could swallow whole villages. The covered market on the Place de la République has given way to an ugly modern version, though local produce is sold including *pâté de fois gras* from small producers. The Musée Bernadotte off the Place de la Libération, offers the interiors of a Napoleonic house. Bernadotte went from being a soldier, to Marshall of France to king of Sweden by an unlikely series of events. The **Musée de Beaux Arts** off the Cours Bosquet is undistinguished, save for the Cotton Exchange in New Orleans, by Degas.

19

Oloron-Ste-Marie and Lescar

This short, 100km, circular route visits one of the small historic towns of the regions, plus a haven of history and quiet stranded in the suburban sprawl of industrial Pau. In between are some surprisingly rural countryside and villages.

The N134 heads south from Pau, crossing the Gave de Pau, taking a right fork at Gan (8km). **Oloron-Ste-Marie** (Hotels/Rest.) is reached in a further 25km (train link with Pau and its regional/national connections. Market Tuesdays and Sundays am). The Tourist Office is at Place de la Résistance, 64400. Tel 59 39 98 00.

Oloron is a curious place, split between two centres by the Gave d'Aspe. Technically, it is two cities, each with a former cathedral and combined only in the 19C. It is instantly attractive and though it carries rather more through traffic than necessary, it offers a quieter stay than Pau. The two halves of the town are dramatically different, the higher town, surrounding the church of Ste-Croix, formed the nucleus of a castle of the counts of Béarn and Oloron, hence its difficult ascent and splendid views.

The lower town, across the river, known as the Quartier Ste-Marie, surrounds the cathedral church that has given its name to the whole town. The distance between the two may make you consider driving. Follow the road for the town centre. In the first square, Place de la Résistance (Tourist Office), the traffic sorts itself out. Take a left and once over the secondary Gave d'Ossau, another left will find a small car park. From here, you can climb up to **Ste-Croix**. The tiny quarter leads straight to the church, occupying the dominant position over the river (it is also possible to park at the west front but the one-way system is difficult to fathom).

The church is Romanesque, with a three-apsed east end, transept, crossing tower and aisled nave. The roof seems huge. The exterior at the east end is very restored. Enter via the damaged Romanesque north door. The interior is inevitably gloomy, though the nave is better lit. From the crossing, the plan is clear. The single-bay chancel is barrel vaulted, as are the transept arms. The apse and the transept chapels have semi-domes. The three-bay nave is also barrel vaulted, while the aisles have half-barrels or quadrant vaults, abutting the main span. The most famous feature of Ste-Croix is above your head and may require a torch. The crossing carries an Islamic-looking ribbed dome in eight parts, supported on scalloped squinches. With Spain a mere mountain away, that would seem the obvious source (see below, Jaca). There is much Romanesque decoration though sadly not in the apse painting, which is 19C. The original capitals hereabout include the Temptation of Christ, Adam and Eve, Cain and Abel, and Abraham and Isaac. The big Baroque altarpiece in the north transept makes its presence felt. The crossing capitals include the Adoration of the Magi, the Baptism of Christ and the Death of St. John the Baptist. The nave sculpture is notable but cruder.

From the north door, the Rue Dalmais has some interesting period houses, including a medieval tower, the Tour de la Grède, which has twin arches on the street and windows on the first floor, all c 1220.

If you intend walking to Ste-Marie, then the shortest route is via the steep Rue Labarraque, cross the river to the Place de Jaba, and take the Rue de Révol. Otherwise drive (parking at Ste-Marie). Apart from the attractive riversides, the town in between is nothing special.

Ste-Marie sits in a square and is more urban that its pair. It is also bigger and more complicated. The east end, higher than the rest, is 14C and has an apse, ambulatory and radiating chapel design, all canted sides, tracery and flyers. The transept is bitty, as is the rest of the building. There is a fortified tower over the south transept, and a 14C treasury adjoining it. The nave has lots more flyers and odd, port-hole clerestory windows. Somewhere within all the additions and lean-tos stands the Romanesque church that goes with the west door.

Oloron-Ste-Marie has a justly famous **door**. It is not spectacular in terms of quality nor iconography, but it is both human and fun. It stands beneath a tower-porch, which itself looks Romanesque but which cuts rather badly into the door design. The door is divided in two, with a central trumeau, and unusually, twin sub-tympana cut into the base of the main tympanum. The door jambs have columns and the arches are sculpted. There are additional sculptures stuck in the wall. The quality of the material is instantly appealing—polished Pyrenean marble that has taken on the gleam of age. It cuts well, and survives. On the base of the central column are twin Saracens in chains, a reference to the Crusader exploits of the patron, Gaston IV, count of Béarn and Oloron, died 1131. The central tympanum depicts the Deposition of Christ, while lions occupy the sub-arches. The inner order of the main arch has charming scenes of local life—salmon fishing, hunting, cheese making and viniculture. The outer order has the Elders of the Apocalypse playing instruments. Either side are, on the left, a monster eating a man, and on the right, the famous equestrian figure of Gaston IV. This is a magnificent work, and a rare, almost free-standing piece of Romanesque sculpture. Note the horses' eyes, which are rather sinister. On the upper wall are figures said to represent the guards ordered by Constantine to protect the Holy Places of the Christian World. The whole ensemble is difficult to date, but is perhaps c 1150.

The dark **interior** is not easy to read. Basically, the nave has two periods of Romanesque, the earlier including the aisle walls, forming part of the church begun by Gaston, then the later inner arcades, which are a rebuild from the end of the 12C. It is not helped by the smashing of much of the earlier work by the addition of side chapels, nor by the erection of a Gothic rib vault over the nave. This has also knocked the building sideways. The nave piers look c 1200, and are arranged in two double bays. The aisles are very messy, and the vaults much later, but the responds at the west end belong to the same date as the west front, c 1150. Something strange happens at the east end of the nave, which has off-centre arcade arches. Perhaps there were formerly towers over the aisles here. The transept announces the intentions of the 14C—to demolish the lot and start again. This scheme saw the entire reconstruction of the east end, a start on the transept and a transformation by stealth of much of the nave aisles. On the north side where nave meets transept, the added chapel has a fine late Gothic triradial vault, with triangular vault segments that reflect the eccentric placing of vault supports. The choir is odd: one bay leads straight into the canted apse, it has no middle storey, is immensely tall and displays an entirely whimsical choice of pier design. Why the supporting columns vary one to the next is unclear but by the time you reach the choir you are ready for anything. The aisle and chapel vaults are skilfully united.

The few fittings include a 16C hanging sanctuary lamp and carved chair nearby. To the north of the organ is a 'Murillo' Assumption, perhaps in both senses. Next to the Treasury door, are a pair of 17C semi-naked ladies in vocal poses—'Who Me? Why Me?'. The Treasury has odds and ends, some vestments and a 17C Nativity. The immediate area around the church has shops, cafés, and some picturesque corners.

A country route may be followed by returning to the Place de la Résistance, and turning left on the D9 for Lacq. This lovely road winds through wine country, rolling and verdant, with little or no traffic (the local wine is, as they say 'interesting'). At 20km you approch **Monien**, a village clearly on the up—it boasts a one-way system *and* a set of traffic lights.

Head into the tiny centre for the unmissable **church**. The west tower of Monien rears up like some multi-storey château. It has nine storeys and is vastly out of proportion for the little church. It dates from the 16C and represents an important cross-over piece, when church and domestic architecture are so similar as to be interchangeable. It also happens to be a most beautiful piece. At the foot, the west door has damaged sculpture, apparently re-used from an earlier tower. Scenes include Adam and Eve, and the Presentation at the Temple. Within, the entrance is mixed late Gothic and early Renaissance. The spacious interior has a north arcade carried on fat piers and a simple vault, all nicely toppling over. The south chapel has almost gone. The opposite north chapel remains from an earlier church and has a multi-ribbed tierceron vault. The altarpiece is Baroque, the lectern swivels with a squeak and a dog sleeps eternally beneath the pulpit of c 1600.

Take the D34 for Lasseube but at Cuqueron (2.5km) turn left on the D229 for Arbus, passing through **Parbayse**, a farm-village of rustic simplicity. At Arbus (6.5km) pick up the D2 by turning right and head for 5km towards Pau, where a junction with the D501 heads north, crossing the river, the main N117, the railway and out-of-town furniture centres to arrive at **Lescar** (4km). The Tourist Office is at Place Royales, 64230, tel 59 81 15 98. You enter the old town by staying on the one-way system as it heads west, drive up the hill and as the road swings right and then left, an instant right turn heads through a medieval gate and into another world. Do not worry if you miss it first time, just go once more round the whirlpool and try again.

Lescar is an ancient place, formerly the capital of the Béarn. It was the centre for the pre-Roman *Vernarni*, while in Roman times it was *Benehar-*

num, though this stood down in the valley. A bishopric was established here in the 6C but in c 850, the town was sacked by the marauding Norman Vikings. A new town was established on the hill-top, commanding fine views of the valley, ignoring the odd factory and power station. The cathedral became the burial church of the kings of Navarre but was savaged by the Huguenots. The present building reveals a messy history but is worthwhile.

Park as soon as you see the church. The hill-top town virtually consists of a loop surrounding the former cathedral. There are some fine old houses—the Tourist Office south of the church occupies a late Gothic town house—and good views.

The **cathedral** dates from the 1120s, with many later additions. The general view of the south side reveals all. The apse is 1120s, highly decorated though very restored. The nave is Romanesque in its lower sections, 17C above. The evidence of burning is everywhere. The north door is dated 1627. The west front is entirely 17C. By the south door, is an inscription commemorating the original builder bishop who died in 1141. No trace of the monastic buildings remains. The interior is unexpectedly bright. The spacious nave has four bays and a 17C barrel vault. The aisles have low, transverse arches, carrying barrel vaults set at right-angles to the nave, very 12C Cistercian, as at Fontenay or Fountains. The crossing is a 17C rebuild, complete with rib vault, though the east capitals are Romanesque. The short barrel-vaulted chancel has side entrances into the flanking chapels. Here there is an outbreak of sculpture, some of it very fine. Capitals adorn the wall arcades, the windows and the semi-domed side chapels. Some of the lowest sculpture looks restored but most of it must have been covered up before the French Wars of Religion. The intact capitals (see the main apse wall aracade) are immensely classicising, and the figures act predominantly as corner volutes. There are numerous biblical scenes and the odd head has been restored. Beneath your feet is another rarity, a 12C mosaic design with scenes of hunting. The quasi-late Roman style may be crude but it has the simple directness of the Bayeaux Tapestry. An inscription records the donor, Bishop Guido.

The altarpiece is of course Baroque, while the crossing has rather fine stalls complete with misericords and tall figures in niches, all post 1600. The nave altar seats and lectern are very flashy. The nave begins with a complete 17C bay, after that, a series of deliciously fraudulent capitals.

From Lescar it is possible to return to Pau on the D945 (8km). Alternatively, when reaching the intersection of the N134 at 5km cross over, and continue south east through the outskirts of the town until the route runs out at the D943 (5.5km) where a left on that road takes you to **Morlaàs** (7km). This little town has a huge church, famous for its Romanesque sculpture. The church was begun by Centulle V, Count of Béarn, in expiation for a consanguinial marriage to Gisla. It was founded as a priory, and soon given to Cluny. Although severely damaged by the Huguenots and horrendously restored both in the 17C and 19C, it still contains much that is worth seeing.

The church (Ste-Foy) has a simple plan though wonky in execution. A straight row of three apses at the east end, plus little flanking structures that mask the brief transept. The nave is long, and incorporates the base of a stocky tower, virtually lost. Most of the nave dates from after 1600, indeed, after 1850, excepting the west door.

The striking west front of Monien church

The west front of Morlaàs was intended to be marvellous. It is now sad but still interesting. Only the doorway of the Romanesque church survives, now set into a massive fragment of west wall. It follows the layout of Oloron-Ste-Marie, only here everything is increased. The central trumeau rests on squatting figures, the tympanum has inset scenes beneath arches, the jambs have columns and figures and there are many more orders within the main overarch. The iconography features Christ in Majesty with the Evangelistic symbols (modern copy, see below), with the Flight into Egypt below right and the Massacre of the Innocents on the left. The jamb figures are all by Viollet-le-Duc and are good of their kind: famously contorted figures of Atlantes hold up the encircling arches which are themselves treated to all sorts of decoration—vegetation, the Elders of the Apocalypse, ducks and daisies etc.

Inside, the church seems derelict and the modern wooden vault over the nave threatens collapse. Only one section of the medieval clerestory remains towards the south west angle. The chancel is barrel vaulted. The east apse has wall arcades with Romanesque capitals, painted in part, possibly original. The floor has another mosaic, recalling that at Sorde-l'Abbaye which could be Roman, Romanesque or Recent. In the north chapel are remains from the Romanesque west tympanum and a Christ in Majesty. In the south chapel are a 17C Virgin and Child and scenes of Moses.

From Morlaàs, the D943 returns directly to Pau in 13km.

20

The Passes of the Pyrenees and Spain

171km round trip, one-way to Col du Somport, 111.8km

Pau is ideally situated for a trip to the mountains. The Pyrenees form both a natural frontier and an invitation to penetrate deep into their lush and spectacular passes. For those who have never seen them, they may come as a complete shock. Green and well watered on the French side, they are barren and majestic on the Spanish. The following route combines the two nearest and finest routes, which can be linked by crossing into Spain, making a round day-trip. As an added bonus, the cross-country road begins at the Spanish city of Jaca, just over the border, but is very difficult to reach from any part of Spain. From Pau it is simple. That Jaca possesses one of Spain's foremost Romanesque cathedrals and a stunning museum of medieval art is an added incentive.

A full day should be allowed for the whole trip. The passes are worth seeing for themselves, and there are many picturesque villages en route. A number have been included here. Starting first thing in the morning will allow time to visit Jaca, where the museum closes at 13.30, the adjacent cathedral at 14.00. There is plenty of time for lunch, before a leisurely return on a different mountain route. The main purpose of the exercise is to see the scenery which is never less than marvellous. The mornings can be very cool until quite late.

Head south from Pau on the N134, passing Oloron-Ste-Marie (33km) where Spain is signposted as a the continuation of the same road. The route soon enters the foothills of the mountains, following the valley of the Gave d'Apse. At 18km, **Sarrance** is signposted just off the road in a magnificent setting. The centre is a tiny square fronting the church, with a tumble of houses, a fountain, and a washing tank. It looks like the curtain-up of some Viennese operetta. The **church** of 1609 is very ambitious, with a Borromini-style façade and big tower. Inside it is a true village church, filled with simple folk art, though a regional pilgrimage centre of some renown. The big interior looks like a series of stage sets, all brightly painted. Notable features include the bull's head motif, strange, painted 3-D carvings, which are apparently a local speciality (see the men fishing), bizarre confessional boxes and some rather ill-advised paintings. The art objects within the church hint at the contents of the museum of sacred art behind the building. Unfortunately, you may have to leave before its 10.00 opening time.

From Sarrance, the valley gets tighter and the river starts to rush. At 6.5km, the village of **Bedous** (Tourist Office, 64490 Bedous. Tel 59 34 33 14) marks a small but worthwhile detour. Head into the village and cross the central square before the church. The exit right of the building (notice the small plastered château) finds a little D237 to **Aydius** (6.5km). This is one of the prettiest detours of the day, a winding narrow road through inpene-trable woodlands, streams and waterfalls—in places the water jets straight from the rock-face beside the road. At the end, the little village has an Alpine air, with houses skittering down the valley sides. Park and walk awhile. The **church** is placed on a ledge so that you come eye to eye with its slate roof. The building is unremarkable but the setting superb. The narrow interior is brightly painted, as is the local sculpture. The pulpit is 17C while the confessional boxes house a collection of brooms. The setting of the cemetery might cause heart-failure.

Return to Bedous and the main road, and head once again for Spain. In 6km, a turning right leads to **Lescun** (D239, 5.5km). This detour enters a different landscape, now grey-faced, sheer and exposed. Lescun has a simple hotel for true peace and quiet, while the little church has village simplicity, a double gallery across the west end, a marvellous shining floor of local stone, a Baroque altarpiece with rather more architecture than is good for it and a fine Louis XIII chest doubling up as an altar.

Once more on the main road, the valley gets deeper though the driving no harder. At **Etsaut** (5.5km), you enter the Parc National des Pyrénées. Signs abound offering hotels, nature trails and bears. Sadly, the likelihood of seeing any furry friends is slight—they are near extinction. Try not to run them over. In another 3.5km **Fort de Portalet** swings into view, a tiny village and ruined castle impossibly perched half-way up a cliff. The road winds another 15km to the **Col du Somport** and the international border, which has long been vacated. Attention should be paid to sheep and goats which wander freely, and to the last 8km of French road, which requires attentive driving until it is upgraded. You may find lorry loads of granite hereabouts which can be a nuisance.

The contrast between the French Up and Spanish Down could not be greater. Where have the trees gone? The lush grasses, the steep-sided valleys? Now all is bare, the vistas huge and sun-bleached, the road a great deal better. The new road to Jaca, N330, will not detain you long.

Jaca is reached in 32km. On entering the town, park as soon as a low-lying Renaissance fort comes into view to your right. It is clearly marked as it is still a barracks. Take any of the unpromising lanes opposite and you are in the old town. You will hit the **cathedral** within a block or two (signposted *cathedrale romanica*). For a full description of Jaca see Blue Guide Spain, but the following offers a brief resumé. The cathedral is Romanesque and late Gothic. It was begun in 1076 by Bishop Garcia and King Sancho Ramirez, founder of the city. The shell of the early building survives well; see the south east apse, very well preserved, the short transept, south porch, nave and voluminous west porch. The church contains one of the great collections of Romanesque **sculpture** in Spain—no Huguenot spoil-sports here. The main east apse is an 18C rebuild. The south porch is an odd piece, housed in a loggia-like structure. The capitals here are stupendous if grubby, and date from c 1120. The west door is housed beneath a great barrel vault. It features lions on the tympanum beneath an early-Christian symbol, but there are too many excellent capitals to mention each one.

The **interior** needs a clean (there are lights). The plan is straightforward. The aisled nave was vaulted late in the Middle Ages, though it retains a fine set of Romanesque **capitals**. The aisle vaults are varied and attractive, and the upper vault, though essentially Gothic, seems to contain an early Renaissance clerestory design. The Romanesque church was either barrrel vaulted with no clerestroy, or it had an open wooden roof. The crossing has a ribbed dome of Islamic inspiration. The transept chapels are Romanesque, notice the decorated string courses of the north chapel repeated at three levels. The chancel is Baroque. The huge numbers of fittings cannot be covered here, but note the late Gothic tombs and screens, early Renaissance set-pieces and Baroque altars.

From the north west door of the nave, the **Diocesan Museum** may be visited (closes 13.30, accepts payment in French francs). This is exceptional and should not be missed. Housed in the cloisters and monastic buildings, the museum features medieval finds from Jaca and its region. The cloisters were rebuilt in the 17C but retain a rustic charm. They offer fine views of the church. The museum includes important Romanesque sculpture, some from the earlier cloister on this site. One wall is filled with 12/13C carved Madonnas, while a number of 12C metal screens are also shown. The most exciting display must be the complete cycles of Romanesque and later wall paintings lifted from churches in the diocese. Most important is the near complete church cycle from Bagües, dating from the late 11C. It offers a rare chance to see what a Romanesque church should have looked like, and includes a Genesis cycle with the Childhood of Christ below, while opposite are Old Testament scenes—Noah, the Miracles of Christ, andthe Marriage Feast of Cana. The apse contains Resurrection scenes. Not all the scenes are in strict order, some skip across the church while others drop a register. The style is graphic, with strong outlines and very free brush-strokes. The collection continues with a further 15 cycles of various dates and condition. Later exhibits include panel paintings of the 15/16C. and a wealth of other material.

Jaca has little else to offer except lunch and shops (the Spanish eat lunch late). The fort is open at odd times and has a fancy gate.

To return to France, take the C134 and head east along a flat, open road. At 14km, a left takes a short-cut to Beuscas (15km), where a reasonably good road, C136, heads north for Col du Pourtalet and France (33km). The last few km to France are being improved. Lorries are not allowed on the French section of this road. Crossing the frontier at 2165m, the French road

The Romanesque Cathedral at Jaca

could be better, but the landscape changes as surely as it did before. You are quickly back in narrow, green valleys, where streams tumble and rocks overhang. At 11km a side road on the right leads to the mountain railway at **Artouste**, a popular scenic excursion. The road continues on its enchanting way, offering occasions for parking (keep well off the carriageway) where sitting on a rock or paddling in the streams may prove irrestistible temptations. However, the water is very fast and very, very cold.

At 16km from Artouste, the turning right goes to Eaux-Bonnes (see below) while through Laruns, a right turn leads to **Béost** (3km). This tiny, picturesque village is worth exploring. It has a château and a church merely inches apart, the church with crude Romanesque capitals. There is a camping site in the village. The D934 then returns to Pau in 36km, joining the D134 at Gan.

21

The Col d'Aubisque, St-Savin and Lourdes

This 145km route is not for the faint-hearted. The mountain road along the corniche between the Col d'Aubisque and the Col du Soulor offers some of the finest scenery in Europe but needs a strong nerve and good driving skills. It must not be attempted in bad weather, nor is it possible 'out of season'. If the mountain-tops are clearly visible from Pau, then go, otherwise, wait for another day. This route goes one-way over the mountains, taking advantage of the inner side of the road. It continues to the lovely village of St-Savin, which is not technically in Aquitaine. Return via Lourdes and a splendid grotto.

The route from Pau follows the N134 for 8km to Gan, where the D934 to Col du Pouralet heads left for Spain. At 29km, Laruns (see above), after which the D918 heads uphill for Eaux-Bonnes. The road is steep and twisty for 4km, when suddenly, you arrive almost beneath the first buildings of the town. **Eaux-Bonnes** has fallen upon hard times. Hotels, some derelict, line the long sloping central gardens. There are still working hotels and restaurants but its hey-day was clearly yesterday. It is still a centre for winter sports. The Tourist Office (64440 Laruns. Tel 59 05 33 08) occupies a curious circular tower structure in the middle of the park, and posts up expected weather conditions for the mountain routes. Read them.

The next 12km will test anyone's driving ability and stamina. A twisting road cut into the rock face, sheer drops of thousands of feet, difficult passing, goats, horses, all make for slow but spectacular going. Stop only at designated places.

At the **Col d'Aubisque**, there are parking spaces, a café, and one of the great views of Europe. The road onwards may be closed without warning. It descends gradually from 1870m to 1474m at the **Col du Soular** (10km) and thence, to the village of Arrens (8km) at only 878m. Now the worst is over. **Arrens** is a typical mountain village, seemingly sunk into the ground. The little church has a peasant doorway, featuring Christ in Majesty. **Aucun** is similar (3km), where the rustic church has a 12C apse and a big, sloping roof. In 9km, you arrive at **Argelès-Gazost** (Hotels/Rest.), a regional resort for winter and other mountain and water sports. The Tourist Office, off the pretty central square, also has weather reports. The D921 heading south branches at the petrol station (on the right-hand side, in the suburbs), where the D101 winds picturesquely to St-Savin (3km).

St-Savin (Hotels/Rest.) lies on the western slopes of the Gave de Pau. The road enters the village around the apse of the abbey church which is the main attraction of the place. The little village has a rambling square with erratically placed timber and stone buildings, extremely picturesque, albeit of slight architectural interest. The modest hotel on the left commands a fine view. The **abbey church** is Romanesque (closed at lunchtimes). It has a bold east apse, rather plain transept and nave, and remains of a cloister and a chapter house against the north side. The apse has some rubble additions, perhaps part of a fortification scheme. The 12C work has wall arcades with Romanesque capitals and decorated corbel tables. The whole east end is battlemented. The remaining exterior is very simple, except the tower, which turns polygonal and has angle buttresses and a stumpy spire, 14C.

The **interior** is big and plain, with little architectural decoration. The short choir leads to the semi-domed apse, the transept also has apsidal east chapels, while the nave is barrel vaulted. The crossing may have carried a ribbed dome like Oloron, though now only the squinches survive, and the existing rib-vault is, perhaps, later. The west door is very damaged. It retains some primitive and possibly renewed animal carvings and a bad Christ in Majesty with the Evangelistic symbols. Christ is dressed as a priest.

The lack of Romanesque capitals within the church comes as a surprise and a disappointment, though the 12C holy water stoops in the form of caryatids are interesting. There is also a rare painted and gilded wooden tabernacle from the 14C while behind the High altar is a painted cycle of the Life of St. Savin, 15C(?) with 18 panels. The altar itself contains the tomb of the saint, and has an arcaded design in Pyrenean marble, c 1200. In the nave, are a 13C Crucifixion, a 16C organ loft and a 17C pulpit.

In the chapter house, a six-bay vaulted building, is a small treasury with metal-work and architectural fragments. It is open occasionally.

Above the village (signposted) is the house of the Black Prince, a modest late-medieval building with a machicolated donjon, modern extensions and wonderful views (open in season, not Mondays). Also signposted on the south-east skirt of the village is the tiny Pilgrimage Chapel, la chapelle de Piétat, an 18C trilobe design, filled with peasant art and paintwork. Near the pulpit, is an earlier survival with sections of medieval paintings. There are wonderful views from the shaded churchyard.

To the south from St-Savin, run two immensely scenic routes, the Gorges de Luz and the Gaves de Cauterets.

The return to Pau may be made on less spectacular but easier roads. From St-Savin, return to Argelès-Gazost, and take the D313 to Lourdes, which is reached in 13km (at the entrance to the town, a funicular up the Pic du Jer, at nearly 1000m, and futher in, the same to Le Béout, 791m, both very popular outings).

Lourdes (Hotels/Rest.) is one of the most famous places in France, indeed, the entire world. Pilgrimages to the site of Bernadette's visions of the Virgin are more popular than ever. Previously, Lourdes was the site of a small castle, sitting on a prominent rock and little else. Now it is one of the most offensive and distressing places that it is possible to imagine. It is not the sick that make it so, far from it. Their strength and courage and the willing assistance of the more fortunate is inspiring, but the town has fallen victim to a commercialism that is totally repellent. To say that Lourdes is Blackpool without the tower would be to insult that Lancashire resort. Nothing can prepare the casual visitor for the horror in store. If you have been able to park, which is most difficult, and to survive the plastic piety (no longer as pious as of old—it is amazing just what a plastic Virgin can be made to do) and have made it to the sacred enclosure, there are more shocks in store, this time aesthetic.

The basilica and its enclosure is hectic. Large signs warn against pickpockets. The double-storey **church** defies description, the lower church, begun in 1869, is a pseudo-Byzantine bunker of unbelievable ugliness, while the upper church, 1871, in suburban Victorian Town Hall Gothic, is another unrivalled example of bad taste. Note the great number of votive plaques from the period of the defeat by Prussia, coincidentally the year the upper church was begun. One great irony is that no facilities exist within either church for the disabled, not even to enable them to get upstairs.

In the grounds, quite literally, an entirely different experience awaits. The huge underground basilica of St. Pious X is truly magnificent, both in scale and design. It is based on a giant oval plan, roofed in concrete, with vast ramps curving around the walls, the whole supported by colossal V-shaped concrete supports. It was designed in 1958 by Pierre Vago. The scale is unimaginable. Huge lorries cruise the aisles, there are 20,000 seats, and the great processional routes illustrated with illuminated stations of the cross. Everything is of Cecil B. de Mille proportions. The building is simply staggering. Go to station number eight for the best views.

The castle (lift to summit) houses a local collection of Pyrenean life and culture. It commands fine views (and manages to rise above the commercial squalor below).

Escape from Lourdes on the D937 to Pau. At **St-Pé-de-Bigorre** (10km), is a fat Romanesque church of puzzling appearance. It began life as a Benedictine abbey in 1022, founded by the duc of Gascony on the site of a miracle. It was consecrated in 1096, by which time it was Cluniac. In the 12C a second church was built, reusing sections of the old, but effectively pushing the crossing further west. St-Pé was burnt by the Huguenots in 1569, shaken by earthquakes in 1660, and suffered the collapse of its central dome in 1661. Almost by premonition, a new, simpler church had been begun within the choir space of the old. This was completed in 1681. The monks were thrown out in 1791, and for a time the church was used as an army workshop. In the 19C a new church was built on to the west end of the truncated 17C building. It is little wonder that the present appearance is puzzling. The three-apsed east end belongs to the first church, though the main apse is a restoration. After only one short bay, the work becomes 17C until the present west end and the short tower. The tower stands over what was the south transept arm of the 12C church. The present entrance east of the tower formed part of the south aisle of the extended choir. When you enter, you stand in 12C work, and the baptistery to your left, was part of the 12C transept (damaged Romanesque wall arcades and capitals). Once into the church, you are in a fairly dull 17C aisled interior, but the east apses of both aisles are 11C.

Among the fittings, the 17C stalls with scenes of St. Peter are very fine, as are the 14C Virgin of St-Pé, in the south apse, and in the preceeding bay, an Annunciation salvaged from the old church. On the north east pier of the nave is the Key of St. Peter, evidently medieval, and along the north wall, St. Anthony of Padua, preaching to the fish at Rimini.

From St-Pé it is 3km to the famous **Grottes de Bétharram**, straddling the border of Aquitaine, and perhaps the best of all such underground excursions. Open every day from Easter to mid-October (closed midday) they are very popular. The management advises early morning arrivals in high season, though arriving at the end of the afternoon can be equally successful. Wait at the car park for instructions. The cave interiors can be damp underfoot. The 'great hall' features huge interiors wandering off in several directions, with spectacular rock formations, imaginatively lit. You proceed through numerous halls and passages, perhaps rather more than you wished to see. Memorable are the catwalks above racing streams, the 'boat' across a small underground lake, and the white-knuckle train ride through tight, twisting tunnels. Those of a nervous disposition should not sit at the front. The tour, in several languages, lasts about 50 minutes. You exit via a wonderfully old-fashioned tea-room and shop.

From Betharram, pick up the D937 for Pau, which is reached in 30km.

INDEX